D1707364

On the Edge of Empire

On the Edge of Empire
Four British Plans for North East India, 1941–1947

Edited by
David R. Syiemlieh

www.sagepublications.com
Los Angeles • London • New Delhi • Singapore • Washington DC

First published in 2014 by

SAGE Publications India Pvt Ltd
B1/I-1 Mohan Cooperative Industrial Area
Mathura Road, New Delhi 110 044, India
www.sagepub.in

SAGE Publications Inc
2455 Teller Road
Thousand Oaks, California 91320, USA

SAGE Publications Ltd
1 Oliver's Yard, 55 City Road
London EC1Y 1SP, United Kingdom

SAGE Publications Asia-Pacific Pte Ltd
3 Church Street
#10-04 Samsung Hub
Singapore 049483

Published by Vivek Mehra for SAGE Publications India Pvt Ltd, typeset in 10.5/12.5 Sabon by RECTO Graphics, Delhi and printed at Saurabh Printers Pvt Ltd, New Delhi.

Library of Congress Cataloging-in-Publication Data

On the edge of empire : four British plans for North East India, 1941–1947 / edited by David R. Syiemlieh.
    pages cm
  Includes bibliographical references.
    1. India, Northeastern—Politics and government—20th century. 2. Tribes—India—Assam—History—20th century. 3. Britain—Colonies—History—20th century. I. Syiemlieh, David R. (David Reid) editor of compilation.
    DS483.75.O56   954'.1—dc23   2014   2013043664

ISBN: 978-81-321-1347-8 (HB)

The SAGE Team: N. Unni Nair, Alekha Chandra Jena, Anju Saxena and
            Dally Verghese

For Maxine, Colin and Reuben

Thank you for choosing a SAGE product! If you have any comment, observation or feedback, I would like to personally hear from you. Please write to me at contactceo@sagepub.in

—Vivek Mehra, Managing Director and CEO,
SAGE Publications India Pvt Ltd, New Delhi

Bulk Sales

SAGE India offers special discounts for purchase of books in bulk. We also make available special imprints and excerpts from our books on demand.

For orders and enquiries, write to us at

Marketing Department
SAGE Publications India Pvt Ltd
B1/I-1, Mohan Cooperative Industrial Area
Mathura Road, Post Bag 7
New Delhi 110044, India
E-mail us at marketing@sagepub.in

Get to know more about SAGE, be invited to SAGE events, get on our mailing list. Write today to marketing@sagepub.in

This book is also available as an e-book.

Contents

Preface

Studies in British imperialism remain a dominant theme in the history of North East India. In the closing years of the British rule, a secret plan was conceived and discussed at the highest levels of administration for setting up a Crown Colony which would comprise the hill areas of the North East India and the tribal areas of Burma. The plan could not be implemented for various reasons but for the most part because it had come up rather later in the day. My interest in the history of North East India drew me to study these plans, first mooted in 1941 and discussed by the Governments of India, Burma and Britain through to 1945 when it was closed. The research was conducted in libraries in the region, Delhi and archives and libraries in the UK. A number of articles were then published on this subject. The plan has been referred to in many other publications. What is of concern for me, as a historian, is that several scholars have made reference to the Crown Colony Plan/Protectorate without reading the actual texts. Secondary references have been used in writing about these plans as the original documents were not easily available for research. Consequently, there have been chronological, factual and interpretational inconsistencies.

While I am still interested in putting together a volume on the plan and its fallout, it occurred to me that it would be of tremendous interest to many to place in a single volume, four of the British plans for the hill people of the region in the years before and shortly after Independence. What has been done in this volume is to place an introduction on the geographical, administrative and colonial contexts of four British plans. There is a link between the note of Sir Robert N. Reid, Governor of Assam, 1937–1942; the note of his Secretary, James P. Mills; the tract of Reid's successor Sir Andrew G. Clow, Governor, 1942–1947 and that of Philip F. Adams, who in turn became Secretary to the Assam Governor after Mills. There appears to be a strand of thought between that of Reid and Mills, for they would have often discussed the matter of the hill tribes. All four were members of the Indian Civil Service and all four served in various capacities in the North East. However detailed the plans were and their significance as documents for the future of the hill tribes of the region, apart from that of Reid, they were not taken up seriously by the government considering the changing international situation, the Indian freedom struggle and political situation that prevailed and the fast-moving events towards the transfer of power. All four plans were of a confidential nature. The four officers left their notes perhaps not mindful whether there would be discussion and policy decisions on them. It is the disregard of these notes by the Assam and Central Governments, much of which could not be implemented and yet the perspective from which the four British officers wrote these plans that academia and policymakers will find interest.

Robert N. Reid, the Governor of Assam, 1937–1942, first put across the idea that the hill people of the region should be given special attention by the British Government. Within his note of 1941 is the concept of the Crown Colony for North East India and the hill region of Burma. The note makes a detailed study of how the hill people were governed with suggestions for another and different phase of British administration. Reid's successor Sir Andrew G. Clow, the last British Governor of Assam, disagreed with Reid on many issues. His long note is a detailed review of the administration of Assam tribes. Both Reid and Clow had James P. Mills as their adviser. Mills' own note, quite different from that of the governors', puts in perspective the future of the hill tribes of the region in a self-governing India, for by the time he wrote his note, it was clear that the British did not have long to stay in India. Philip F. Adams took over from Mills. He remained as Secretary to assist Sir Akbar Hydari, the first Indian Governor of Assam. His short note is a useful reference of the British mind on the hill tribes. Adams subsequently left India for service in East Africa.

The title of the book, *On the Edge of Empire: Four British Plans for North East India, 1941–1947*, is symbolic of the location of the North East and the period in time this history narrates. The introduction provides a background of the administrative machinery and the political activity in the hills before and leading to Independence and after. It makes reference to the careers of the British officers and gives a gist of their views on the subject. It then brings up the story to the transfer of power from Britain to India and the effects this had on the North East. This is followed by the four notes on the administration and future of the hill and tribal people of North East India. No change has been made to the original texts.

Acknowledgements

Many institutions and persons have encouraged me in the publication of this volume. The Charles Wallace India Trust and the Indian Council of Social Science Research provided funds for data collection from archives and libraries in the UK. To these institutions, I owe gratitude for their support. I gratefully acknowledge the permission given to conduct research at the India Office Library and Records, now part of the British Library, with permission from the British Library Board to reprint the notes of Reid, Mills, Clow and Adams and the waiver of fees. I spent some exciting months over several winters researching in this library and the Cambridge South Asia Archives, two repositories having impressive collections on India. I owe the libraries and their staff much for all their support. Thanks are also due to Sandra Powlette and Jackie Brown, Permission and Key Account Managers with the British Library, London. Gratefully acknowledged is the support of Derek Perry and KOI HAI for use of the group image of Sir Robert N. Reid at Haflong, and Winifred Assan and Susannah Rayner and the Archives and Special Collections, SOAS Library for the inclusion of the image of James P. Mills. Grants from the Special Assistance Programme, Department of History, North-Eastern Hill University enabled me to visit the National Archives of India and the Nehru Memorial Museum and Library. The collection of the North-Eastern Hill University library was extremely useful.

Among those who have taken interest in my research, Professors J. B. Bhattacharjee and Imdad Hussain are remembered for their friendship and encouragement. Dr C. J. Thomas of the Indian Council of Social Science Research-North Eastern Regional Centre (ICSSR-NERC), Shillong, has been a friend and collaborator in our work for the Social Sciences in the North East. The support he provided is gratefully acknowledged. I recall the discussions on the Crown Colony Plan and the events in the North East before and after Independence with Chan Chai Fong of Tokyo University and Yusuf Ali, the former chief secretary, Arunachal Pradesh. Their understanding of the issues kept the interest in me to bring out this compendium. SAGE Publications have been very patient and did not give up on me. My thanks in particular go to Sutapa Ghosh, Alekha Chandra Jena and Anju Saxen of SAGE India for their administrative and technical inputs. My wife Maxine and sons Colin and Reuben have been very patient with all my travel, academic and writing assignments. I dedicate this volume to my family for all we have shared and their encouragement to write this book.

The Khasis express gratitude with the word *Khublei*—God bless you. To all these institutions, family and friends I say with the highest regard, *Khublei*.

David R. Syiemlieh
Member
Union Public Service Commission

Introduction

David R. Syiemlieh

I

North East India was brought under British colonial rule over the 19th century. Colonial sub-imperialism, the extension of exiting European possessions to expand into their environment,[1] started in North East India with the annexation in 1822 of the Garo foothills along Mymensing and Goalpara. This followed the annexation of Assam in March 1826 after the defeat of Burma in the first Anglo–Burmese War and the signing of the Treaty of Yandaboo. Soon after followed political control over the Khasis after their defeat in the Anglo–Khasi War of 1829–1833. Cachar was annexed in 1832 and the Jaintia Kingdom in 1835. Upper Assam was returned to Purandhar Sinha, the Ahom ruler in 1833. The territory was again taken over by the British in 1838 after Purandhar Sinha failed to meet British expectations. Annexation continued unabated despite Queen Victoria's assurance in her Proclamation after the great Indian mutiny that there would be no more annexations following that upheaval of 1857–1858. What remained to be annexed were the hills of present-day Arunachal Pradesh, the Naga Hills and the erstwhile Lushai Hills. The Naga Hills are inhabited by numerous Naga tribes and spread over much of the hills stretching on both sides of the Patkai range. By the last quarter of the 19th century, the Nagas were brought under the British rule. Similarly, the Lusheis inhabiting what is today Mizoram were brought under colonial rule in the last decade of the 19th century.[2] These hill tracts were incorporated into British India.

Nagas and Chins on the other side of the watershed were also brought under colonial subjugation. Their hills were placed under the Burma administration. Before the turn of the 19th century, the divide had been made between what was to constitute British India and British Burma. British imperial expansion and policy over what was the homeland of numerous tribal communities, therefore, was responsible for eventually giving the people on both sides of the dividing line their Indian and Burmese identities.

The hills that came under the direct control of the Raj were categorised by the Government of India Act, 1919, as Backward Tracts. While the majority of the tribes acquiesced with the term, the Khasi–Jaintia were unhappy being put into this category.[3] Consequently, the 1935 Government of India Act applied a different nomenclature for the tribal areas. The hills were categorised as either Excluded Areas or Partially Excluded Areas. The Excluded Areas which included the Naga and the Lushai Hills Districts were placed under the executive control of the Assam Governor. The Partially Excluded Areas including the Garo, Khasi–Jaintia and the Mikir Hills Districts came under the control of the Governor and were subject to ministerial administration, but the governor had an overriding power when it came to exercising his discretion. No act of the Assam or Indian legislatures could apply to these two hill divisions unless the governor so directed. He was empowered to make regulations for the hill districts which had the force of law. The administration of these hills was his "special responsibility". With no representatives in the Assam Assembly (other than the Partially Excluded Areas, which sent one legislator each), political activity above their village and local level could hardly have existed.

Within the region were the 25 Khasi states, Manipur and Tripura. The Khasi states were nominally under the administration of their chiefs (*Syiems, Lyngdohs, Sirdars* or *Wahadadars*) in durbar with only a supervising attention from the Deputy Commissioner of the Khasi and Jaintia Hills District who doubled as their political officer. With much of Manipur State in the hills around the Imphal Valley, that state's political agent, stationed in an impressive residency in the heart of the capital town, was vested with certain special responsibilities in respect of the administration of Manipur tribals. Tripura never appeared to have had a tribal policy despite the tribal Maharaja.

There was yet a third area in the North East inhabited by tribals. Along the watershed between Burma and further north in the hills reaching the eastern Himalayas lived Nyishi, Galo, Shedrukpen, Monpa, Mishing, some Naga tribes, Singpho and other tribal groups of this once inaccessible and remote stretch of land who were "unadministered" as the official term went. Their hills were only occasionally visited by the British in punitive expeditions and survey operations. The Naga Tribal Area and the Tirap Frontier Tract were technically and for practical purposes outside British India. There was a statutory boundary between these two frontier tracts and the adjoining districts of the province. While this boundary had been defined, by an oversight no similar notification was issued for the northern boundary of the Assam province and it was, thus, assumed that the whole territory up to the Indo-Tibetan frontier was de jure an excluded area and so theoretically formed part of the province. However, this interpretation was contrary to the administrative position because while the Government of India treated the area as tribal and unadministered, treaties of 1862 and 1874 with the tribes of these hills refer to them as "foreign" with a distinction made between "the boundary of the Queen and your country" and the limits of British territory were fixed at the foothills.[4]

The non-regulation pattern of administration operated in the region. First applied to the Mal Pahariyas of Chota Nagpur and then to the Garos by Regulation X of 1822 and later elaborated by a series of official administrative measures including the Inner Line Regulation of 1873 and the Scheduled Districts Act, 1874, the system was characterised by a simple procedure of administration.[5] The full provisions of law and administration were not made applicable to the tribes inhabiting these hills. For instance, the income tax and registration of land was not made applicable. In time the non-regulation system was adapted for all the hill tribes of North East India as and when they came under the British rule, other than those residing in the "native states".

This pattern of administration was also applied to the tribals of Chota Nagpur, Jalpaiguri, Darjeeling, Chittagong hill tracts of Bengal, Kumoan in the North West Province and in certain districts of Sindh. With their subjugation by the British, steps were taken by the colonial administration to give to these hill people a "paternal" government which allowed them to exercise their own genius in the management of themselves, with just that amount of control from above. Traditional leaders were encouraged to continue their age-old and traditional administration under the new dispensation. Their traditional hierarchical structure remained. The colonial administration permitted their chiefs to continue their authority over their respective villages under the watchful eyes of the district authorities. In the British India villages, the Khasi *Sirdar*, the Naga *Goanbura*, the Mizo *Lal* and the Garo *Nokma* assisted the administration in collection of revenue, house tax and other functions for which they were paid a share of the collection. The Naga *Goanbura*s were each given a distinctive red blanket as a symbol of their authority. This form of indirect administration operated in the hills whereby the chiefs became the local props; if such a term is appropriate, to describe the relationship between the rulers and the traditional heads of villages.

The British rule over the hill people of the North East superseded centuries' old political isolation of the hill people and introduced a pattern of administration to suit imperial policy. An important feature of this administrative pattern was the integration of distinct tribal areas into a district or subdivision named after the predominant tribe. In the process of acquisition and consolidation of British administration over these hills, several of their indigenous institutions and customs were conveniently allowed to become defunct. On the other hand, certain other institutions and laws were introduced which were alien to tribal traditions. Generally, however, and in line with the British policy of non-interference with the traditional forms of governance of the people, customs in their life and culture and governance got sanction without being spelled out in any detail.

The politics of the Indian National Congress, the All India Muslim League and other political parties of the Assam legislature did not have any effect in these hills. The British policy of exclusion and segregation of the hill tribes kept them out of touch with the political, cultural and other developments in other parts of India.[6] However, it was not long before political consciousness emerged in the hill districts. It started with the Jaintia Durbar in 1900. From the second decade of the last century, political activity in these hills increased in view of the constitutional reforms Britain offered India. The participation of several hill tribes as Labour Corps in the war of 1914–1918 exposed them for the first time to peoples and places far from their homes. Naga political activity began with the establishment of the Naga Club in 1918. This was followed by the more hectic political maneuverings of the Khasi National Durbar set-up in 1923 and the Federation of Khasi states formed in 1934. The pace of political activity increased sharply shortly before the independence of India. Garos were brought together in 1946 by the Garo National Council. The Mizos with popular initiative formed the Mizo Union in April that year.

II

British administrators have left behind several accounts of people, culture and history of the North East. This genre of literature has been widely used by scholars to understand the history of the region, the functioning of the colonial administration, the colonial mind and perspectives in their governance of this region within the colonial state. Here, I am reminded of the address made by my senior colleague Milton Sangma to members of the North East India History Association at its 15th Annual Session in 1994. His presidential address underscored the significant contribution made by the British administrators to our understanding of the region.[7] Whereas much of the early literature written by the administrator has been fruitfully used by scholars, several writings published towards the closing years of the British rule have not been made use of in any large measure. There could be two reasons for this. Firstly, many British reports were not available for research because of their location in repositories not easily accessible to Indian scholars. Secondly, research on the closing years of colonial rule relating to North East India is only now finding some interest among historians.[8]

Among several reports and accounts published between the years 1941 and 1947 written with the perspective of working out plans for the future administration of the hills of North East India and in an independent India, four stand out prominently because of their author's positions in the administration, their details and their intent. The four notes published in this book are those of Sir Robert N. Reid, Governor of Assam 1937–1942; that of his successor Sir Andrew G. Clow, Governor of Assam 1942–1947, James P. Mills, the Advisor to the Government of Assam for Tribal Areas and States and his successor and fellow Indian Civil Service officer Philip F. Adams. Their notes and related papers had been carefully collated from various repositories. These facilitated my research on the last years of the British rule over the region. Several papers emerged from the study.[9]

Robert Reid[10] had long been associated with administration in Bengal as an Indian Civil Service officer before he took over as Governor in 1937 of what was then the composite province of Assam. A prolific writer, he wrote extensively of the region. His first and rather lengthy piece with which we are interested was *A Note on the Future of the Present Excluded, Partially Excluded and Tribal Areas of Assam* which was published in confidential nature in early November 1941. Some 50 copies were printed at the Government Printing Press, Shillong. A year later, he wrote *History of the Frontier Areas Bordering on Assam* (Shillong, 1942). This was an update of Alexander Mackenzie's *A History of the Relations of the Government with the Hill Tribes of North East Frontier of Bengal* (Calcutta, 1884). An unpublished manuscript is with the British Library, India and Oriental Collection. Titled *Assam and the North East Frontier of India*, Reid penned this after his retirement and returned home in 1946. Before his death in 1964 he had put together his autobiography *Years of Change in Bengal and Assam*. The book was published posthumously.

The 22-page *A Note on the Future of the Present Excluded, Partially Excluded and Tribal Areas of Assam*, with which we are concerned, first makes a review of the administrative history of Assam and the hills which were attached to its administration. He provides a detailed account of the background of the Khasi, Jaintia, Garo and Mikir Hills administration as Partially Excluded Areas and the Naga and the Lushai Hills as Excluded Areas. Mention is also made of the Tribal Areas between India and Burma. He drew his information from the *Census of India*; the Memoranda to the *Indian Statutory Commission* and its *Report* of 1930; the *White Paper* of 1931, Government correspondence and the Government of India Act, 1935. Reid says that the experience of 1937–1941 of the working of the arrangements 'has been on the whole not unfavourable'. He found no difficulty in administrating the Excluded Areas and he was quite clear that these areas had benefited greatly by not being placed within the control of the Assam Ministry and the Legislature. He was satisfied also that their exclusion had not stood in the way of prospects of progress and development which the Government of India in 1932 sought to ensure by including them within the control of both the ministry and legislature.[11] The case of the Partially Excluded Areas was different. He says he was always careful that the responsibility of administration of this category of hills lay with the ministry but he ensured that he was always kept aware of what was going on so as to be able to fulfil his special responsibility in the governance of these hills.[12]

About the future of the hills of Assam, Governor Reid argued that their future should be decided by the British Parliament. 'It cannot be left to Indian political leaders with neither knowledge, interest nor feelings for these areas', he wrote.[13] Building up his argument and "main premise", he quoted L. S. Amery, the Secretary of State for India and Burma who remarked on 3 March 1941 of Burma and her separation from India: 'that separation was the natural consequence of the introduction of self-government, for in her racial type and her culture, as well as in her geographical position, Burma belongs not to India, but to the easternmost of the great southward projection of the main bulk

Asia, the Indo-Chinese peninsula'.[14] This applied just as closely Reid continued, to the tribes inhabiting the Partially Excluded Areas, the Excluded Areas and the Tribal Areas. He notes that when one 'emerges from the hills into the plains of Assam one enters a different world, whereas the boundary between our hills and the Burma hills, is artificial as it is imperceptible'.[15] Reid also used the idea of John Hutton, Deputy Commissioner, Naga Hills District, in his memorandum to the Indian Statutory Commission that the tribal areas had interests which conflicted with those of the people inhabiting the Assam plains and that the introduction of provincial self-government raised the necessity of some form of protection for these areas until they would reach a position to stand on their own feet either as an integral part of the Assam province or as independent units of the federated whole. This impression of the Governor was formed in part after a second visit he made to Aizawl in December 1940, where he got the sense that the Mizos, 'the most alert and quick witted of the hill tribes and a race that takes keen interest in the outside world', were uncomfortable being labelled as "Excluded" or "Backward" and could not tolerate the idea of being swamped by the Indians.[16] Reid saw a way out of this situation by reviving the idea Hutton had given to the Indian Statutory Commission in 1928 of a North East Province or Agency embracing the entire hill fringe from the Lakher land in the south of the Lushai hills in a crescent shape to the hills of present-day Arunachal Pradesh. Included in this concept would be the Chittagong Hill Tracts, the areas inhabited by the Nagas, the Chins and the Shans States of Burma, the Khasi states and Manipur. A footnote mentions the possibility of including Sikkim, in the proposed Agency. The entire thrust of Reid's Note then follows: 'I would put his under a Chief Commissioner and he in turn would, I imagine, have to be divorced (as is Burma) from the control of the Government of India (presumably a federal body by then) and put perhaps under some appropriate department at Whitehall.'[17] Reid did not suggest the location of the headquarters of the proposed agency other than again referring to Hutton's "evidence" to the Joint Committee in which he suggested:[18]

I think it would be impossible to put the Assam districts directly under a Burma administration because of the difficulties of language and of the distances of communication through the hills, but I do think you could establish a centre somewhere near Manipur, for instance, from which, it would be possible to administer as Commissioner or Chief Commissioner, under the Burma Government, a block of frontier districts of Assam and North-West Burma.

The form of polity Reid envisaged for the Agency would be the operation of tribal institutions of local self-government. He admitted if this scheme were to take operation, finance would be difficult, but he found precedence for this in the history of the Crown Colonies. As to how such a province should be manned, he believed the Burma Frontier Service could be expanded to handle the administration of the Agency. The Governor felt the arrangements could be made by treaty guarantee and the imposition of a control over each community which would be adjusted to its state of development and which would be decided after reviewing each particular case. The amount of control would undoubtedly, he stressed, have to be considerable for a time, but he pointed out again 'it is essential that it should come from Whitehall, and not from India, to which the hill tracts are entirely alien'.[19]

Reid mentions that what he had proposed was only a tentative proposal in broad outline. Much detail would have to be filled in. Supposing it were decided, for whatever reason, that the plan he had outlined were impracticable, he felt it was necessary to consider alternatives. Reid recommended:[20]

I trust that sufficient has been said to prove that to place the Hills under the control of the Ministry of Assam as now constituted is utterly impossible and unworkable. A workable intermediate arrangement, though I would not myself advocate it, might be found in the formation of a Province of the Assam Valley only and in placing the hills under that, if they must be placed under a Provincial Government without any of the safeguards that at present exists.

As early as 1941 Reid was envisioning a constitution in the future in which the "backward areas" of Central India would require special protection. He did not see a similar situation for the "Mongolian areas" which in his opinion 'do not, and cannot, form part of India, and to recognize the fact is to recognize the necessity for special treatment'.[21]

The Governor-General Lord Linlithgow was amongst the first to receive a copy of Reid's confidential note. He thanked the Governor for the "valuable note" and informed that he would be sending a copy to L. S. Amery, the Secretary of State for India.[22] After reading the note, Amery commented:[23]

> Supposing that Pakistan does come off, there will be possibility of two Muslim areas, the whole of the states, Hindu British India … and finally at least an important primitive hill tribe area such as that which Reid has very interestingly outlined in the memorandum which reached me by the last mail.

So impressed was Amery of the plan that he gave a copy of the note to Reginald Coupland to be used by the Oxford Professor for writing the third and final volume on the constitutional problem in India. Amery, however, cautioned Coupland:[24]

> I do this on a confidential basis on the understanding that they will not be quoted and do not represent the official view of the Government concerned or this office. It would however, do no harm, I think if the broad idea suggested by Reid were publicly ventilated it you feel it is attractive.

Coupland did just this. He suggested in *The Future of India* the amalgamation of the Burma and India tribal areas and to be separated in some way from the Governments of India and Burma.[25] This first published opinion changed what originated as a private and confidential report into a scheme that wrongly took Coupland's name.[26]

The Burma Government was then functioning from a Simla hotel after it was forced to evacuate Rangoon following Japanese advance into Burma. When given a copy of Reid's note, the Burma administration found the plan both attractive and difficult to implement. The issue of amalgamating the hill areas of Burma and India was discussed at the meeting of the Committee on Scheduled Areas between 5 and 11 December 1942. One lone voice spoke for amalgamation and separation of the tribal areas. Four others listened attentively for four days while C. W. North of the Burma Foreign Service argued in support of implementing the plan. A vote was then taken whether the Scheduled Areas of Burma should be amalgamated in whole or in part with similar areas outside Burma to form a North East Frontier Agency. Four members voted that the amalgamation should not be resorted to; North gave a dissenting opinion. The Chairman of the Commission of Scheduled Areas of Burma, H. J. Mitchell, had prepared, shortly prior to the meeting referred to, a long confidential note on the subject which may have been read by other members and influenced their decision. Mitchell concluded his note by saying that the proposal for amalgamation of the Scheduled Areas of India and Burma into an agency administered from Whitehall should be dropped.[27]

The Governor of Burma Sir Reginald Dorman-Smith thought differently. He took a personal interest in the scheme. Dorman-Smith initially wanted the scheme extended to the hill areas under his charge, despite the decision taken by the Commission on Scheduled Areas. He was to admit later that he had gone wrong flirting with Reid's plan and that it had resulted in a delay in his Government's explanation to the frontier people of Burma what their reconstruction plans would be.[28] By August 1945, the proposition for a separate agency was dropped by Burma to prepare for other plans with the return of Government to Rangoon. In India though, the Crown Colony somehow continued to draw the attention of the last of the British administrators. There is an interesting reference that Lord Wavell, the Governor-General of India, was credited with taking to London a plan for a province to be solely ruled by Britain.[29] Could this have been the proposal for the North East Protectorate/Crown Colony?

What was the response of the hill people who would have "benefitted" from continued British rule? Since these plans were of a confidential nature the simple tribals knew little of its origins, development and collapse. When they did get wind of it there were mixed feelings. While Reverend L. Gatphoh, representing the Jaintia Hills in the Assam legislature hoped his hills would come into the colony/protectorate,[30] his friend, colleague and minister in the Assam Government, Reverend J. J. M. Nichols-Roy, who had returned on a Congress ticket from the Shillong Constituency, took the opposite stand. In his memorandum to the British Cabinet Mission, Nichols-Roy wrote that for some time rumours were afloat "all over India" that the British government wanted to form a new British protectorate with the hills of Assam. He informed, 'The people of these hills who are educated and who have had experience in this political rule are greatly against such a rule.' He went on to add: 'When the whole of India will get Independence,' he told the Mission, 'the hill people of Assam should be connected with the Province of Assam.'[31] Three Garos, Emonsing M. Sangma, Ganram R. Marak and Singdon K. Sangma, had only one purpose for their delegation to the British Parliamentary Delegation. They said that they were 'filled with dismay to hear the rumours that there is a plan of some British officials in Assam to exclude our districts from Assam and India'.[32] They opposed the plan as undesirable and demanded that their hills join with Assam and India. Japfu Phizo, the Naga leader, said some years later, 'Naga leaders stood against the scheme of colony because it would go against the interest of other eastern people.... We had to fight against the scheme for a long time.'[33] The Mizos of the Lushai Hills despite the stand they would later take on their union with Burma, voiced their disapproval and turned down the proposal through their Mizo Union. The party favoured autonomous status for the Lushai Hills within the province of Assam. The Mizos who had then just begun a movement to abolish *Lalship* (chieftainship) realised that any call for Mizo independence as well as continued British administration would only perpetuate that institution.[34] The opinion of the Burma tribes is not known.

By the middle of 1946, the plan was wound up.[35] By then the British had come to realise that it was ill-timed and conceived too late for it to take shape. Some were convinced that had the suggestions been made in the early 1930s, the Crown Colony could perhaps have been made possible by 1935. There were, no doubt, many advantages in support of the plan but the problems were far too many. Moreover, had the British pressed for its creation, their intentions would have come under suspect by the new Indian leadership.

III

James Philip Mills (1890–1960) was born on 18 February 1890 at Oak Lea, Norbury, England. Educated at Winchester College and Corpus Christi College, Oxford, he entered the Indian Civil Service (ICS) in 1913 and like J. H. Hutton before him, spent much of his administrative career in the Naga Hills. A civil servant with long experience in the region, he had served for several years in the Naga Hills, first as a subdivision officer and later as the district's deputy commissioner. He fruitfully used his administrative experience to author two monographs on the Nagas, *The Lhota Nagas*, 1922 and *The Ao Nagas*, 1926 and a number of articles on the anthropology of the region. In 1930, he became Honorary Director of Ethnology, Assam. Two years later, he was promoted as Secretary to the Government of Assam. An important assignment he held for several years was Adviser to the Governor of Assam for Tribal Areas and States. It was in this capacity that Mills wrote his note on the North East which became one of several studies by British officials before their political control of India came to a close. He retired from the ICS in mid-1947 just before India's independence. Using his service as colonial administrator and his interest in anthropology built up during his service in India, in 1947 he joined the faculty of Anthropology in the School of Oriental and African Studies, University of London, serving the institution till 1954.

As Adviser Tribal Areas and States (1943–1947), Mills advised both Sir Robert Reid and his successor, Sir Andrew Clow, the last British Governor of Assam. What motivated Mills to write and then publish a "secret" document *A Note on the Future of the Hill Tribes of Assam and the Adjoining Hills in a Self-*

governing India is nowhere explained. Perhaps he did not fully agree with what Reid had argued in his note, though it was rumoured in the India Office in London that Reid owed a great deal to Mills' inspiration; perhaps he found Reid's successor Andrew Clow's insensitivity to the tribal communities of the region a matter of concern. Perhaps he too felt that he should put in print his thoughts on the future of the tribal communities and their administration. Mills completed writing *A Note on the Future of the Hill Tribes of Assam and the Adjoining Hills in a Self-governing India* on 21 September 1945. Within a month, copies of his note were printed at the Assam Government Press, Shillong. Much had happened in India since Reid brought out his note. Mills wrote his note close to the end of the war and following the British Government's assurance that India's independence was a matter of time. Earlier the Cripps Mission 1942, despite its recall, had set in pace the advance of India's freedom. Following this, the Quit India Movement had given the British a rude shock of the potential of the Indian freedom struggle. In this background, Mills' note spoke of the future of the hill tribes in a self-governing India.

In the opening lines of the introduction, Mills says that his note dealt only with the position of the hill tribes when India would attain independence. No attempt was made to consider what modifications of policy may have been feasible or desirable within the framework of the Government of India Act, 1935. Writing in late 1945, he evidently envisioned Indian Independence in the not too distant future. 'Writing about my friends', he closes the introduction, 'whose welfare I seek above all else and (to) that extent I can be called biased'. The note has a section on the "Average Hillman", "the Khasi", there is a long section on local self-government and its development in the hills of the region; he traces the historical past before taking up their future. In Chapter 6, Mills echoed Reid's belief: 'There is no question of the tribes of the North Eastern Frontier being Indian.... Racially they are no more Indian than are the Burmans to whom they are akin.'[36] Then follow sections on religious background, increasing divergences, the geographical factor and the analogy of

Burma. He takes up the views of the hillmen and their future by referring to a representation of the hill tribes of Manipur dated 27 February 1945 and Naga meeting at Kohima on 10 April that year expressing their reservations of coming within a democratic constitution and suggesting the constitution of an administrative unit comprising the hill districts of Assam and the neighbouring hill tracts under the British Crown.[37] Mills then in a very short chapter takes the views of Robert Reid advocating separation of the hills from India. The idea had by then also been projected by, and he mentions Reginald Coupland, who as we have seen was wrongly credited for initiating the Crown Colony Plan.[38] Mills makes an interesting observation that Indian writers had seriously considered the full inclusion of the tribals of Central India in any new constitution. He was not aware of any writer contemplating the inclusion of the "Mongoloid block of North East India".[39]

The Governor's Secretary presented three possible alternatives. First, the inclusion of all the hills in Assam, which to his mind, was clearly impossible. Under the second alternative, the choice appeared to lie between 'the two extremes of excluding only some of the present tribal areas and including only the present Partially Excluded Areas'. He expressed a hope that all the hill tribes would eventually join Assam and be united under one government and 'it may be argued that to postpone the union of any now is to make the ultimate union of all more difficult'. He favoured that the union of all the hills be done at the same and appropriate time. The third alternative he discussed was that of temporarily excluding all the hills from Assam and according to them special treatment was designed on the lines of indirect rule to develop those indigenous institutions which still survived and to fit the tribes for eventual union with the province of Assam.[40]

If the hills were to be separated from the plains, Mills continued, the two alternatives appeared to form a province composed of districts, frontier tracts, agencies and states or to form a union of states from the outset. He strongly favoured the second alternative. Giving an outline of the scheme he desired, he suggested that homogenous areas could be termed "States" such as an "Abor State" covering all the tribes included under the term; a "Lushai

State" and a "Khasi State" which interestingly could include the
Garos and the Jaintias. Within this union of states would be sub-
states, a term borrowed from the Burma context where small or
intermingled tribes had been combined in a single sub-state. Full
use would be made of existing customs and institutions such as
the village councils by keeping power in ordinary affairs as local
as possible. There would be a gradation of levels of administration from this level to the Sub-state Council, the State Council
and the Governor's Council. Mills preferred the use of the term
union of states rather than province because it was likely to facilitate the inclusion of existing states which in a province would be
reduced to the status of districts or not be permitted to continue
in the ordinary sense. Moreover, the term "state" might engender a feeling of responsibility and cohesion of the people. With
regards to staff each state would require a political officer with an
additional political officer in the larger states. Two officers with
the status of commissioners for the charges North and South of
the Brahmaputra would oversee the administration. The object
of the administration being to guide rather than to govern, Mills
wanted the administrative staff to be as small as possible. In line
with the principle of paternal administration, the aim ought to
be indirect rule rather than administration.[41] For several reasons
Mills ruled out Shillong as the possible capital of the union of
states including the possibility of Shillong remaining the capital
of the Province of Assam and the difficulty of having an airstrip
nearby. Imphal appeared to him to offer better advantages. The
states' headquarters could be reached by air. Tripura and Sikkim,
if included, could be reached, Mills believed, with equal ease.
The 'Naga State would be within close reach and communication
with Burma, with which relations were likely to become closer,
would be easy.'[42]

Mills concluded his note that the union of states must be under
the control either of His Majesty's Government (HMG) or the
Government of India or as a possible compromise the Indian
Government might be given a form of mandate. He realised that
HMG might decline either to fund the union of states or to face
the political outcry (in India) with continued British control over

the hills. He felt that there were practical advantages of treating the union of states as a colony (after the precedents of the South African Protectorates of Basutoland, Bechuanaland and Swaziland) and till such time as they would sufficiently advance to unite with India the idea should not be rejected out of hand.[43] Governor Andrew Clow who had the advantage of reading both Reid's and Mills' notes had much to say, contrary to their views.

IV

While Mills was at work on his note, Reid's successor, Sir Andrew Clow, too was writing *The Future Government of the Assam Tribal Peoples*. Printed on 17 December 1945, the 52-page tract—the most detailed of the four notes we are concerned—was published around the middle of his term as Governor. When Clow took over as Governor in May 1942, Reid was dismayed that his successor was disinclined to see the future of the hills in the same light as he did. The Governor's position on the hill tribes and their future emerged early during his tenure. A recent book on the Shillong Raj Bhavan mentions that when Clow arrived in the Government House, the air was thick with what he called "fantastic ideas" about crown colonies and protectorates. The view Clow held from the start was that the plains and hill districts of Assam were so interdependent that their administrative separation would be injurious to both.[44] He pursued this belief to the hilt.

Clow outlined in the "preface" of the document that assuming Indian self-government at a very early date the question would arise what arrangements would be feasible and appropriate for the tribesmen of Assam. The aim throughout the tract had been to analyse the complicated situation and the possibilities these offered rather than to present a cut and dried case for any particular solution to the difficulties. Clow acknowledged his debt to John Hutton's note to the Indian Statutory Commission and Reid's and Mills' notes discussed earlier.[45] In Chapters 1 to 3, an

effort was made to set out a description of the tribes, the existing system of government and what concerned him as five preliminary factors, each of which raised issues of importance with
bearing on the soundness of any scheme that might be devised.
These preliminaries were the actual and potential scope of tribal
institutions, the capacity of the tribes for self-government, the
desires of the people concerned, the extent of cohesion among
the tribes and the relationship of the tribes with the outer
world.[46] Clow saw a possibility of fusion of the hills and plains
of Assam. The fusion he argued had gone some distance and the
Government of India Act, 1935, could be considered an endorse-
ment of the idea.[47] Chapter 5 focused on demolishing Reid's
and Mills' "grandiose plans" of a Crown Colony/Protectorate/
Agency. 'It seems most unlikely', he wrote:[48]

> the British Government which is prepared to set India and Burma on
> a self-governing footing should now undertake the administration and
> financial responsibility for a patchwork of sparsely populated hills
> lying where these hills do. Indian opinion would be equally strongly
> opposed to the constitution of a foreign territory with its natural
> boundaries. To ask an Indian government to contribute towards the
> maintenance of the imputed member would be regarded as adding
> insult to injury.

Apart from political difficulties, Clow had other reservations to
such a scheme being implemented. Geographically the proposed
colony, he wrote, would have a "fantastic shape" and would
completely lack cohesion. Economically, it would be isolated and
its interests would almost certainly be ignored by both India and
Burma, 'so that it would have to relapse even further into an economic self-sufficiency of a primitive type'. Administratively, there
would be difficulties in securing and retaining suitable cadres of
officers. The proposal, moreover, would involve a postponement
of responsibility in government and an actual step back for the
Partially Excluded Areas in their political and administrative
advance.[49]

To put things briefly, Clow's conclusions were that the northern hills—present-day Arunachal Pradesh and part of the Naga

Hills—should be treated as they were then, as a federal agency. He wrote that to include the other of the "Assam Hills" in the agency "would be the worst solution". The choice for the hills could be confined to two possibilities: a merger of the hills and plains of Assam in a manner which would conserve tribal rights and would recognise in an effective manner the different needs and outlooks of the two areas and the constitution of separate provinces for the hills and the plains with some administrative links. In either case, tribal institutions would have a place in the constitution and would exercise a considerable measure of local autonomy.[50] The Governor was aware that before the choice would be made, many fresh considerations would appear which would give weight to one of the alternatives or which might suggest something different. To his mind if a choice would have to be made he would opt for the first of the two alternatives. Shortly after he had completed the draft of *The Future Government of the Assam Tribal People*, Clow wrote to the Governor-General Lord Wavell and conveyed to him that after considerable hesitation he had come in favour of the first alternative. The two arguments, in particular, that appealed to him were: it would keep the hill tribes and plain tribes together and in the long run there was no future for the Assam hills in separation from the plains. He further went on to say that both the Khasi states and Manipur could be fitted into any scheme that was devised.[51]

The mind of this administrator and his understanding of the delicate situation of the future of the hill areas of North East India after 1945 is very well put across in the closing paragraph of the document:[52]

Assam is never likely to be as homogeneous as other provinces. The plains people are not so divided as those of the hills, but they are far from being a single people such as can be found in many equally large or larger areas in India. But this great collection of peoples, in hills and plains, have been set in a particular well-demarcated corner of the world and their welfare will depend on their proving able to live together. Assam should look to her diversity and to her capacity for toleration, which is greater than that of other provinces, to provide her strength.

Sir Charles Pawsey, the Deputy Commissioner of the Naga Hills from 1937, felt a need for the hill tribes to be given some say in their future administration. He believed that they should be allowed to run the administration of their own hills in their own way; they must be given security of land tenure; they must be protected from the rapacity of money lenders; they must have their freedom that they enjoyed under the British. He said it would be 'immoral for the British to hand the Nagas over to the tender mercies of the Assamese'. Pawsey had no "ideal plan" for the hills but he would agree with some form of interim government, with a steady building up of tribal councils to take the place of British officers, who should be retained for a number of years.[53] Clow's own desire was 'to see the Nagas and the other tribes cooperating with the Assamese in a regime acceptable to both'. By then the Nagas had become more vocal concerning their future. It is in reference to this that Clow wrote to Pawsey: 'The British are definitely going and the Naga idea of ten years' interim government if it means government by Britain, is a chimera.'[54]

The hill tribes had many options for their political future. The "native states" were free to associate with one or the other of the Dominion Governments, to federate among themselves or to stand alone. The British India territories could amalgamate, join Assam or ask for independence. The Naga Hills Tribal Area being unadministered was technically independent and at liberty to negotiate its own terms—or bide for time. There was by then no illusion of British permanence in India. The tribesmen, as will become apparent, were given very little to say in these matters. Clow completed his five years as the last British Governor of Assam on 4 May 1947. He put his thoughts down rather succinctly in a note he wrote before handing over charge to Sir Akbar Hydari, the first Indian Governor of Assam:[55]

> The trouble of course is that we have not the time we would like, and that in the past we tended to assume that we had much longer. The main thing now is to get the tribal people thinking within the limits of the practical, and my own profound conviction is that they should plump for cooperation and get the best bargain they can.

V

Philip Francis Adams arrived in India as a young ICS officer on 14 December 1937 and was among the last of the cadre of officers recruited for service. The war years put a halt to recruitment for this "steel frame" of the Indian administration. He was for several years attached to the Assam administration and posted as assistant commissioner of the Naga Hills District in charge of the Mokokchung Subdivision. Together with Charles Pawsey, the deputy commissioner, they were responsible for the administration of these hills during the entire war years. Pawsey was knighted for the splendid effort of administering the hills during the difficult war years. Adams received a Master of the British Empire (MBE). Adams was for several months Adviser to the Governor of Assam, a position he filled after Mills put in his papers. We may assume that it was while he was in this office and perhaps working on the same table that Adams wrote *Some Notes on a Policy for the Hills Tribes of Assam*. The 19-page tract was printed on 5 August 1947, 10 days before India's independence, by which Adams had resigned from service.

Adams' note, quite unlike those of Reid, Mills and Clow, does not go into any detail and makes little reference to any one of the hill people. In this delightful and insightful note, he sums up much of what the policy for the hill tribes should be. He makes no reference to the other three notes. It is as if a personal last line before demitting office. He writes in his introduction that the future of the "backward people", including the tribals of the North East, had suffered considerably from the lack of any coordinated and consistent policy towards them. In the absence of any central authority over them, the policy towards these people had been left to the provinces concerned. The consequence according to him was that they received somewhat sporadic attention being overshadowed by other political and administrative questions.[56] Adams classified three objectives towards a policy for the hill tribes. He first turned his attention to the political objectives. He observed that the tribes of Assam are a distinct racial stock and they in no way formed a cohesive political unit. To this situation was the reality that all the hill districts were deficit areas and were in no position to manage the cost of administration. Surrounded as they were by more prevailing neighbours, Adams believed that it would be impracticable, even if desirable by some sections, to establish the hills as independent areas. To his mind, union of the hills with Burma was impractical other than those contiguous to that frontier. Communications was linked with India. Moreover, Burma would not in all likelihood take on the responsibility to bear the cost of the administration of these hills. Adams was very practical. By the time he wrote his note, preparations were on for the transfer of power from Britain to India. 'Everything points to the conclusion that the union or linkage must be with India,' he wrote.[57] And like Clow, he suggested that arrangements be made to allow the cultural and racial differences of these areas with those of the plains within a framework of political unity. Adams was of the view that the hill communities should be integrated with India and placed within the Assam administration and that the Centre coordinate the policy.[58] Adams appeared to have an idea of the social problem of tribal societies undergoing change and the need to have a study on the communities before policy be implemented. He was of the opinion that as long as the administration lacked detailed knowledge of the communities, the administration could do little more than guide its main lines of development.[59] To his mind, the economic objective was to raise the standard of living of the people to the maximum having regard to such social considerations as policy would determine.[60]

Adams felt it was necessary that each tribe be considered individually before determining the policy towards them. To collectively form a policy towards them would not have the desired effect. He suggested that the tribes be given political and administrative training to develop unity among the tribes and that delegation of authority be delegated slowly. Citing examples of the pace and the effect of change in Africa, Russia and Turkey, Adams was personally not for gradual but rapid change and development.[61] The agency to assist in this process he believed were the village councils. He used an interesting expression to "constitutionalise autocracy" by reviving or developing conciliar activity. Above these councils could be advisory councils for all the hill areas.

Adams suggested in this note, using the Lushai chiefs as an analogy, that the chiefs' positions were being diminished and that the chiefs were trying to get government support to maintain their privileges while decreasing their obligations. Adams wrote that government should constitutionalise the chiefs' positions by giving recognition to the elders and that instead of the chiefs being recognised as village authority they should be the chiefs in council.[62] This was not done for any of the tribes in the adjustment with the transfer of power. Today, the Khasis are debating on the issue of giving constitutional recognition to their traditional chiefs the *Syiems*, *Lyngdohs* and other functionaries.[63]

Towards the close of the note, Adams suggests that as the provinces would in all likelihood not be able to bear the cost of administration of the hill areas, this responsibility should rest with the central government. Adams called for a coordinated approach to the administration of the Tribal, Excluded and the Partially Excluded Areas though they were at different degrees of advance. Taking a position as spokesperson for the people it would be preferable that all the peoples come under one administration and not divided between the centre and the provinces.[64] He goes on to say that an advisory department should be created to coordinate policy, provide technical assistance and advise on particular problems. It would be necessary that the provincial administration coordinate and implement the hill policy. He advocated the creation of an advisory committee for the hill areas to formulate and review policy and to make recommendations for the future. To this committee should be added representatives of the hill people and of the government. This could be the start of a Hills Council. Underscoring all what he wrote Adams concluded his note that it was essential 'that if progress and development is not to be delayed government must, at the earliest possible date, arrive at a settled policy toward the hill people of Assam'.[65]

VI

All four officials were very concerned with the future of the hill people in an independent India. Reid had used the term "federal" for India which indicates that he could foresee the transfer of power. By the time Mills and Clow wrote their documents, the stage had much advanced towards independence. Adams' note was not intended for the British Indian administration. Published only 10 days before India's independence, it was meant for the Indian state to ponder and implement. None of the authors, however, make mention of political consciousness in the hill areas other than passing references to the establishment of political associations. Much less, indeed nothing is said of the Indian freedom struggle in Assam and political activity of this form in the hills. Two of the authors focused attention on the separation of the hills from Assam and from both India and Burma. The tribal response to the scheme was different to different tribes.[66] Archibald Ian Bowman, who was briefly attached to the Lushai Hills administration, informed Reid that he had not the chance of seeing the Governor's scheme, 'though I heard a lot about it—it was very popular with the people I worked among but I gathered from Sir Andrew Clow that it had been scrapped'.[67] The timing of the idea and attempts to implement it were not opportune given the fact that India was on the verge of getting independence and that Burma too would benefit from the collapse of colonial rule. Other than the utopian plan, much of what else was suggested was not taken for consideration by the Indian Government such as the well-advanced discussions to amalgamate the tribal inhabited areas of the two administrations, to demarcate the Indo-Burma border on ethnic lines, the suggestion to have a referendum or plebiscite to the hill people to decide their future or the idea to allow the Lakhers to join Burma. Tribals, particularly the inhabitants of the "Naga Tribal Areas", were not informed and taken into confidence of their future. Here lay the seeds of future problem and discontent.[68]

The clubbing together of the hill areas with Assam after 1947 would continue for only some years. Clow's alternative, as time was to show, was not the better of the two choices. Mills with some foresight had suggested the formation of small states. His "Abor State" has in time become the larger Arunachal Pradesh. Likewise, the suggestion he gave of a "Khasi State" to include the Garos and Jaintias has taken shape in Meghalaya. Similarly, the "Lushai State" and the "Naga State" have become Mizoram and Nagaland. It is also interesting to note the reference to Sikkim. The Himalayan state has joined the seven states of the North East for special attention and funding under the North Eastern Council. All four officials were concerned that the traditional institutions of governance should be cherished and used. Of late there has been a resurgence of the institutions. There is an ongoing debate in the region both appreciating and questioning the role of the traditional institutions of governance.

As India's independence drew near, agreements were reached in early July 1947 between Sir Akbar Hydari, the Governor of Assam and the heads of the 25 Khasi states on the necessity of maintaining the unity of India by the states joining the Indian Union for defence, foreign affairs and communication.[69] A few days before Independence, they signed the Standstill Agreement. The chiefs agreed that from 15 August 1947 all existing arrangements between the province of Assam and the Indian Dominion on the one hand and the Khasi states on the other should continue to be in force for a period of two years or until new/modified arrangements would be arrived at.[70] Getting the states to sign the Instrument of Accession proved a difficult job for the Governor. Twenty chiefs signed the Instrument of Accession at his official residence on 15 December 1947 and some force and tact got the remaining five to do the same in the early months of 1948.[71] Generally, the Khasi states had no desire to join Pakistan. The *Syiem* of Cherra, it is reported, did flirt with the local authorities in Sylhet before signing the Instrument of Accession but was warned by Hydari against playing the game. Many of the Khasi chiefs felt that their states had much to lose with the implementation of the Radcliffe Award because the new international boundary with East Pakistan along Sylhet and Mymensingh districts was based on geographical and not ethnic considerations. The Khasi states abutting on Sylhet had much of their territory along the foothills and into the Sylhet plains. Their *hats* were located along what would become the boundary. The *Syiem* of Nongstoin's resistance and eventual acceptance of the Instrument of Accession, however, did not stop his nephew from making an appeal to the United Nations Organisation, concerning the way in which Nongstoin, one of the larger of the Khasi states, was intimidated into joining India.[72] Pakistan, in the meanwhile, had embarked on a virtual economic blockade of the Khasi and Jaintia Hills. The producers of oranges, pineapples and *tezpat* found no market for their produce in Pakistan. The export of rice into the hills was stopped. Such trade restrictions had an adverse effect on the economy as most of the produce were perishable items. The object of the blockade was to put pressure on the hillmen and create among them a feeling that they could be better off in Pakistan. The Indian Government immediately came to the rescue of the producers by constructing an airstrip, which enabled the produce to be airlifted to Calcutta and by dispatching much-needed rice.[73]

The Khasi states had acceded to India but could take no decision to merge their states. Sardar Vallabhbhai Patel visited Shillong during 1–2 January 1948. His meeting with the chiefs ended in a stalemate over the merger issue, for they said that only a duly constituted durbar of the states could decide on such a move. Sixteen months later, the Khasi States Constitution making durbar was inaugurated on 29 April 1949. In July that year, J. J. M. Nichols-Roy's stand for including the district within Assam was put to test against the *Syiem* of Jirang's demand that the Khasi and Jaintia Hills should form one united administration outside Assam which was possible under the provisions of both the Instrument of Accession and the Draft Constitution of India. The vote went with a 46–40 decision in favour of the chiefs.[74] Nichols-Roy had then only one alternative—to use his position as minister in the Assam Government and membership of the Constituent Assembly to undo the defeat in the smaller constitution-making durbar.

Meanwhile, all was calm in the Garo Hills, which did not appear to have had any strong popular reaction or support to independence, partition or incorporation into Assam. Only one person reacted sharply to the demarcation of the border with East Pakistan. Mikat Sangma had been educated at Calcutta. Returning home after his education he proclaimed himself chief of the southern parts of the Garo Hills. Failing to get the title recognised, he was charged with sedition, arrested and imprisoned. He escaped, took to the hills, collected a band of followers and demanded that the frontier of East Pakistan with the Garo Hills should be withdrawn 30 miles into the Mymensingh plains.[75] Nothing came out of Sangma's brave stand. Partition separated and continues to separate one large segment of the Garo tribe from those living in Mymensing District of East Pakistan from the sizeable group in the hills. Here too there was serious disruption to life and trade between the hills and the plain areas.

The transfer of power to Burma in 1948 and the better bargaining position given to the Burma hill tribes gave encouragement to parts of frontier India to look for incorporation into Burma. There were a number of opinions for the people of the former Lushai Hills. Some sought an independent state; other wished to remain in India as the Mizo Union had expressed, if only for a period of 10 years; while others hoped that the Lushai Hills could be tagged with the Chin Hills of Burma.[76] The Mizos were quite content to be under the British rule but had to consider their future in the event of British withdrawal. Many of their leaders wrote to the powers that were in Britain in a last bid to express their concern for being left to look after their own destiny. The Secretary of the Lushai Chiefs Council wanted to opt for Burma and so did Lalbiakthanga, the President of the United Mizo Freedom Organisation.[77] Similar views were expressed by "a Lushai" who wrote in *The Manchester Guardian*:[78]

> If is absolutely out of the question for us to be allowed to remain under British rule or if there are no means of receiving help or

protection from the British Government, and if Indian authorities are not genuinely considerate to our case, it seems inevitable that we shall somehow or other desire to link ourselves with Burmese people who are more akin to us by custom and heredity. Such desire would not be a mere whim nor would it be meant as an act of disloyalty to the new India. It might be the only way open for us.

It is difficult to believe that 'when the country became independent, the Mizo people joined most heavily the big family of diverse people which constitutes the great Indian nation'.[79] In these hills, 15 August 1947 was not celebrated with any fanfare. A suggestion by volunteers of the Mizo Union to have a procession to mark the occasion was resisted by dissidents in the party. Not a single tricolour was raised anywhere for fear of those advocating independence and incorporation with Burma.[80] A meeting was convened on 14 August at Aizawl by Leonard Peters, the Superintendent of Lushai Hills, which some 50 accredited leaders of the Mizo political parties attended. There they accepted the fait accompli of the inclusion of their hills into India, with a demand that they should be allowed to opt out of the Union within a period of 10 years and that the Chin Hill Regulation and Bengal Eastern Frontier Regulation should continue to operate for them.[81]

The Naga National Council (NNC) set up in 1946 claimed even in its inception to represent the various Naga tribes. It emerged when the Nagas, just as other tribal groups in the region, were galvanised into political activity to have some say in what seemed an uncertain future. It was to this group of educated Nagas led by prominent Aos and Angamis that Jawaharlal Nehru, the prime minister of the interim government, addressed a letter. He appealed that the Nagas should merge with Assam. He assured that Naga tradition and custom would be honoured and that they should not have a fear of being swarmed by the people from other parts of the country.[82] On 19 February 1947, this Council met at Kohima to discuss their future. Copies of the memorandum drawn up at this meeting were sent to the Viceroy, to the British Prime Minister and the Secretary of State for India. Lord Simon and Winston Churchill also received the appeal. It sought to present the case of the Naga people for self-determination with 'financial provisions for a period of 10 years, at the end of which the Naga people will be left to choose any form of government under which they themselves choose to live'.[83] Mountbatten and Clow were sympathetic to the appeal. The Governor admitted that the Council was self-constituted and was 'as representative a body as can be found of the more educated Nagas'. His superior interpreted the memorandum to mean 'an interim form of British Government'.[84] Such concern was not shown in London where the memorandum was shelved without any acknowledgement from the prime minister or the secretary of state, 'presumably because doubts have expressed as to whether the NNC was fully representative of the Nagas.'[85]

A second memorandum was drawn up on 19 May. This clarified that the 10-year interim government might be a government conducted by the Nagas themselves with full legislative, executive and judicial powers and that the guardian power might, for defence, position such a force as might be required.[86] By such time factionalism has set in with several aspirants for the post of standard bearer. One leader who differed in the line of approach of the Naga National Council was Zapu Phizo. In July, he led a deputation to Delhi with the ultimatum that the Nagas would declare independence from 14 August 1947. It must have come as a surprise to Phizo and his friends that Mahatma Gandhi, whom they met on 19 July 1947, recognised the Naga right to independence outside India.[87] Meanwhile, back home the larger faction had come to an understanding with Sir Akbar Hydari in what is called the "Nine Point Agreement". The NNC discussed the administrative and constitutional changes with the Governor over three days in late June. The agreement recognised 'the right of the Naga to develop themselves according to their freely expressed wishes'. According to the last article of the agreement, it was open to the Nagas after the expiry of the 10-year period of the agreement to ask either for its extension or for a new agreement regarding the future of the Naga people.[88]

Akbar Hydari had wanted some breathing time within which a final agreement could be reached. This was never to be, for no sooner had the Naga representatives signed the document when accusations were levelled that the wording of the ninth article had changed substantially in meaning between what was agreed to in discussion and what appeared in the document.[89] There was nothing in the controversial clause that suggested that the Nagas participation in India was temporary. The government interpreted the agreement to mean that the Nagas could ask for revision with the framework of the Indian Union only after 10 years. One section of the NNC interpreted the clause to suggest that they could ask for independence, another supported the agreement on the ground that it was a first step towards self-government.

In this background, it was not possible for the Nagas to have celebrated Indian independence "with great excitement and enthusiasm", as one is made to believe.[90] Southern Angami, Manipur Nagas of the North Cachar Hills through the President of the "Naga State" declared their independence from India from 14 August and had even started negotiating with Pakistan.[91] Phizo too had threatened that the Nagas would secede. These developments, no doubt, cautioned Delhi's policy towards the Nagas. The one serious lapse, however, on the part of Delhi was to incorporate the Naga Hills and the other tribal districts within Assam, instead of considering some of the suggestions discussed earlier in this note. Indian independence had its repercussions across the Naga Hills into Burma where the Nagas were restive. The unnatural division along the watershed had witnessed the relative advance of the larger Naga tribe in the North East hills of India to forcefully press that they be heard. Nagas of Burma could see these developments and consequently wished to unite with their fellow Nagas across the border.[92] Despite the official stand to amalgamate the Naga inhabited areas, this was lost sight of when the transfer of power took place. Nothing was done to amend an accident in history. The time was just not opportune to settle this issue.

These demands for a special status for the Nagas in independent India also had their repercussions across their hills into neighbouring Manipur. In the Manipur tribal areas, political awakening had just about coalesced. The tribe there took advantage of the winds of change to suggest the incorporation of their hills into the contiguous Naga and Lushai Hills districts. In this the Maos got a leader in Athikho Daiho who launched a no-tax campaign in the Naga-dominated areas. South Manipur with its Kuki people allowed the Mizo Union to spread its influence into their hills and demand for the integration of all Mizo peoples into one administration.[93] Nonetheless such legitimate wants could not be given to them for the complexities of realigning state's boundaries had not been considered at that point of time.

Two months before partition, Muhammed Ali Jinnah received a letter from R. Ahsan of the Calcutta District Muslim League. Ahsan lamented: 'The loss of Calcutta and Assam is terrible.... If we get the excluded areas of Santhal Parganas, Khasi and Jaintia Hills, Lushai Hills and Naga Hills, we will get room for expansion.' The letter had an enclosure relating to the India Plan in which it was stated that the Khasi–Jaintias Hills, Garos Hills, Naga Hills and the Lushai Hills should be given the option to join Pakistan or Hindustan. It put forth two reasons. 'Because the tribals were not Hindus and Congress did not represent them and as they were demanding separate electorates, it was only the League that was in a position to meet their aspirations,' Ahsan said. Secondly, as the areas inhabited by the tribals was a special charge and obligation of the British Government, 'Britain owes it to the poor tribals ... to give them protection.... The British Government is morally, constitutionally and legally bound to protect them. The tribals are a trust of civilisation,' he wrote.[94] This together with the plans for placing Assam and its hills for handing over territories to Pakistan were matters of serious concern for Assam. Fortunately, Assam had in Gopinath Bordoloi, its Premier, a man who stood up to counter the claims of the Muslim League for including Assam in Pakistan. Earlier the Assam Legislative Assembly, fearing Assam would be tagged to Bengal, adopted a resolution moved by Bordoloi expressing strong resentment over the Cabinet Mission proposal to place Assam in

Section C. Assam and its hill districts would be linked with India. The threads were strong enough to prevent a breakaway.

Meanwhile, the subcommittee of the Indian Constituent Assembly on the Assam Tribal and Excluded Areas with Bordoloi as chairman and with Nichols-Roy, Rupnath Brahma, the Bodo tribal leader, A. V. Thakkar, a social worker among the Central India tribes, and B. N. Rau, the constitutional adviser to the Constituent Assembly, as members was touring the hill region to assess the tribal situation. Among other information, Bordoloi was concerned with what he learned: 'We are really pained', he said,[95]

> to learn that the former Governors of Assam and their supporters have been advocating in England and in other places for a Crown Colony to be formed with the entire hill region of Assam and the northern hill region of upper Burma. After going through the administrative files, I have fully come to understand that the then rulers in Delhi made a plan to form such a Crown Colony because they foresaw the possibility of such a colony. The separatist tendency was firmly rooted in the minds of the hill people.

Bordoloi reiterated the separatist tendency of the hill areas again in the Constituent Assembly when the Sixth Schedule was taken up for discussion.[96] Apparently, Bordoloi's policy towards the tribes at that time was to integrate them in a Gandhian way. The Report of the Bordoloi Committee expressed concern that the hill people had not "assimilated" with Assam.[97]

The response of the hill people of North East India towards partition and independence were, therefore, varied. Nagas took advantage of the emergence of East Pakistan to negotiate with India. Some of the Khasi states realised they had much to lose in joining India but found that it was the only situation open for them. To some extent, the Mizos were brought nearer realities and their hope of getting finance from India and being left alone to spend it was shattered when the Advisory Committee of the Constituent Assembly visiting Aizawl bluntly told them that they could not expect to secure education in an India from which they were separated.[98] Tribals in Manipur and Tripura were beginning to speak for themselves and expected a better deal in India. The Garos expected no problem in joining Assam. The tribals of present-day Arunachal Pradesh, to the north of the Brahmaputra valley, did not have any say in the matter. There political activity had not even begun. In part this was the effect of the British policy of treating them as beyond the line of British administration. By 15 August, all these hills had been incorporated into India. The integration of the region into the Indian Union, however, was not quite complete until Tripura, Manipur and the Khasi states signed their Instruments of Accession and merger agreements with the new Indian Government. Tripura was the first "native state" to accede to India. The merger took place on 9 September 1949. Manipur signed the merger agreement on 21 September 1949 but it was officially announced on 15 October 1949. The Khasi states had refused to sign the instrument of merger. The revived Federation of Khasi States, meanwhile, had taken shape and had begun operating under the provisions of the Instrument of Accession. Despite their representation to the Constituent Assembly and the continued dialogue with the Central authorities, they found to their surprise that from 26 January 1950 their hills had become a district of Assam.[99]

Tripura and Manipur became Union Territories in 1950 and evolved their own policy towards their tribals. The Garo, Khasi, Jaintia, Mikir, North Cachar and Lushai Hills were provided District Councils to safeguard their forest, land and tradition. The Sixth Schedule provided these tribals the opportunity to take care of their fears and aspirations. Only the Nagas wanted to have nothing to do with the provisions of the Schedule for the situation there was still very fluid.

These hill people could have lived peaceably in Assam but for the attitude of some Assamese legislators. Hardly had the British left when Assam's representatives in the Constituent Assembly advanced assimilation views. Strong protests were raised by them in the Assembly when the Sixth Schedule was taken up for discussion. Kuladhar Chaliha saw in the Schedule that the 'British mind is still there. There is the old separatist tendency and you want to keep them away from us', he is recorded to have said.[100] His friend, Rohini Kumar Choudhury, had forgotten that only 30 years earlier Assam's leaders had called for removing the hill areas from the province because they were backward and deficit areas. 'We want to assimilate the tribal people', he said, 'we were never given that opportunity so far'.[101] They were strangely ignorant that their friend in the Constituent Assembly, Nichols-Roy, had some years earlier submerged his Khasi identity when he referring to "we Assamese" in their reaction to the province being placed in category C of the Cabinet Mission Plan 1946.[102] The tribals did not want to be assimilated in this fashion. It would not be long before the cordial relations between the Assamese and the hill people would end.

VII

For various reasons the four plans were not implemented. They failed to influence policy shortly before and at the time of the transfer of power from Britain to independent India. They never had full public support. However, we are only today realising the very perceptive and detailed thought that went into the mind and the writings of these officials, many of whom left their service soon after the transfer of power. The Crown Colony/Protectorate Plan continues to play on the minds of some groups. What also becomes apparent in the policy towards the hill people of the region was the lack of appreciating the tribal mind and lifestyle by the new rulers of India. Moreover, the administrative transition from what had been in operation for long to that under the new dispensation was all too sudden. That the hill people were unprepared for what was to come there is no doubt. The Mizos, and more so the Lakhers, could have been asked if they wanted a referendum to decide which dominion they would opt for. The boundary between the Khasi and Jaintia Hills and even the Garo Hills and Sylhet and Mymensing districts of East Pakistan did not take the local situation into consideration. The border issue continues to remain sensitive along the Indo–Myanmar and Indo–Bangladesh frontiers. These will continue to be problems as long as people who belong to a common and shared tradition remain separated.

It is unfortunate that despite the serious issues of the inclusion or separation of the hill areas in the Indian union, few national leaders personally visited the region to dialogue with the tribal leaders. Nehru had last visited the region in December 1945. Vallabhhai Patel made a hurried visit to settle integration issues. Bordoloi's connection we have noted. Tribal leaders who earlier interacted with district administrators were drawn into discussions with politicians and high-government officials. Some had perforce to go to Delhi as did Nagas and Khasis. In October 1952, Nehru made a tour of the North East. His secret note after the tour apart from several other points had this advice:[103]

> There is a tendency in Assam for what is called integration of these tribes and for the establishment of a homogeneous State. This really means merging in a cultural and like sense the tribal people into the Assamese. I think that this is not desirable movement and instead of achieving its objective, will lead to conflicts and difficulties. There is bound to be a process of assimilation, but this will have to be developed by itself through education and contacts without any special effort. Indeed, the effort should be in retaining their individual culture, much of which is certainly worth retaining. They have an innate sense of art and are a strong and virile people. It would be a great pity if in this respect they were brought down to a lower level, even though they may advance in some other ways.

That the Naga armed struggle has become the longest effort faced by the Indian Government is in large part due to the mishandling of the negotiations in the months shortly before and after Independence. It has become a legacy of independence and partition. After many years of struggle by the Nagas and the continued negotiations over these 50 years and more the peace process appears to be moving ahead towards an amicable solution. A new concern has emerged. Meitheis and Khasis are going back to the process of the integration of Manipur and the 25 Khasi states into the Indian Union. They have raised a number of pertinent questions on the use of intimidation, sovereignty and other issues.

It is the hope of many in the region today that the events of 1946–1950, which have caught up with the present, should not be a cause to disturb the lives of the people. Indeed, the aftermath of independence and partition for the people of the region has been traumatic for many. To be fair to the Indian state, the quality of life, security and special provisions the Constitution has provided for the tribes inhabiting the North East Hills is far more comfortable than that experienced by the hill people in the neighbouring states. A concerned and sincere policy for the region, all-round development and continued dialogue will provide hope for tomorrow.

NOTES AND REFERENCES

1. D. K. Fieldhouse. 1976. *Economics and Empire 1830–1914*. London: Weidenfeld and Nicholas, pp. 80–81; 173–175.
2. There are numerous histories of British expansion into the region. Among these may be read, Edward Gait. 1906. *A History of Assam*, Calcutta: Thaker Spink and Co.; H. K. Barjpujari. 1990–1993. *A Comprehensive History of Assam*, vols. 1–5, Publication Division Government of Assam, Guwahati; H. K. Barpujari et al. 1977–1980. *Political History of Assam*, vols. 1–3, Guwahati; Priyam Goswami. 2012. *A History of Assam Yandabo to Partition 1826–1947*. Delhi: Orient BlackSwan.
3. D. R. Syiemlieh. 1989. *British Administration in Meghalaya: Policy and Pattern*. New Delhi: Heritage Publishers, pp. 181–187.
4. D. R. Syiemlieh, 'Response of the North Eastern Hill Tribes of India towards Partition and Independence', *Indo-British Review: A Journal of History*, XVII(1): 27.
5. For details on this pattern of administration see the relevant chapters in, J. B. Bhattacharjee. 1978. *The English and the Garos*. New Delhi: Radiant Publishers and D. R. Syiemlieh. 1989. *British Administration in Meghalaya: Policy and Pattern*. New Delhi: Heritage Publishers.
6. S. K. Chaube has a critique of this policy in *Hill Politics in Northeast India*. 1999. New Delhi: Orient Longman, pp. 11–30.
7. Milton S. Sangma, Presidential Address, *Proceedings of the North East India History Association, Fifteenth Session*, Doimukh, 1994, pp. 1–22.

8. For an update of the research on the history of the region see, D. R. Syiemlieh. 2000. *Survey of Research in History on North East India 1970–1990*. New Delhi: Regency Publications.

9. 'The Crown Colony Scheme for North East India 1928–1947: An Analysis of Official Views', *Proceedings of the NEIHA*, Second Session, Dibrugarh, 1981, Shillong, 1982, pp. 172–178; 'The Crown Colony—Protectorate for North East India: The Tribal Response', *Proceedings of the North East India History Association*, 11th Session, Imphal, 1990, Shillong, 1991, pp. 206–211; *Response of the North East Hill Tribes of India Towards Partition, Independence and Integration: 1946–1950*, Prativa Devi Memorial Lectures, Guwuhati University, 2003, pp. 1–27; 'Before We Go Home: Three British Plans for North East India 1941–1945', *Proceedings of the North East India History Association*, 26th Session, Aizawl, 2006, pp. 252–264; 'The Crown Colony Plan for the Hills of North East India: Concept to Collapse', Sajal Nag, et al. (ed.). 2007. *Making of the Indian Union: Merger of Princely States and Excluded Areas*. New Delhi: Akansha Publishing House, pp. 242–248.

10. For an autobiography, read Robert N. Reid. 1966. *Years of Change in Bengal and Assam*. London: Ernest Benns Ltd with a Foreword by Ian Stephens. Also, refer to Daralin Suting. 1993. 'Sir Robert Neil Reid in North East India: a Biographical Sketch,' M. Phil Dissertation, NEHU.

11. Note, p. 12. The references from this text and subsequent notes of Mills, Reid and Adams are from the pages of their original texts.

12. A Note on the Future of the Present Excluded, Partially Excluded and Tribal Areas of Assam, p. 13.

13. Ibid., p. 14.

14. Ibid.

15. Ibid., pp. 14–15.

16. Ibid., p. 15.

17. Ibid., pp. 16–17. The footnote on this page reads:

> There is much to be said for including Sikkim in the proposed Agency. Firstly, this state is essentially Mongolian and Non-Indian and secondly, the political officer there is the channel of communication between the central government and the Governments of Bhutan and Tibet, both of which countries have long frontiers with Assam. It is obviously advantageous that the political officer in Sikkim should be in constant touch with and under the control of, the head of the Agency along the frontier of which questions with Bhutan and Tibet are constantly arising.

18. Cited by Reid, Note... pp. 16–17.

19. Ibid., pp. 17–18.

20. Ibid., p. 22.

21. This is the closing sentence of the note, p. 22.

22. India Office Library and Records (IOLR), London, Reid Collection, MSS Eur E/178/4(g), letter dated 5 January 1942.

23. Ibid., Amery Collection, MSS Eur F/125/11, Amery to Linlithgow, 24 March 1942. J. B. Bhattacharjee had this to say in his Presidential Address *World War II*

& India: A Fifty Years Perspective at the Modern History Section, Indian History Congress, Gorakhpur Session, 30 December 1989–1 January 1990, p. 32:

> The historians of Modern India have also missed a parallel development in the north-east which, if it had matured, could have resulted in another partition, alongside the birth of Pakistan. I am referring to so-called "Crown Colony" scheme propounded by the Governor of Assam Sir Robert Reid and a few British officers.

24. Ibid., LP& J7/6789, Amery to Coupland, 30 July 1943.
25. Reginald Coupland. 1943. *The Future of India*, Part III. London: Oxford University Press, p. 164.
26. For instance, see the section 'The Crown Colony' in S. K. Chaube, *Hill Politics in Northeast India*. 1999. New Delhi: Orient Longman, pp. 76–79.
27. IOLR, M/4/2803, 'The Scheduled Areas of Burma', a confidential note prepared by H. J. Mitchell, 20 March 1942.
28. IOLR, M/4/2803/Dorman-Smith to Pethick Lawrence, 13 August 1945.
29. IOLR, L/P&J/&/6787, Extract from a private and confidential letter from L. S. Amery to Lord Wavell, dated 10 August 1945.
30. *U Salonsar*, 1(26): 3, 31 December 1980.
31. J. J. M. Nichols-Roy. 1946. *Hill Districts of Assam: Their Future in the New Constitution of India*, Memorandum submitted to the British Cabinet Mission, p. 5.
32. IOLR, L/P &J 21/3115A, Memorandum of the People of the Garo Hills, Assam, India, to the Chairman of the British Parliamentary Delegation, 25 February 1945.
33. A. Z. Phizo to C. Rajagopalacharya, 22 November 1948 cited in V. K. Nuh, *Nalaland Church and Politics*, Kohima, p. 90.
34. S. K. Chaube, *Hill Politics in Northeast India*. 1999. New Delhi: Orient Longman, p. 175.
35. The fate of the Crown Colony for the hills of the North East and the hill areas of Burma was sealed in a minute of the secretary of state for India and Burma, dated 6 May 1946, IOLR, L/P&J/7/6787.
36. J. P. Mills. 1945. *A Note on the Future of the Hill Tribes of Assam and the Adjoining Hills in a Self-governing India*. Shillong: Assam Government Press, p. 9.
37. Ibid., p. 13.
38. Ibid., pp. 13–14.
39. Ibid.
40. Ibid., p. 17.
41. Ibid., pp. 18–20. The note developed in more detail the pattern of administration on pp. 21–33.
42. Ibid., p. 33.
43. Ibid.
44. Imdad Hussain. 2005. *From Residency to Raj Bhavan: A History of the Shillong Government House*. New Delhi: Regency Publications, pp. 115–116.
45. Clow. 1945. *The Future Government of the Assam Tribal Peoples*. Preface. Shillong: Government Printing Press.

46. Ibid., pp. 15–22.
47. Ibid., pp. 23–27.
48. Ibid., p. 29.
49. Ibid.
50. Ibid., p. 46.
51. Ibid. and IOLR, L/P&J/7/6787, Clow to Lord Wavell, 23 October 1945.
52. Clow, *The Future Government of the Assam Tribal Peoples*, p. 47.
53. Cambridge South Asia Archives, Pawsey Papers, Box 1, No. 5, Clow to Pawsey, 26 April 1947.
54. Ibid.
55. Ibid.
56. P. F. Adams. 1947. *Some Notes on a Policy for the Hill Tribes of Assam*, Shillong, p. 1.
57. Ibid.
58. Ibid., pp. 4–5.
59. Ibid., pp. 5–6.
60. Ibid., p. 6.
61. Ibid., pp. 7–9.
62. Ibid., pp. 13–14.
63. Read Bengt G. Karlsson. 2011. *Unruly Hills: Nature and Nation in India's Northeast*. New Delhi: Orient BlackSwan, Chapter 5: Indigenous Government, pp. 245–288.
64. Ibid., pp. 17–18.
65. Karlsson. 2011. *Unruly Hills: Nature and Nation in India's Northeast*, p. 19.
66. For details of this, see D. R. Syiemlieh. 1990. 'The Crown Colony—Protectorate for North East India: The Tribal Response', *Proceedings of the North East India History Association*, 11th Session, Imphal, pp. 206–211.
67. IOLR, Bowman Collection, MSS Eur F. 229/19, letter from Bowman to Reid dated 15 June 1947.
68. Several other notes of the last of British administrators on the theme of the future of the hill tribes of North East India include two other papers by J. P. Mills, 'A Note on Schemes of Tribal Self Government', 1 June 1946 and 'The Excluded and Partially Excluded Areas of Assam', 22 March 1947; John H. Hutton's, 'Problems of Reconstruction in the Assam Hills', Presidential Address at the Royal Anthropological Institute of Great Britain and Ireland, 1945.
69. A discussion concerning this appeared in *Ka Synjuk Lang ki Hima Khasi*, August 1947, pp. 1–3. Also, see D. Das (ed.). 1973. *Sardar Patel's Correspondence*, Vol. V, pp. 42–43, Ahmedabad: Navajivan Publication House.
70. L. L. D. Basan (comp.). 1948. *The Khasi States Under the Indian Union*. Shillong, pp. 1–3.
71. For full detail of this episode, see D. R. Syiemlieh. 1989. *British Administration in Meghalaya: Policy and Pattern*. New Delhi: Heritage Publishers, pp. 192–194.
72. IOLR, L/P&J/7110635, R. W. Selby to H. A. Rumbold, 13 April 1948; *The Sunday Statesman*, 28 March 1948. The enduring contribution of the late R. T. Rymbai, assistant to the political agent, Khasi Hills, at the time of the integration of Indian states into the Indian Union, was a series of articles 'Integration of the Khasi States', which came out in four parts. See, *The Shillong Times*, 21–24 April 1997.

40   David R. Syiemlieh

73. For an account of the economic effects of partition, see L. S. Gassah. 1984. 'Effects of Partition on the Border Marketing of Jaintia Hills', in J. B. Ganguly (ed.), *Marketing in North-East India*, 65–67. Guwahati: Omsons Publications; A. R. Choudhury. 1972. 'Sylhet and its trade with Highland Neighbours', *The Second Convention of Trade, Commerce and Industry* (Souvenir, p. 42. Shillong; Nari Rustomji. 1971. *Enchanted Frontiers*. Bombay: Oxford University Press, p. 110; D. Das (ed.). 1973. *Sardar Patel's Correspondence*. Ahmedabad: Navajivan Publication House.
74. L. G. Shullai. 1975. *Ki Hima Khasi*. Shillong: L. G. Shullai, pp. 11–13.
75. Gabrielle Bertrand. 1958. *Secret Lands Where Women Reign*. London: Robert Hale, pp. 114–115.
76. S. K. Chaube, *Hill Politics in Northeast India*. 1999. New Delhi: Orient Longman, pp. 161–163; Lal Rinawma. 1986. (unpublished). 'Political Development in Mizo Hills 1935–1965'. MPhil Dissertation, NEHU, p. 41.
77. IOLR, L/P&J/7/10635. Letter from Ch. Ngrura, Secretary Lushai Chiefs Council to Lord Listowel, 17 October 1947; Telegram from Lalbiakthanga, President United Mizo Freedom Organisation to Lord Listowel and Thakin Nu, 9 September 1947.
78. IOLR, L/P&J/7/10635. Cutting from *The Manchester Guardian*, 3 March 1948.
79. L. B. Thanga. 1978. *The Mizos*, Guwahati: United Publishers, p. 166.
80. Lal Rinawma, "Political Development in Mizo Hills 1935–1965", unpublished M. Phil dissertation, NEHU, 1986, pp. 43–44; in A. C. Ray, *Mizoram: Dynamics of Change*, Calcutta, 1982, p. 124.
81. Ibid., and S. K. Chaube, *Hill Politics in Northeast India*. 1999. New Delhi: Orient Longman, pp. 162–163.
82. IOLR, L/P&J/7/10635, Memorandum of the Naga People for Self-determination and an appeal to His Majesty's Government and the Government of India. There appears to be some connection with this appeal and that of the Mizos of September 1946, the Secretary of the Naga National Council T. Sakhrie was present in Aizawl when the Mizos first mooted this idea. The content of this letter of the Naga people and many others relating to the Naga political demands, the disturbances in the 1950s–1960s and coming to more recent peace initiatives, the Atlanta Meet 1997 and the effort of the Churches to bring peace to Nagaland have been published. Refer to V. K. Nuh (comp). 2003. *The Naga Chronicle*, New Delhi: Regency Publications.
83. M. Alemchiba. 1970. *A Brief Historical Account of Nagaland*. Kohima: Naga Institute of Culture, pp. 166–168.
84. Nicholas Mansergh (ed.). 1981. *The Transfer of Power, 1942–1947*. London: Her Majesty's Stationery Office, No. 210, Lord Mountbatten to Lord Listowell, 24 April 1947.
85. Ibid., No. 134, Pethick Lawrence to Lord Mountbatten, 12 April 1947.
86. See, Asoso Yonuo. 1974. *The Rising Nagas*. New Delhi: Vikas, p. 168.
87. S. K. Chaube, *Hill Politics in Northeast India*. 1999. New Delhi: Orient Longman, p. 144. It is not certain whether Phizo made a second visit to Delhi or he remained there for some days to lobby for the Naga cause. The government apparently was worried of his presence there. Hydari's telegram to Nehru of 5 August suggested that the delegation 'be completely ignored as they represent unimportant minority. Suggest your warning Mahatmaji and Sardar Patel

against giving them any encouragement'. See, D. Das (ed.). 1973. *Sardar Patel's Correspondence*, V(22). Ahmedabad: Navajivan Publication House.

88. Asoso Yonuo, 1974. *The Rising Nagas*. New Delhi: Vikas, pp. 173–174.

89. See, T. Aliba Imti. 1988. *Reminiscence: Impur to Naga National Council*. Mokokchung: T. Aliba Imti, pp. 67–68.

90. M. Alemchiba Ao. 1972. 'Problems of Re-adjustment to a New Situation (with Special Reference to the Naga Tribe)', in K. S. Singh (ed.), *Tribal Situation in India*, p. 482. Simla: Indian Institute of Advanced Study.

91. CSAA, Stewart Papers, Box 2, Letter from Elizabeth Stewart to her parents, Letter dated 15 August 1947.

92. IOLR, M/4/2847, Monthly Reports of J. W. McGuiness, Deputy Commissioner, Naga Hills District, Burma for June–August 1947.

93. N. Rustomji. 1971. *Enchanted Frontiers*, Bombay, pp. 106–110: Asoso Yonuo, 1974. *The Rising Nagas*. New Delhi: Vikas, pp. 370–371; S. K. Chaube, *Hill Politics in Northeast India*. 1999. New Delhi: Orient Longman, pp. 194–195.

94. Z. H. Zaidi. 1994. *Jinnah Paper: Pakistan in Making*, 3 June–30 June 1947, First series, Vol. II, National Archives of Pakistan. Islamabad: Oxford University Press, p. 52.

95. Parag Chaliha. 1958. *An Outlook on North Eastern Frontier Agency*. Calcutta: Assam Sahitya Sabha, p. 57; Sitaram Johri. n.d. *Where India China and Burma Meet*. Calcutta: Thaker Spink, p. 238.

96. *Constituent Assembly Debates*, Vol. IX, 1967, New Delhi, p. 1011.

97. S. K. Chaube. 1999. *Hill Politics in Northeast India*. New Delhi: Orient Longman, p. 92.

98. IOLR, L/P&J/5/140/ Clow to Wavell, 2 May 1947.

99. D. R. Syiemlieh. 1989. *British Administration in Meghalaya: Policy and Pattern*. Delhi: Heritage Publishers, pp.194–205. For a personal account of what happened in those years, read Webster Davis Jyrwa. 1997. 'A Story Retold: The Khasi States after British Rule, I and II', *The Shillong Times*, 28 May and 29 May.

100. Constituent Assembly Debates, Vol. IX, New Delhi, 1967, p. 1008.

101. Ibid., p. 1005.

102. Pushapalata Das. 1991. 'Assam Deserves Greater Attention', in Nagen Saikia (ed.), *Assam and the Assamese Mind*. Jorhat: Asam Sahitya Sabha, pp. 88–89.

103. Jawaharlal Nehru. 1952. A Note by the Prime Minister on his tour of the North-Eastern Frontier Areas, Secret, Delhi: Government of India, p. 5.

A Note on the Future of the Present Excluded, Partially Excluded and Tribal Areas of Assam

Sir Robert N. Reid

For purposes of the Constitution Act, 1935, these areas, in terms of the Government of India (Excluded and Partially Excluded Areas) Order, 1936, are

Excluded Areas—

The North-East Frontier (Sadiya, Balipara and Lakhimpur) Tracts.
The Naga Hills District.
The Lushai Hills District.
The North Cachar Hills Subdivision of the Cachar District.

Partially Excluded Areas—

The Garo Hills District.
The Mikir Hills (in the Nowgong and Sibsagar Districts).
The British portion of the Khasi and Jaintia Hills District, other than the Shillong Municipality and Cantonment.

Beyond the administered portion of the Sadiya and Balipara Frontier Tracts (but within the "McMahon Line" of 1914), and outside the administered boundary of the Naga Hills and lying between that district and Burma, is an immense tract of country over which we exercise, within the frontier of India though it be

Sir Robert N. Reid, Governor of Assam (seated in the centre) at Haflong 1942

only the most shadowy control. Relations with this tract were, before 1937, the concern of the Local Government subject to the control of the Central Government, but they are now specifically the concern of the latter, the Governor being the Agent of the Governor-General. Their ultimate fate must be bound up with that of the excluded areas, and their great area (some 28,000 square miles, equal to that of the present Totally and Partially Excluded Areas of the Province), the identity of the countries with which they march and their importance from the point of view of strategy and international politics[1] are factors which cannot be overlooked.

2. Before narrating the history of the process by which the areas with which this note deals attained their present constitutional status, it is worth while to touch briefly on the changes which have occurred in the last 100 years in the plains districts of Assam, among or around which the Excluded, Partially Excluded

---

[1] Problems arising out of the Sino-Japanese War and the World War of 1939, have underlined the importance of the North-East Frontier in its relation to Tibet, China, Burma and Japan.

and Tribal Areas lie. The principal feature in the development of this period is that the plains have become, and are still becoming, increasingly identical in culture with India proper, with the result that the contrasts between the plains and the hills, instead of diminishing, have increased. Taking the Surma Valley first, Sylhet, being essentially part of Bengal, has always been Indian. Up to about 1837 the plains of Cachar, however, were a very sparsely populated and essentially Mongolian area under the rule of the Kachari Raja, with his capital at Khaspur. He always had a number of Bengali advisers around him and gave grants of land to some, but the population as a whole must have been very similar to that of the North Cachar Hills today. Bengali settlers poured into the district when British rule gave good and peaceful government, and it is now in the truest sense of the word a Bengali colony, the plains portion of Cachar district, i.e., the Cachar Sadr and Hailakandi subdivisions, being now entirely Indianised.

In the Assam Valley the process of what may be termed "Indianisation" has taken place at a somewhat later stage. In the later reigns of the Ahom dynasty, towards the end of the 18th century, a number of Indians were brought in, but the main bulk of the population was for long what we now call "Plains Tribals". In recent years, however, i.e., since the year 1905 or thereabouts, Muslim immigrants, mainly from the Bengal district of Mymensingh, have tended to flock into this Valley in ever increasing numbers. Mr. Mullan in Chapter III of his Census Report of 1931 describes the invasion as the most important event in the last 25 years, destined "to destroy more surely than did the Burmese invaders of 1820 the whole structure of Assamese culture and civilisation", and foretells that "in another thirty years Sibsagar district will be the only part of Assam in which an Assamese will find himself at home". The Census of 1941 showed a Mussalman population in the Assam Valley of 1,304,827. In 1901 it was 248,842. In 40 years, therefore, it has multiplied itself by very nearly 6 times. This unceasing invasion from Bengal is clearly bound ultimately to have a substantial effect on the relations between the plains and the still Mongolian hills and to separate their interests more and more widely as time goes on.

3. Let us now examine the course of the prolonged discussions which finally emerged in the Government of India Act of 1935. Under the heading "Recommendations" at pages 99–101 of the "Memoranda" prepared for the Indian Statutory Commission in July 1928, the Government of Assam gave their opinion as to the future of the Backward Tracts as follows:—

> ".........The Government of Assam.........are convinced that......... the Backward Tracts should be excluded from the Province of Assam in the new constitution.........These areas have nothing in common with the rest of the Province. There is no sympathy on either side and the union is an artificial one, resented by both parties. The Backward Tracts are, with certain safeguards, brought within the reforms and the control of a Council in which they cannot be effectively presented. On the other hand the Council and indeed the rest of the Province generally resent the burden which the administration of these areas places on the provincial revenues, and fear that their own political growth and material development are impeded or may be impeded by their being yoked to the Backward Tracts. The Backward Tracts, where there is already a deficit, cannot expect to obtain from the Council the funds which their development may require. On the other hand it would be unreasonable to make all expenditure in these areas non-voted, so long as there is a deficit which has to be made good from the revenues of the rest of the Province.
>
> 38. The existing restrictions on the powers of the Legislative Council to legislate for the Backward Tracts and on the executive control of the popular Minister emphasise the artificiality of the political union. Yet these restrictions are necessary, because the Backward Tracts have not, and cannot for many years hope to have, effective representation in the Council, and because they must be allowed to develop on their own lines and be protected against exploitation and the subversion of their rules and customs by a different civilisation which would be unsuited to them in the present state of their development, and in which they would be unable at present to distinguish the good from the evil.
>
> 39. Another point is that it is necessary that these areas should be administered by British Officers. The tribes would in fact resent as a breach of faith, and might refuse to submit to, any other authority. Yet the progress of Indianisation in, and the provincialisation of, the services will make it impossible to provide the officers required for these areas from the Assam cadres, unless special provision is made

for them and the cost of administration is not debited to provincial revenues.

40. For these reasons the Government of Assam are convinced that in the interests both of the Backward Tracts and of the rest of the Province the present artificial union should be ended. The Backward Tracts should be excluded from the Province of Assam and be administered by the Governor-in-Council, as Agent for the Governor-General in Council, and at the cost of Central revenues. If it be contended that the charge of these areas cannot reasonably be transferred from the provincial tax-payer to the general tax-payer of India, it may be stated in reply that the Naga Hills, Lushai Hills, and the Sadiya and Balipara Frontier Tracts are frontier districts occupied to protect India as well as the Province from invasion and attack, and that, though for the moment the North-East Frontier may not be a serious menace to the peace of the rest of India, there was a time not long ago when attention was directed to that frontier, and the time may soon come when that frontier will become no less, if not more, important for the defence of India than the North-West Frontier, the administration of which is a charge on Central revenues."

The Assam Government had previously (page 78 of the "Memoranda") enumerated the Backward Tracts as the—

Lushai Hills,
Naga Hills,
British portion of the Khasi and Jaintia Hills,
Garo Hills,
Mikir Hills,
North Cachar Hills,
Lakhimpur Frontier Tract,
Sadiya Frontier Tract,
Balipara Frontier Tract,

in fact all the areas subsequently classified as either Excluded or Partially Excluded[2]. A paragraph (paragraph 41) was however

---

[2] The constitutional future of the unadministered areas was not, of course, specifically discussed, it being assumed that their ultimate destiny would be the same as that of the administered Backward Tracts of which they form the hinterland.

devoted to the question of whether the British portion of the Khasi and Jaintia Hills district (i.e., mainly the Jowai subdivision) should not be included within the constitution. The then Minister for Local Self-Government, Mr. Nichols-Roy, a Khasi, advocated this. But the rest of the Government on either side, were opposed to this. They did not believe it would be in the interests of the people as yet, and they were not prepared to admit them on privileged terms, such as would be necessary to protect them until they became politically further advanced. The Government view was that the Khasis would "maintain their individuality and secure their development more certainly by exclusion than by inclusion in the Province of Assam under the new constitution".

When formulating these views, the Government had before them a valuable note[3] recorded by Dr. J. H. Hutton, C.I.E., who was for many years Deputy Commissioner of the Naga Hills, as well as one by Mr. N.E. Parry, I.C.S., who had had experience both of the Lushai and the Garo Hills. Dr. Hutton showed how the hill people neither racially, historically, culturally nor linguistically had any affinity with the people of the plains, while the administration was wholly on different lines. He considered that the true solution of the question of their administration (page 116) was "the gradual creation of self-governing communities, semi-independent in nature.........for whose external relations alone the Governor of the Province would ultimately be responsible.

Mr. Parry (page 122) offered two alternative possibilities, (*a*) a Hill Division under a Commissioner directly under the Governor, any deficit in its budget to be made up by the Imperial Government; (*b*) a North-East Frontier Province to comprise backward tracts, both of Burma and Assam, under a

---

[3] Dr. Hutton recorded three notes on this subjects, all of which repay study—

    (*a*)   On 17th March 1928 (at pages 111–22 of the Assam Government's Memoranda prepared for the Indian Statutory Commission).

    (*b*)   On 6th July 1930 [at pages 31–34 notes in Assam Secretariat, Proceedings Political (Reforms) A. December 1930, Nos. 1–3].

    (*c*)   On 18th September 1935 (at pages 7–9 notes in Assam Secretariat, Proceedings Political A, December 1936, Nos. 1–30).

Chief Commissioner, the deficit, if any, to be met as an (*a*) from Imperial Funds.

4. The Indian Statutory Commission touched on the question in paragraph 94 of Volume I "Survey" of their Report, and few will demur to one observation which they make and that is that "if progress is to benefit and not to destroy these people, it must come about gradually".

They dealt with the subject in more detail in Chapter 2 of Part III and Chapter 2 of Part IV of their second volume "Recommendations". The most important pronouncements in that volume are perhaps these—

> "128.........They [i.e., the inhabitants of the Backward Tracts] do not ask for self-determination, but for security of land tenure, freedom in the pursuit of their traditional methods of livelihood, and the reasonable exercise of their ancestral customs. Their contentment does not depend so much on rapid political advance as on experienced and sympathetic handling, and on protection from economic subjugation by their neighbours.

> 129. The responsibility of Parliament for the Backward Tracts will not be discharged merely by securing to them protection from exploitation and by preventing those outbreaks which have from time to time occurred within their borders. The principal duty of the administration is to educate these peoples to stand on their own feet, and this is a process which has scarcely begun. It is too large a task to be left to the single-handed efforts of missionary societies or of individual officials. Co-ordination of activity and adequate funds are principally required. The typical backward tract is a deficit area, and no Provincial Legislature is likely to possess either the will or the means to devote special attention to its particular requirements. Expenditure in the tracts does not benefit the areas from which elected representatives are returned. Moreover, the most extensive tracts (if Burma be left out of account) fall within the poorest Provinces. Only if responsibility for the Backward Tracts is entrusted to the Centre, does it appear likely that it will be adequately discharged."

"We have no doubt whatever," they said in a subsequent paragraph (131), "that for the really Backward Tracts such as those of Assam.........the alternative of complete exclusion must be adopted." They even went so far (paragraph 172) as to suggest, as a corollary to making the Backward Tracts a Central responsibility, that there might be a Member of the Governor-General's Executive Council charged with this portfolio either by itself or combined with other duties. Their views therefore coincide in great measure with those put forward by the Government of Assam in their Memoranda of 1928.

The Assam Government commented on this portion of the Report in their letter No. Rfm. 8/8801-P.A.,* dated the 12th August 1930, and the proposals made therein were naturally based on "the assumption that Parliament would be in a position to ensure, through the agency of the Government of India and the Governor, the peaceful development of the excluded tracts". The Local Government were unanimous in recommending the exclusion of the—

Naga Hills.
Lushai Hills.
North Cachar Hills.
Mikir Hills.
The three Frontier Tracts.

As regards the Garo and the Khasi and Jaintia Hills, the Governor and the Finance Member of Council wished to exclude them, while the two Ministers and the Indian Members of Council wished to include them. It is interesting to observe that in noting on this problem the present Prime Minister of Assam, Sir Muhammad Saadulla, said on the 7th July 1930, that he was agreeable to the total exclusion of all Hill Districts except the Garo and the Khasi and Jaintia Hills from the Reforms "or even from the Province".

In paragraph 40 of this letter mention was made of "an interesting suggestion that the hill districts on the Burmese Frontier should be united under one administration": the suggestion is

---

*Assam Secretariat Proceedings Political (Reforms) A, December 1930, Nos. 1–3.

made that the Central Government might "desire to enquire whether it would not at least be desirable to combine with the administration of the Backward Tracts in Assam that of the Arrakan, Chittagong and Pakokku Hills Tracts, the Chin Hills and the area inhabited by the Rangpang Nagas on both sides of the Patkoi": and the conclusion is reached that "the proposition that a North-East Frontier Province, or at least some unified form of administration for the portions of Assam and Burma which adjoin, has.........great attractions". These remarks are based on a second note recorded by Dr. Hutton on the 6th July 1930. It gives in outline the essentials of what I would advocate today, and I think that experience of the 1935 Constitution Act has only strengthened the case for some such solution of the problem. An extract from that note is as follows:—

> ".........A much more attractive alternative would be the forma-tion of an Agency or Commission to combine the Hill Districts of Assam with the adjacent districts of Burma. The districts which I would suggest for this purpose are, starting from the Bay of Bengal, the Hill Tracts of Arrakan, Pakokku and Chittagong, and the Chin Hills, the Lushai Hills and the North Cachar Hills, the Naga Hills, the Mikir Hills, the parts of the Upper Chindwin District, and the hill areas administered on the west bank of the Chindwin from the Upper Chindwin District, and the Hukong Valley, together with the Sadiya and Balipara Frontier Tracts, the Lakhimpur Frontier Tract, the States of Manipur and Tripura and the isolated Shan States of Thangdut on the west bank of the Chindwin. The Garo Hills would, in this case, become a sacrifice and a Partially Excluded Area for the sake of the geographical cohesion of the remainder. It might be neces-sary also to omit the Balipara Frontier Tract and the Sadiya Frontier Tract west of the Dihang, leaving the Abors, Miris and Daflas as a totally Excluded Area under Assam and including the Mishmis in the North-East Frontier Province. This would give a province of some 16 districts which could support a cadre of its own without excessive difficulties in the matter of leave. It will also be a province for which it would be extremely easy to recruit in Europe, which is not likely to be the case with any province in which service under a reformed Local Government is normal. The other advantages of such a solution of the problem of the Assam Backward Tracts are many. From the Arrakan Hill States northwards Maghs, Mros, Kukis, Lakhers, Chins,

Nagas of all sorts, Khamtis and Western Kachins are found on both sides of the so called watershed, having common customs, common languages and living under precisely similar social conditions. All these tribes, at present divided between two administrations would gain enormously by consolidated treatment, and sentiment, which is at present parochial as a result of divided administration, would easily be transformed into a tribal consciousness covering a much greater area—a decided advance towards the ideal which the Commission seems to have in view. All these tribes, again, have not perhaps a common religion, but a common basis of religion, if Animism may be so described. Neither the Burma nor the Assam tribes show any marked tendency to adopt the religion of their neighbours to the east or to the west. All these hill areas have a common system of taxation which is not based on land revenue and which, owing to difficulties of survey, probably never can be. All of them have the same educational problem and the problem of the vernacular scripts already alluded to. All of them are at present administered on much the same lines and on lines entirely different to those followed in the regulation districts of the Provinces of which they respectively form part. Incidentally it may be pointed out that the separation of Burma forecasted by the Committee may complicate the present method of settling the many inter-tribal disputes which take place between the inhabitants of Assam and the inhabitants of Burma and which are settled by regular boundary meetings of the officers concerned.

The constitution of such a Province would also greatly facilitate the treatment of the frontier question. China at present may be a negligible quantity, but should she ever recover from her internal disorders the question of the Chinese frontier is likely to become very much more important than it is at present and the advantages of having under one administration both the frontier and its bases from the ninety-second to ninety-seventh degree of longitude would be considerable. At present the Assam Frontier Tract covers this section of the frontier, but the areas to the south of it, including the Hukong Valley, are administered by Burma. The proposed hill Province would be triangular, with its base on the frontier and its apex on the Bay of Bengal, replacing an irregular frontier on which a narrow strip of Assam overlaps an intrusion from Burma.

As regards expense, the Secretariat staff required would be so small that the cost of a Chief Commissioner and a Secretary would hardly exceed that of the two Commissioners (Assam and Burma) required under separate administration.

The advantages of the formation of such a province may be put concisely as follows:—

(1) The provision of an opportunity for political advance on corporate tribal lines as distinct from the present position in which no corporate future for different tribes can be envisaged which involves more than that part of many tribes which resides on the Assam or Bengal side of the present frontier. The separation of Burma from India on lines of the present frontiers will permanently divorce portions of tribes which naturally should comprise a single unit. Incorporated into a single Province there would be opportunities of advance not dissimilar to those of the North-West Frontier Province, while separated from the people of the plains on both sides, the pace will not be unduly forced by a more advanced neighbour.

(2) The possibility of the consolidation of an incredibly polyglot[4] area into a uniform administrative unit with ultimately a common language (English) for official purposes.

(3) The possibility of obtaining and maintaining a proper provincial cadre, recruited for the Province as a whole instead of borrowed from time to time from neighbouring areas and liable to inconvenient transfers to and from entirely dissimilar administrative areas, which means that officers unsuited to hill administration are sent there to benefit their health or sometimes that the hills are used as a penal settlement for officers whose services are unprofitable in the more vocal plains.

(4) Facility for the proper treatment of the question of frontier defence between longitudes 92° and 97°.

Two objections are likely to be made to such a proposal; one is a question of communications and another that of the language in general use. With regard to the communications, the Assam-Bengal Railway on the west and the Chindwin river on the east provide an easy enough method of getting from one end to the other of the Province

---

[4] The polyglot character of this area does not diminish its homogeneity as much as might perhaps be inferred from Hutton's remark. The large number of different languages spoken in this area are all, except the Khasi language, of the Tibeto-Burman, family and a speaker of one can usually learn another with the greatest ease. The sharp difference is not between one language and another within this family, but between any single one of the family and the Sanskritic languages of the plains of Assam.

outside the hills. Inside the hills there are through communications between the Lushai Hills and the Chin Hills, between the Manipur State and both of these districts, between the Manipur State and the Burma-Somra Tract, between the Naga Hills and Burma-Somra Tract, and between the Sadiya Frontier Tract and the Hukong Valley. The statement in the Statutory Commission's Report (paragraph 95 at the bottom of page 77, Volume I) that Burma's land frontier forms a practically impassible barrier is incorrect, and its frontier on the Assam side and such communications as there are already could be easily and effectively amplified. The natural capital of this Province would be Imphal in the Manipur State which has already excellent communications with the Assam-Bengal Railway on the west and needs only permanent bridges and a widening of the track to give adequate communications with the Chindwin on the east.

As regards language, it is true that Assamese is used on one side and Burmese on the other, but the difficulty to be surmounted seems no greater that that surmounted in the case of the Provinces of Bihar and Orissa, or of Eastern Bengal and Assam, as it would not be necessary for officers employed in the hills to read or write in either the Burmese or Assamese vernaculars; all that would be required of them would be colloquial tests in these two languages. The initial difficulties would naturally be met by the posting of Burma officers to the one side and Assam officers to the other."

5. The angle of approach to the general question had however to be changed when, as a result of the Round Table Conference, the British Government formulated the plan embodied in the White Paper, of which the leading features were a Federation, responsibility with safeguards at the Centre and autonomy in the Provinces. The matter was again referred to the Provinces in letter No. F-71/31-Reforms, dated the 2nd June 1931, by the Government of India. Assam replied on 29th July 1931 in their letter No. 4533-A.P. Their views they expressed were agreed on by both sides of the Government. These views differed from those expressed in 1930, in that, while retaining the—

Naga Hills,
Lushai Hills,

North Cachar Hills,
Three Frontier Tracts,

as excluded, they were now, in the words of paragraph 16 of their letter, "prepared to risk the introduction of the Mikir Hills (these were previously recommended for total exclusion), the Garo Hills and the Khasi and Jaintia Hills into the new constitution, subject however to certain safeguards and restrictions, the Governor being empowered to bar unsuitable legislation, and to prevent encroachment on the indigenous system of land tenure, taxation and customary law". In making this recommendation, the Government of the day committed themselves (paragraph 14 of their letter) to the very doubtful statement that the inhabitants of the Khasi and Jaintia Hills and of the Garo Hills were "in point of fact as civilised and as educated as their neighbours in the plains districts", a view which scarcely squares with that expressed at the end of the same paragraph that, unless the Governor were given certain "powers of interference and restrains", these two districts should be wholly excluded.

The question of the Mikir Hills gave them even greater cause for hesitation, but, while admitting that the Mikirs had been neglected and exploited in the past, they came to the conclusion that the balance of advantage might lie in allowing the Mikir Hills, subject to the limitations that could be imposed by the Governor, to be included in the Sibsagar and Nowgong districts (paragraph 15).

6. The 6th Schedule to the Bill which was presented to Parliament showed the—

Three Frontier Tracts,
Naga Hills,
Lushai Hills,

as excluded, and the

North Cachar Hills,
Garo Hills,

Mikir Hills,
British portion of the Khasi and Jaintia Hills,

as partially excluded.

It will be observed that the North Cachar Hills, instead of being classed, as recommended in our letter No. 4533-A.P.* of July 1931, as totally excluded, were now put in the partially excluded category. This is related to a bigger question of principle which was the subject of discussion between the Government of India and the Secretary of State in 1932. While accepting the inclusion with restrictions and safeguards of the Khasi and Jaintia, Garo and Mikir Hills, the Government of India in their letter No. 16, dated the 12th May 1932† (paragraph 8), expressed themselves as against the total exclusion even of the Naga, Lushai, North Cachar Hills and the three Frontier Tracts, and in favour of some sort of partial inclusion (paragraph 15), which they thought "might avoid the disadvantages of total exclusion and at the same time secure to these areas better prospects of progress and development". Their proposals (paragraph 17) in brief were that the administration of the Excluded Areas should be vested in the Governor, but "means would be provided whereby the Provincial Ministry and the Legislature would be associated with the Governor without prejudice to his personal responsibility".

Fortunately for these areas, the Secretary of State as the reply to the Government of India contained in his letter No. P. & J. (C) 1896, dated the 1st July 1932, shows, had no doubts on how the Frontier Tracts and the Naga and Lushai Hills should be treated (paragraphs 3 and 4). "There would be no justification", he said, "........for placing the control of them in any degree in the hands of a legislature, composed of persons who have no knowledge of their needs, and outlook, or of Ministers responsible to it.

Paragraph 4.—The Secretary of State is clearly of opinion that these facts must be recognised without compromise or equivocation, and that, in relation to these tracts of Assam, the jurisdiction

---

*Assam Secretariat Proceedings Political A, September 1931, Nos. 130-38.
†Assam Secretariat Proceedings Political B, December 1936, Nos. 1138-89.

of the Provincial Legislature.........and of Ministers, should be entirely excluded".

The Secretary of State had doubts regarding North Cachar. He thought the portion mainly inhabited by Nagas and Kukis might be attached to the Naga Hills District and the rest taken out of the totally excluded category. Inquiries were made on this point, and at first the Government of Assam found the difficulties in the way of carrying out the Secretary of State's suggestion so great that they advised, in their letter Pol. 2169/8497-P., dated the 1st September 1932, that they preferred to stick to their previous proposal, i.e., total exclusion. The Secretary of State, in his letter of the 12th October 1932, said that in view of the difficulties pointed out by Assam, he was prepared to treat the North Cachar Hills like the Nagas and Lushai Hills and the Frontier Tracts. Meanwhile, however, the Local Government had been pursuing further investigations and in their letter No. 989-Fr., dated the 11th January 1933, they reported that in view of certain further facts which had been elicited they had changed their views and wished now to recommend that the North Cachar Hills "as a whole should be included in the New Constitution subject to certain safeguards and restrictions........" Apparently one of the main considerations that moved them was that the alternatives of—

(1) being excluded, and attached to the Naga Hills District, or

(2) of remaining as part of Cachar District and being included,

were put to the local people and the Local Government were led to believe that opinion generally favoured the latter. In actual fact, the opinion which favoured remaining as part of the Cachar District was entirely Kachari. Their sentiments were worked upon and they were deliberately told that there was a danger of their "motherland" being divided, Khaspur, their last capital, being just over the border in Cachar Sadr. Be that as it may, the Government of India supported this fresh recommendation and the Secretary of State accepted it in his letter No. P. & J. 2679, dated the 21st, February 1933.

7. 1935 saw the final phase in constitution making. In response to a certain movement in England on the part of Members of Parliament who were not satisfied as to the treatment accorded to Backward Tracts, the Sixth Schedule was omitted from the Bill, it was decided to take power to determine the classification of such areas by Order-in-Council, and further consultation with authorities in India was initiated. In referring the matter to the Government of India in his telegram No. 1103*, dated the 5th April 1935, the Secretary of State intimated that he would be urged to transfer (among others) the North Cachar Hills and Mikir Hills from the partially to the wholly excluded category. On being referred to, the Government of Assam advised that the Secretary of State might yield as far as the North Cachar Hills were concerned. They were less agreeable to the transfer of the Mikir Hills, expressing the opinion that the area was populated by a homogeneous tribe, the election of a representative was possible, while, geographically, "their total exclusion breaks the Assam Valley in two". (This was something of an overstatement on which Dr. Hutton's subsequent comment was that "whether they are totally included or totally excluded will not make the slightest difference to the life of the plains *mauzas* which surround them"). They also said that if the Mikir Hills were transferred to Part I, i.e., the Totally Excluded Area category, there was no reason why other hill districts should not be placed in it too and there was no knowing where the process might end. They apparently had in mind the Garo Hills (whose case for exclusion was certainly a strong one). A little later, in June 1935, came a request for each Provincial Government to carry out an examination *de novo* of this problem. This was done and the Assam views were submitted in their letter No. 3044-Fr.*, dated the 9th October 1935. They were satisfied once more that the—

---

*Assam Secretariat Proceedings Political A, December 1936, Nos. 1–30.

Naga Hills,
Lushai Hills,
Sadiya Frontier Tract,
Balipara Frontier Tract,
Lakhimpur Frontier Tract,

should be wholly excluded. They recommended that the North Cachar Hills should be replaced in the "Excluded" category. Thirdly, they adhered to their previous view that the Garo Hills, the Khasi and Jaintia Hills, and the Mikir Hills should be partially excluded. The following extracts from the letter of the 9th October indicate the reasons for their attitude:—

"In the opinion of the Local Government the question of whether the Garo Hills and the Mikir Hills should be Totally or Partially Excluded Areas is the only matter on which there can be room for doubt in the whole of the present reference and after reconsideration of the problem in the light of the observations of the Secretary of State the Local Government are definitely of opinion that it is now too late to attempt to upset the whole balance of the scheme for the reformed Provincial Legislature by transferring the Garo Hills and Mikir Hills from the partially excluded list to the totally excluded list. In the first place the scheme of delimitation of constituencies proposed by the Local Government provides for two 'backward area' seats for the Garo Hills and one 'backward area' seat for the Mikir Hills out of the total of 9 seats allocated in the Fifth Schedule to the Government of India Bill to 'representatives of backward areas and tribes' in the Assam Legislative Assembly.........Unless therefore the Government of India Act is amended the total exclusion of the Garo and Mikir Hills would result in a surplus of three backward area seats which are not required elsewhere and which were originally included in the scheme on the assumption that the Garo Hills and Mikir Hills would return representatives to the reformed Legislature. It might conceivably be possible to utilise one of these surplus seats by allocating it to the Manipuris of the Surma Valley, but to fit in three such seats would be at the best more patchwork and would definitely upset the whole balance of the present inter-valley distribution of constituencies.

Furthermore, it has been found quite practicable to devise a suitable system for obtaining representatives from both the Garo Hills and the Mikir Hills, the proposal of the Local Government being that the franchise in both areas should be confined to village headmen. These proposals have been published and representations have actually been received from certain Garos objecting to such a limited franchise and demanding a franchise based on house tax. The total exclusion of the Garo Hills and the Mikir Hills at this stage would therefore lay the Local Government open to the very just accusation of having raised false hopes among the people of these areas. In fact the main objection of the Local Government to the total exclusion of the Garo Hills and Mikir Hills is that it is now too late to make any change.........."

... The Garo Hills and the Mikir Hills are not frontier districts or districts in which armed rebellion or acute internal dissension are to be feared. They are situated in the heart of the Province and they must evolve on lines similar to the rest of the Province. Change must come and all that can be provided is that such change comes gradually and in accordance with the capacity of the local tribes to adopt themselves to it.

There was strong local opposition to this view and it was shared by Sir Walter, Scott, though his was the only dissentient voice in the Cabinet. The Cabinet also had before them a third valuable note recorded by Dr. Hutton on the subject on 18th September 1935. Extracts from his references to the Garo Hills and the Mikir Hills are as follows:—

"2. *The Garo Hills*—The case of this district was probably confused from the start owing to suggestion that the frontier districts from the Lushai Hills to the Sadiya Frontier Tract and westwards to the Bhutan border should form an independent administration directly under the Government of India. The Garo Hills and the Jaintia Hills would then have had to be included in Assam proper in order that the two valleys should not be territorially separated by an area administered by the Central Government. Since this suggestion came to nothing there seems to be no case at all for the partial inclusion of the Garo Hills. That district is in many ways more backward than some (e.g., the Lushai Hills) which are to be totally excluded. The attempt to represent, it on the Reformed Council is almost farcical and there is no reason to suppose that the district as a whole either understands it or desires it, and the nominated members who were the best Garos who could be found to represent the Backward Tracts in the existing constitution proved incapable of contributing anything towards its working. The Deputy Commissioner has adequately emphasised the extreme contrast in social organisation, customary law and tribal sentiment between the Garos of the hills and their neighbours in the plains. The Commissioner makes the very important point that the zemindars who own land within the Garo Hills will undoubtedly launch a campaign of exploitation if they feel that they can rely upon indifference on the part of the administration, while it is possible that a democratic administration in Assam would afford not merely such indifference but definite sympathy with the zemindars rather than with the Garos. The general position therefore with regard to the Garo Hills is not that there is a possible case for its exclusion but that it is quite impossible to find any argument even for partial inclusion in the Reforms.........

3. *Mikir Hills*[5]—Here the two Deputy Commissioners concerned with this area do not entirely agree as to how it should be treated. The Deputy Commissioner of Nowgong, rightly in my opinion, considers that the Mikirs should be totally excluded: the Deputy Commissioner of Nowgong is personally acquainted with the Mikir Hills. The Deputy Commissioner of Sibsagar says that a case for total exclusion has not been made out, but he is himself completely unacquainted with either the Mikirs or their habitat, and has to admit that it will be difficult to find a suitable person to represent them on the Council. On this point the Deputy Commissioner of Nowgong is illuminating. He points out that expenditure on the Mikirs, if partially excluded only, will be votable; that the Mikir Hills are outside the scope of Local Boards; that they are so backward that they will not be able to raise any voice in matters that affect them even vitally; and that they will probably be unable to secure anything at all in the allotment of funds for purely local purposes. He thinks that any member they return will probably be some one put up by a party in the plains, and points out that attempts to 'carpet-bag' the Mikir constituency are already being made. The Commissioner agrees with the Deputy Commissioner, Nowgong, in recommending the total exclusion of the Mikir Hills. An objection has been made to the total exclusion of the Mikir Hills on

---

[5] Though the Mikir Hills cover an area of over 4,000 square miles no officer is posted in them and they are left to the charge of two District Officers already sufficiently occupied with ordinary plains administration. They pay proportionately more in taxes and receive less in amenities than any other area in the Province. Under the scheme proposed in this note neglect of this kind would be remedied.

the ground that it splits up the Assam Valley into two. This objection appears to me completely invalid. No communications run through the Mikir Hills and whether they are totally included or totally excluded will not make the least difference to the life of the plains *mauzas* which surround them. I see no reason why they should not, if necessary, remain within the administration of the District Magistrates of Nowgong and Sibsagar respectively and still be totally excluded, though I agree with the Commissioner of the Surma Valley that it would be very much better to form a combined charge of the Mikir Hills, which could probably be placed under a Sub-Deputy Collector with headquarters at Mohengdijua or, as he suggests, at Dimapur. I do not think the Deputy Commissioner, Naga Hills, would raise any objection to the transfer of that part of Dimapur *mauza* which lies west of the Dhansiri river, since Kohima is no longer dependent on bullock carts for transport. If, however, the Mikir Hills be totally excluded I should be inclined to include with them the *mauzas* of Barpathar and Sarupathar which it was proposed to include in the representative system. Those *mauzas* might remain in the Excluded Areas until the Development Board has finished its work, when they could be incorporated in Golaghat subdivision, if they so desire. That the hill portions of the Mikir Hills Tract should be totally excluded is, I think, a view with which any one who knows them will agree. The Mikirs are in some ways the most backward tribe in Assam and they are totally unfitted to protect themselves against exploitation. Only recently the Deputy Commissioner, Nowgong, found that in some villages the Mikir inhabitants were being oppressed and systematically milked by foreign money-lenders and shopkeepers, who had come and squatted there for that purpose without any authority at all. He was able to order these foreigners to leave, but he might have found his position much more difficult if such settlers were able to bring pressure on the administration through representatives in the Council. As in the case of the Garo Hills the real position seems to be not so much that a case has been made out for total exclusion as that no case for inclusion can under existing circumstances conceivable be made."

Be that as it may, the Government proposals were accepted by the Government of India in their despatch No. 1-Reforms, dated the 24th December 1935, to the Secretary of State, and these conclusions are embodied in the Order-in-Council which is quoted at the beginning of this note.

I have gone into the history of the process by which the final decision embodied in the Order-in-Council of 1936 was arrived at, because it shows that there is nothing new in the proposals which I put forward for consideration and also because it makes clear the varied views which were held from time to time by the different authorities which took part in the discussions, as well as the somewhat inadequate reasons on which recommendations were sometimes based, e.g., in the case of the Mikir Hills, which led to their being given the status of Partially Excluded Areas.

8. The experience of 1937–41 of the working of the present arrangement has been on the whole not unfavourable. I have had no difficulty over the administration of the Excluded Areas, and I am quite clear that they have benefited greatly by not being placed within the control of the Ministry and the Legislature. It is probable (I have no personal knowledge, of course) that these areas may have tended to get rather more personal attention from a Governor than they did in the past, simply because they are now definitely his own responsibility and not one which, as before 1937, he shares with any Member of Council or Minister. I am satisfied also that their exclusion has not stood in the way of those "prospects of progress and development" which the Government of India in 1932 sought to ensure by including them under the control of both Ministry and Legislature.

Financially, I think, they have probably obtained some temporary advantage, though in a paradoxical sort of way. Naturally neither Ministry nor Legislature like spending money on them, but when the Ministry were prepared to spend revenues which did not exist (at least in the eyes of prudent finance) on schemes in the rest of the Province, I was able to claim, and get, a modest proportion of the "new-money" for projects in the Excluded Areas. But the temporary advantages so snatched are obviously fortuitous, and if the extravagance of a Ministry were to bring the Province to the verge of bankruptcy no prudence on the part of the Governor could save the Excluded Areas too from suffering the consequences of such a calamity. If development were shut down in the non-excluded areas the Governor would have to shut it down in the Excluded Areas also, however much, in theory, he could go on charging expenditure as he wished. I need hardly say I have never enjoyed, nor will any other Governor enjoy under the 1935 Constitution, the situation visualised by Secretary of State, Sir Samuel Hoare, when he said in his evidence before the Joint Committee (Answer No. 13453 at page 198 of the Secretary of State's Evidence, Part II) that "He [the Governor] can have what money he wants".

I cannot recall any difficulties arising out of a desire to interfere in the Excluded Areas: even as regards Excise policy there has been no serious attempt to interfere with my discretion.

As regards staff, i.e., the posting of members of the Services to the Excluded Areas, I have had no difficulties. I think the Ministry are generally prepared to accede to requests for British Officers in the hills, partly because on the whole (except in a communal emergency) they prefer to have Indians, especially promoted officers, in the districts that are under their control. Recruitment is a different matter. There has been perennial difficulty in inducing the Ministry to recruit Europeans and Anglo-Indians and hillmen to the Assam Civil Service and Assam Junior Civil Service for employment in the hill districts. They have, of course, no interest in the recruitment of these classes on whose behalf no Members of the Legislature are likely to threaten withdrawal, or promise accession, of support, while they naturally are reluctant to see posts in the Provincial cadres filled by persons who are only intended to serve in the Excluded Areas. I have in fact failed to obtain the recruitment of any Europeans or Anglo-Indians. It is obviously a difficult case to press and it must be admitted that the quality of those already in service does not make it easier.

There are other services, in which the necessity of European or Anglo-Indian officers has never been stressed on administrative grounds, in which somewhat similar difficulties have arisen. Recently, for instance, although the best candidates for seats at the Medical College, Calcutta, were two youths from Excluded Areas the Ministry refused to appoint them. A similar difficulty exists in the Education Service. Though education is of supreme importance to the hills it is extremely difficult to get hillmen appointed to it. Put shortly, in recruiting for Provincial Services a Ministry cannot avoid being actuated to a very great extent by communal and political interests, and can hardly be expected to pay much attention to the interests of Excluded Areas. It is extremely difficult for a Governor to insist on a modification of this policy.

9. The case of the Partially Excluded Areas is not so simple. I have always been careful to take the line laid down in paragraph 80 of the Joint Committee's Report, Volume I, that the primary responsibility of administration lies with the Ministry, but have tried to ensure that I was always kept aware of what was going on, so as to be able to fulfill my special responsibility under section 52 (1) (e) of the Act. Only one Minister has given me trouble over this, Mr. Rohini Kumar Chaudhuri, now in charge of Education. His political principle is, as he explained to me once very clearly, that the Governor should not "interfere" with the Ministry in any way whatever, even where a special responsibility was concerned, and he strongly resented anything which he considered to savour of curtailing Ministerial power. This has made it difficult often for Secretaries to place cases before me, but on the whole I cannot say that even in his portfolio I have had serious grounds for complaint, I refer of course only to matters covered by section 52. Other Ministers have never raised any objection to "Partially Excluded" cases being put before me as a matter of routine and I have never had occasion to query the Ministerial order, as far as I remember, with one exception. That was as regards the application of the Government Excise policy of accelerated reduction of opium rations. I hesitated a long time before agreeing to the application of the order to the Partially Excluded Areas, mainly on grounds of hardship to people in very remote places with no medical aid, but eventually we got agreement. Relations both with the Minister in charge and the Prime Minister, who was consulted throughout, were always cordial and there was none of the suspicion and bitterness displayed by Rohini Chaudhuri.

In the Legislature the Garo Hills have been represented by two Members who carry no weight in the Assembly, while the Mikir

Hills' Member is a man of very little education who I do not think has ever been known to speak and who certainly cannot follow a debate in English. The Khasi Member, Mr. Nicholas Roy, who was a Minister in the pre-1937 Constitution and also a Member of the first Saadulla Ministry (1937–1938), and the Reverend Mr. Gatphoh (a Church of England Minister) who represents Jowai, can complete on pretty good terms with the rest.

I give, of course, only the results of my own experience. Things may be different elsewhere and, in Provinces where the Partially Excluded Areas are numerous and less homogeneous, may have revealed great difficulties. Nor can I say I am entirely satisfied that my immunity from serious difficulty is sure evidence that no defects exist. One great difficulty is that, except by touring and by obtaining the advice of officers whom he can trust—not always readily available, the Governor has no means of ascertaining the needs and troubles of Partially Excluded Areas. Their so-called representatives in the Legislature are usually completely detribalised and inclined to look down upon, and show scant sympathy towards, the humble majority of their communities. They would also hesitate to attempt to approach the Governor direct, even if they felt they had a real grievance to air, as they are naturally closely connected with, and often deeply beholden to, the Ministry. No Member of the Legislative Assembly from a Partially Excluded Area has, in fact, so far as I recollect, ever approached me with a view to obtaining some benefit for his constituency. The situation will be far worse when all Services are provincialised. A Provincial official would then find it extremely difficult frankly to tell the Governor that the advice of his Ministers on some Partially Excluded Area question was wrong and harmful, for he would know that the nature of his advice could not be concealed and that he would almost certainly have to suffer for it later on.

Another defect in the constitutional position which might well, on occasion, assume a serious form, is that Ministers are liable, whether in answer to questions in the Legislature or otherwise, to reveal the advice they have tendered to the Governor on Partially Excluded Area matters, thereby committing themselves and him, before the Governor has had an opportunity of passing orders in his individual judgment. I can recall one such case which for a time gave rise to inconvenience.

10. Now as to the future. This, of course, would have to be decided by Parliament. It cannot be left to Indian political leaders with neither knowledge, interest nor feeling for these areas. In any case, if my main premise of separation from India is accepted, their intervention could scarcely arise. I take as my text what Mr. Amery said on the 3rd of March 1941 of Burma and her separation from India—"that separation was the natural conse-quence of the introduction of self-government, for in her racial type and her culture, as well as in her geographical position, Burma belongs not to India, but to the easternmost of the great southward projection of the main bulk of Asia, the Indo-Chinese peninsula". This applies just as closely to the inhabitants of the Assam Excluded and Tribal Areas, and, I consider, to the Partially Excluded Areas too. When one emerges from the hills into the plains of Assam one enters a different world, whereas the bound-ary between our hills and the Burma hills is as artificial as it is imperceptible. The ethnographical, linguistic and historical facts as regards the races of these tracts have been ably set forth in Dr. Hutton's notes of 17th March 1928, 6th July 1930 and 18th September 1935, and are best studied in the original. I would merely repeat here the following extracts from the portion headed "Conclusions" of Memorandum 86 which he placed before Sub-Committee D, of the Joint Committee (see pages 2367–74 of Volume II—Minutes of Evidence):—

> "The illustrations given above are enough to show that the tribal areas[6] have interests which conflict with those of the people inhabit-ing the normally administered plains areas, and that the introduction of Provincial Self-Government raises the necessity for some form of protection for these areas until they are in a position to stand on their

---

[6] The context shows that the term "tribal areas" here means not only the unad-ministered territory now known as the Tribal Areas, but areas in general where the population is still at the tribal level of culture.

own feet either as an integral part of the Province in which they are found, or as independent units of the federated whole.

Failure to give some protection is likely to lead to the very rapid disintegration of tribal life, particularly in view of the very rapid development of communications in tribal areas, and to the economic ruin of the tribes.........It is hard to believe that most Governors will not have difficulty in withstanding the pressure of their Councils and Ministers, even though the individuals pressing for regularisation of tribal areas are the merest handful of vociferous immigrants, and it would be far safer for aboriginal areas to be excluded entirely rather than partially, so that all the Excluded Areas would be, under their own Provincial Governors, more or less in the position of such Chief Commissioners' Provinces as the Andaman and Nicobar Islands. In some cases they would be safest treated as States for whom, indeed, the Provincial Governor might act as Agent to the Governor-General but which should not be treated as British India at all under the proposed constitution.........

.........the expressed desire of most of the tribal areas is for self-determination, and this could be secured in a number of cases by the creation of petty States on the lines of those in the Khasi Hills or the Kerenni States of Burma. The guidance and supervision of Political Officers would be necessary for some time, but there is no reason why self-governing units should not be fostered, or why the tribal areas should not be allowed freedom to manage their own affairs as petty units of the Federation like the minor States of Western India, unless they preferred, as they might at some subsequent date, to apply for complete incorporation in an adjoining province. Clearly the initial difficulty is one of finance, but the more closely they are administered the greater will be the cost and the cost of administration on political lines would be no greater than that of incorporation into a self-governing province with all its apparatus of elections and representation. Many of them, like the Kolkan in Singhbhum (Bihar and Orissa) retain their original self-governing institutions still intact. It is not suggested that Excluded Areas should be retained precisely as they are. Something must be done to set them on their own feet."

To this I would add the following consideration. In the hill tracts of Assam Muslims and Hindus are almost everywhere confined to the small district and subdivisional headquarters, and there has been no widespread infiltration of members of these advanced communities into a primitive Animist population such as has occurred elsewhere in India. The population of the area we are considering can, for practical purposes, be regarded as a solid block of Animists in rapid process of becoming Christians.[7] The speed of that process is proved by the fact that between 1931 and 1941 the Christian population of the hills of Assam including the Khasi States, has increased from 164,000 to 251,000. We have no right to allow this great body of non-Indian Animists and Christians to be drawn into the struggle between Hindu and Muslim, which is now land will be in the future with ever increasing intensity the dominating feature of politics in India proper. Besides great benefits, the rapid spread of Christianity among the people has brought with it problems enough, and nothing but harm could enure to them if they were thrown in addition into a conflict, the protagonists in which were both equally alien to them and yet in which they would have inevitably to take sides. Palpably outrageous though they are, the claims of Congress to include the hills of Assam in a Hindu *Raj* and of the Muslim League to make them part of Pakisthan are seriously meant. To allow them is to abandon every undertaking on behalf of minorities that has so solemnly been made.

Contact with the plains has not obliterated, it has indeed scarely blurred, the cleavage between plains and hills. I am quite certain that the inhabitants of the Excluded Areas would not now, any more than when the New Constitution was being discussed ten years ago, be ready to join in any constitution in which they would be in danger of coming under the political domination of Indians. Yet, among the Lushais at any rate, the most alert and quick-witted of the hill tribes and a race which takes a

---

[7] Except in the hinterland of the Balipara Frontier Tract there is no considerable Buddhist element in Assam but the inclusion of the Chittagong Hill Tracts in the proposed Agency would bring in a large number of Buddhists, which would be further greatly increased if areas in Burma were added. This Buddhist element would be still more important if Sikkim, with its connections with Bhutan and Tibet, also formed part of the Agency, as is suggested below. Buddhists in India have fully as much right as their co-religionists in Burma to be removed, where geographical facts make it possible, from the arena of the Hindu-Muslim struggle.

keen interest in the outside world, there is a vague groping after something better. They do not want to be labelled for ever as "Excluded" or "Backward" and yet they cannot tolerate the idea of being swamped by the Indian. When I visited the Lushai Hills for the second time in December 1940, this was one of the points that was put to me, and with it was coupled a notion that they might be better off if attached to the hill areas of Burma. The other Excluded Areas are less politically-minded but I have no doubts whatever as to their dislike of the idea of being attached to India under a parliamentary system. Throughout the hills the Indian of the plains is despised for his effeminacy but feared for his cunning. The antipathy to him of the Assam hillman is strictly comparable with that of his cousin the Burman, and merits as serious consideration. The people of the hills of Assam are as eager to work out their own salvation free from Indian domination as are the people of Burma, and for the same reasons.

How then can we formulate a system which will acknowledge these affinities and give the people of these areas the opportunities they deserve and must have, of developing on sound lines towards civilised institutions? Personally, I am in favour of Dr. Hutton's idea, explained in paragraph 3 above, of a North-East Province or Agency embracing all the hill fringe from Lushai (or rather Lakher) land on the south right round to Balipara Frontier Tract on north embracing on the way the Chittagong Hill Tracts of Bengal and the Nagas and Chins of Burma and perhaps their Shan States too[8]. I would put this under a Chief Commissioner and he in turn would, I imagine, have to be divorced (as is Burma) from the control of the Government of India (presumably a federal body by then) and put perhaps under some appropriate department at Whitehall. I cannot do better,

---

[8] There is also much to be said for including Sikkim in the proposed Agency. Firstly, this State is essentially Mongolian and non-Indian and, secondly, the Political Officer there is the channel of communication between the Central Government and the Governments of Bhutan and Tibet, both of which countries have long frontiers with Assam. It is obviously advantageous that the Political Officer in Sikkim should be in constant touch with, and under the control of, the head of the Agency along the frontier of which questions with Bhutan and Tibet are constantly arising.

I think, than quote here Dr. Hutton's answer No. D. 270 recorded at page 2391 of Volume—Minutes of Evidence before the Joint Committee.

> "I think what I proposed to the Government of Assam but it would not meet with approval there, was that there should be a sub-Province of Burma which would embrace the North-East Frontier Districts of Assam with the North-East Frontier Districts of Burma. The people in Assam on the Assam side of the present boundary are much nearer to the Burmese than they are to the Indians. Their languages are exactly the same in some cases as those on the Burma side, and there is no difference of race at all, and there is constant communication, so far as there is any communication at all—it runs across from the Hukong Valley into the Naga Hills on the Assam side. I think it would be impossible to put the Assam Districts directly under a Burma adminis-tration because of the difficulties of language and of the distances and of communication through the hills, but I do think you could establish a centre somewhere near Manipur, for instance, from which it would be possible to administer as Commissioner or Chief Commissioner, under the Burma Government, a block of frontier districts of Assam and North-West Burma."

Such a tract or Agency would cover a large area of territory, i.e.,—

Administered hill tracts of Assam—28,211 square miles.
Unadministered territory—28,460 square miles.
Khasi State—3,694 square miles.
Manipur—8,620 square miles.

To this would have the area now in Burma which, it is sug-gested, should be included. The present area of Assam, exclud-ing Manipur, is 55,043 square miles. But a great deal of the suggested Agency would be uninhabited mountain and forest. Leaving the Burma area out of account, the population of the suggested Province or Agency would be about 2,000,000 *plus* another half million for Manipur, which would also be in the Agency. (The population of the unadministered areas has been estimated at 850,000. This estimate is based on area and cannot claim accuracy.)

The form of policy that I should visualise would be on self-governing lines, in the way outlined in Dr. Hutton's note of 17th March 1928 (*see* page 3 *ante*). Institutions of this kind in the plains are as good as dead, but in the tribal areas they are untouched and working; for a community, however savage, must have some form of government and organisation if it is to function at all, while even in the administered districts these institution are still flourishing, side by side, with a tendency for some cases at least to come to the Deputy Commissioner's Court. Elders or Chiefs with their Advisers settle the majority of disputes, villages have their own funds, and village roads and bridges are kept up by communal unpaid labour. Each village is a self-governing unit, but there are unmistakeable signs of willingness to combine into large units, the Lushai Hills have the nucleus of this. The system there, ever since we assumed responsibility for the country fifty years ago, has been to administer through the Chiefs, and there are Chiefs in various areas who meet in Circle, Subdivisional and, occasionally, District Councils. There is, similarly, in the Naga Hills a system of local committees which is capable of development. The Ao tribe has four "Range Committees" the oldest founded in 1934; the Lhota tribe has a committee founded as far back as 1926 which covers the entire Lhota country; a Sema Committee is in process of being formed. There is therefore something to go upon. The Shan States, I understand, have their own system of self government.

Finance would be a difficulty. As the Simon Commission pointed out at page 109 of Volume II (*see* page 4 *ante*) of their Report, these areas are deficit areas. Given their severance from India, and the ending of the present system whereby they derive such finance as they get from a Ministry which has no responsibility for, and therefore no interest in, their welfare and to whom in turn they can be of no advantage politically or otherwise, the only resort is financing from Imperial sources. There are precedents for this in the history of the Crown Colonies. At the same time there would be a strong case for contributions, both from the

Federal Government of India and from the Local Governments with those territories these lands would march, for a contribution as a matter of frontier insurance.

Addressing the Government of India in paragraph 7 of his letter No. P.J.(C)1896, dated the 1st July 1932, the Secretary of State expressed the view that the special treatment which Assam would require as a deficit Province "should either in whole or in part take the form of a grant towards the financing of the Totally Excluded Areas, and that such grant should at the outset represent the whole annual sum required to supplement whatever revenues may be raised in the areas themselves in order to cover the total cost of their administration". This of course, was not in fact done, and the annual subvention of Rs. 30 lakhs has no such conditions attached to it. The Excluded Areas would have been better off if there had been, but the existing arrangement can hardly be gone back on now. In any case the point would not arise if these proposals for complete severance from India were accepted, except to the extent that the financial needs of the Excluded Areas were taken into consideration when the Niemeyer proposals were framed, and therefore there would be a case for a reduction of the subvention if the "fringe" districts were cut off. I mention the matter to show that the needs and claims of the Excluded Areas were clearly visualised in 1932.

As to how such a Province should be manned, I think there need be no great difficulty. There is, I understand, already a Burma Frontier Service, and this could be expanded. The bigger in fact such a service were, the better. The whole would be placed under a Chief Commissioner and that post would be the "plum" of the service. He would probably need only one Secretary. Whether officers should be interchanged with those serving, say, in similar areas elsewhere, is open to question. I believe the Colonial Services are interchangeable. Dr. Hutton in his evidence before the Joint Committee advocated an All-India Service on the ground that local ones would be too small and so not provide a career within themselves (Page 2379, Volume II – Minutes of Evidence).

The question arises as to whether our aim should from the start be that the components of this block of self-governing communities should be communities of the nature of States with their rights guaranteed by *treaty* and not subject to constitutional changes introduced in the Provinces of India any more than are ordinary States, or something at a lower level of development at the outset, with future progress towards a higher status in the background. It is difficult, if not impossible, to see how otherwise than by treaty guarantee we can keep for the hill tracts the security without which progress is impossible. But such treaty guarantee would be far from precluding the imposition of a control over each community which would be adjusted to its state of development and which could be decided after reviewing each particular case. I would make it quite certain that all possibility of misrule such as has disfigured so many Indian States to this day or the petty inefficiency and dishonesty which characterises the Siemships of the Khasi Hills was eliminated. The amount of control would undoubtedly have to be very considerable for a time, but it is essential that it should come from Whitehall, and not from India, to which the hill tracts are entirely alien.

This is only a tentative proposal in board outline. Much detail would have to be filled in. But I see no other line along which we can fulfil our duty to these primitive peoples. They will *not* get a square deal from an *autonomous* Indian Government and the sequel would be rebellion, bloodshed and ultimate ruin.

11. The formation in administered districts of the Excluded Areas as, for instance, the Naga Hills and the Lushai Hills, of States of the kind I visualise would presumably have to await the introduction of the great constitutional changes promised after the war. In most areas there would be little difficulty. For example, there would be no insuperable difficulty in placing the Lushai Hills under a Council of Chiefs. In the Naga Hills the Deputy Commissioner has for some years visualised development on these lines. His Lhotas, Aos, Western Angamis, Eastern Angamis and so on could manage their own affairs with advice and adjustment. The seed is there. Similarly the Sirdars in the Jaintia Hills (if that

area were included in the proposed Agency) are quite as capable of running little States as are the Siems next door.

In some, if not all, of the Tribal Areas outside our administered control the process might well begin now. The Political Officer, Balipara Frontier Tract, for instance, would be prepared immediately to initiate the formation of an Aka State, seeing that we already recognise an Aka Raja. In the Naga tribal country the greater Konyak *Angs* could be recognised as heads of small States, for each one already has a recognised sphere of jurisdiction. Annexation to the Province would be avoided, while we should insist on reasonable control in return for recognition. In such an Agency of States, each with its own degree of independence adjusted according to its capabilities, Political Officers would take the place of District Officers.

12. The Partially Excluded Areas present a difficult problem. As regards the Mikir Hills I have no doubt whatever. They are still the most backward of the whole lot at that stage in many parts, where the "village", which consists of 3 or 4 houses only, is known by the name, not of the place, but of the headman, because the village site shifts every few years. They are more backward than either the totally excluded Nagas or Lushais. They are much more backward than the partially excluded Khasis. They are more backward than the partially excluded Garos. They ought never to have been "included" and the sooner they are taken out of that category the better.

As regards the Garos, after a long tour in the Garo Hills and a study of the papers, I came to the conclusion that they too ought never to have been included. But they have been included now for four years, and it is possible to point, in proof of their advancement, to the fact that one of their representatives has attained the rank of Parliamentary Secretary. There is material therefore on which to base a sufficiency of colourable arguments which might make one hesitate to recommend their "de-exclusion". But if one looks to their real good the case is different. I have yet to discover that the Garos have derived any outstanding benefit from being "included", or that they have developed any outstanding political sense in these four years, to the extent, for instance, that they could or would claim that the time had come when the franchise should be extended beyond the individuals who now exercise that privilege. The present franchise in these Hills is confined to the "Nokmas", of whom there were, in 1935, 685 in the Garo Hills North Constituency and 804 in the Garo Hills South. The total population of the Garo Hills by the 1941 Census is 223,569, so that a great deal less than 1 per cent of them enjoy the vote. Their representatives in the Assembly have been known to speak, but they are contemptible as far as intellect goes, their venality is notorious, while merit found no place in the considerations which led to the appointment of Mr. Benjamin Momin as a Parliamentary Secretary. If the obvious difficulties of undertaking what would be stigmatised as a retrograde step could be surmounted, I would welcome a proposal to put the Garos into the proposed new Agency. They too are not without the seeds of native self-government and to this day their "laskars" are entrusted with judicial powers.

Geographically the Garo Hills are bounded on the North by the "included" Assam districts of Kamrup and Goalpara, on the West by the Bengal included district of Rangpur, on the South by the "included" Bengal district of Mymensingh, or rather its partially excluded northern fringe, on the East by a portion of the Khasi and Jaintia Hills district of Assam, which consists entirely, or almost entirely, of Khasi States. It might therefore be argued, as it was in the past, that to exclude the Garo Hills would leave it an island in a sea of inclusion. But great rivers separate it from Kamrup, Goalpara and Rangpur, the Mymensingh fringe is of another province, while their Eastern neighbours are not British India at all. The geographical arguments are not really strong in themselves and ought not to be allowed to cause the real advantages of the Garos to be overlooked.

The third area which calls for examination is that which is known somewhat loosely as "the Khasi and Jaintia Hills District", a looseness of phrase which, as will be shown below, is decidedly when it is used as a basis for constitutional conclusions. The Khasis undoubtedly have absorbed education at a great rate, their two representatives are well-educated men, and one has been a Minister. There is obviously much to be said against relegating them to the rather "tribal" state which I visualise. But an analysis of the composition of this area reveals a number of considerations which must not be lost sight of if we are to arrive at a sound conclusion. The Khasi and Jaintia Hills District, which covers 6,145 square miles and contains a total population of 332,251, includes three different constitutional entities.

First, there are the Khasi States, 25 in number and of varying size and importance, covering an area of 3,700 square miles, or more than half the total area of the "district", and with, in 1941, a population of 213,586. These are not British India; they stand outside the Constitution[9]: they have their own form of self-government: and they are therefore obviously suitable areas to be included in the proposed new Agency. They are, as it is, fairly closely supervised by the Deputy Commissioner, Khasi and Jaintia Hills, in his capacity as Political Officer and the Governor is responsible for them as Agent to the Crown Representative.

Secondly, there is the Partially Excluded Area, which is described in the Order-in-Councils as "the British portion of the Khasi and Jaintia Hills District, other than the Shillong Municipality and Cantonment". The largest self-contained block of this is the Jowai subdivision, otherwise known as the Jaintia Hills, which was annexed by the British in 1835. Its area is 2,106 square miles and in 1941 its population numbered 85,807. The rest of the Partially Excluded Area is made up of a few odd islands of British territory the whole aggregating only 336 square miles. In this area the Deputy Commissioner functions as such, and the primary responsibility for the administration rests with the Ministry, subject to the Governor's special responsibility for a Partially Excluded Area.

Thirdly, there are the portions mentioned in the Order-in-Council as outside the scope of that Order, i.e., neither Excluded

---

[9] Seven square miles of Mylliem State covered by Shillong Town are included in the Shillong constituency referred to below, though, of course, the Assam Legislative have no jurisdiction over this little piece of State territory.

nor Partially Excluded, but within the Constitution. These, the Shillong Cantonments and part of the Shillong Town, cover an area of about 3 square miles and a population of about 13,000.

Of the so-called "Khasi and Jaintia Hills Districts" then, with its total area of 6,145 square miles and total population of something like 330,000 persons, only an area of 2,445 square miles or rather more than one-third, with a population bearing a similar proportion to the total, is either "Included" or "Partially Excluded", and can therefore be said to have established a claim to remain inside the Constitution. It returns two Members to the Assembly. One represents the Jowai subdivision with a population of 85,807 and an electorate of 10,700. The other represents a somewhat artificial entity called "Shillong", which comprises (*vide* page 85 of the Assam Electoral Manual) "the British territory of the Shillong subdivision *plus* the non-British areas in which the Municipality and Cantonment exercise jurisdiction" and which covers an area of 346 square miles and has an electorate of 6,200, of whom 3,900 are residents of British India and 2,300 of Mylliem State. There is a long history behind this, but it suffices to say that this constituency contains within it a considerable proportion of non-British electors, as follows:—

British subjects	...	4,300
Non-British subjects	...	1,900

Total	...	6,200

The apparent discrepancy in the details of the figures is explained by the fact that, while all voters residing in the British India part of the Constituency are assumed to be British subjects, of those residing in the States part of the Constituency some are British subjects and some are not.

While the standard among some Khasis is high, I have no hesitation in saying that the bulk of the inhabitants of the Jowai subdivision are no more advanced than those of their next door excluded neighbours, the North Cachar Hills, and they could

therefore conveniently and agreeably join with them as component parts of the new confederacy. In the Jowai subdivision there
is the nucleus of self-governing institutions. But, it will be said,
as in the Garo Hills case, these people now return a Member to
the Legislature and the case is stronger than that of the Garo
Hills because he is an intelligent man and has proved his worth.
Again, the answer must be that the real good of the people must
weigh the heaviest and it is unwise to base policy on individuals.
I have it, in point of fact, on unimpeachable authority, though
not first-hand and therefore I would not use the point beyond a
"mention" that the sitting Member, Mr. Gatphoh has expressed
quite decidedly his regret that his constituency was ever even
placed in the partially excluded category.

This leaves Shillong, and a difficult problem too. If, however,
things were straightened out to the extent that the whole of the
present electorate area *plus* a reasonable "fringe" were converted
into British territory, perhaps there would be no great difficulty
in leaving the Constituency as it is.

But I think that, stated in these terms, there certainly emerges
a good case for adding the bulk of the Khasi and Jaintia Hills to
the proposed new Agency.

13. Incidentally, if this rearrangement of boundaries ever became
fact, I would take the opportunity of severing the unnatural
alliance of Sylhet and Cachar with Assam and returning those
two (or rather one and a half, for the northern subdivision of
the latter, the North Cachar Hills, would already have gone to
the new Hill Province) districts to Bengal—if Bengal would have
them, especially Sylhet, a "deficit district" to the tune of 18 lakhs
annually. The remainder might be too small for a Governorship,
but though that was used more than once, e.g., in paragraph 11
of Assam Government's letter No. 1573-Pol-3860-A.P., dated
the 11th August 1925, as an argument for retaining Sylhet and
Cachar in Assam, I do not think it is really a very relevant one.
That consideration apart, the balance of advantage is all the other
way. A new Assam, small but homogeneous would be a much
happier place than it is now, for "Valleyism" would disappear

and I cannot imagine a greater boon, while to be the head of the administration would be still an attractive as well as responsible post, even if it carried less pay and lower status.

In this connection, I append a note compiled by Mr. J. P. Mills, Governor's Secretary, Assam, which contains an interesting suggestion. It runs as follows:—

"There is one final suggestion in this connection which I should like to make, for at least consideration. It is perhaps more logical and less startling than it seems at first sight. One objection which is quite certain to be raised to the proposal to form a Province of the Assam Valley only is that it would be so small as to be useless. This is a very serious objection indeed, and one which it is essential to forestall. I would do so as follows. The whole political outlook has altered in the last four years. Dominion Status has been promised, and under it it appears to me to be impossible to argue that the Provinces will be any more 'British' India than the States. Therefore, since sentiment is all important in Indian politics, I would go so far as to make the gesture of *offering* to restore the old Ahom kingdom as a State— needless to say on very strict conditions. The chief condition would be that the new State would be deprived of none of the democratic institutions Assam now enjoys; the entire power would be in the hands of Ministers responsible to the legislature. The Raja would be nothing more than a figurehead, and the only branch of the Royal Family surviving is a distant one. But as a figurehead he might well arouse sentiment, and we should get a modicum of praise for restoring past prestige, instead of universal abuse for reducing Assam to an insignificant fragment. The Muslims would not like it, but they and other minorities will have no more protections from Parliament in a Province than in a State under Dominion Status, for States and Provinces alike will only be attached to the Crown by a tenuous thread. I can see no other way in which the objection to the bisection of Assam be met."

I am not prepared at present to hazard a final opinion on this suggestion, in many ways attractive though it be. It would be necessary, if it were ever to be pursued, to obtain opinions on it.

14. Supposing it were decided, for whatever reason, that the scheme I have attempted to outline above were impracticable, it

is necessary to consider the alternatives that present themselves. I trust that sufficient has been said to prove that to place the Hills under the control of the Ministry of an Assam as now constituted is utterly impossible and unworkable. A workable intermediate arrangement, though I would not myself advocate it, might be found in the formation of a Province of the Assam Valley only and in placing the hills under that, if they must be placed under a Provincial Government without any of the safeguards that at present exist. There would at least be a chance that the old Assamese friendly methods of dealing with the hillmen—for the hills and the plains were by no means always at war—might be in part revived. The Assam Valley still contains a substratum of Mongolian population similar to that of the hills, and though, as I have explained, this is being rapidly submerged by the immigrant Muslims from Bengal, the latter have not yet pervaded political, in the way they have pervaded agricultural, life, so that the hills would perhaps not get such a bad deal as they certainly would from the Bengali politicians of the Surma Valley. But this alternative has little to commend it and will have less and less as immigration increases: then it will be too late.

It has been suggested that the areas with which this note deals might be lumped with the "backward areas" which cover so much of the central plateau of India proper and which will undoubtedly require special protection in the Constitution of the future. To this proposal there are grave and obvious objections. The culture of the Mongolian areas is different from, rather than lower than, that of the "backward areas" of India proper, to which they neither historically nor racially belong. There must inevitably be some bargaining with Indian leaders over the future of the "backward areas" of India proper, but to bargain with alien politicians over the future of non-Indian Mongolian areas would be a breach of faith. These areas do not, and cannot, form part of India, and to recognise the facts is to recognise the necessity for special treatment.

A Note on the Future of the Hill Tribes of Assam and the Adjoining Hills in a Self-governing India

James P. Mills

1. INTRODUCTORY

This note deals only with the position of the hill tribes when India has obtained her independence. No attempt therefore is made to consider what modifications of policy may be feasible or desirable within the framework of the Government of India Act of 1935. A reference has been made to the States of Tripura, Bhutan and Sikkim and to the Chittagong Hill Tracts because they are geographically and culturally part of the area under consideration.

I have attempted to present as objective a case as possible, but sympathies (or prejudices) are bound to colour all writing. I consider that all primitive peoples require special protection during periods of change a thousand times swifter than anything they have ever before experienced. This does not mean that they must be put into "human museums", as the phrase goes. That would be both impossible and wrong, for change is inevitable. But it does mean that far from speeding up the change, which will be all too swift of itself, we must be prepared when necessary to do what we can to slow it down to a pace at which its impact will not be destructive. We must not destroy the old, or allow it to be destroyed if we can help it, till we are quite sure what we are going to put in its place. Planned replacement is far more important than planned destruction, and requires far more

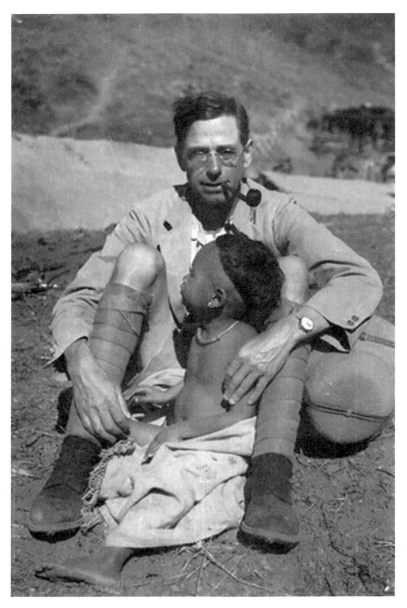

J. P. Mills with a Naga child, photographed sometime in 1936–1937 during the expedition to Pangsha village

detailed study. A tribal culture is a structure which has stood the test of centuries. It therefore cannot be wholly bad, though some of it may seem out of date or even dangerous to us. To demolish it utterly is easy, but the old materials cannot then be used again, and something which embodied much good will have gone for ever. It is surely better to repair it and modernise it as one would a fine old house. But to do this means time and study, for an old beam cannot be cut out till we know what it is supporting and have put in props to replace it.

The danger of unwise, if well-intentioned, legislation is obvious, but it is frequently said that the tribesmen of India do not need protection against deliberate exploitation by Indians. I unhesitatingly say they do. Difficulty of access has so far largely protected the tribes of Assam, but for an account of what has happened elsewhere I would refer to the report I wrote on the subject while on special duty with the Government of India in the Reforms Department in the summer of 1926. It is based on the most reliable information available and I would earnestly ask that it be read by anyone who feels doubt on this point. More recent and fully documented information on the same subject is contained in "Tribal Hyderabad" published by His Exalted Highness the Nizam's Government this year.

I feel above all that a mere negative fear of harming the tribesmen is not enough. To it must be added a positive desire to help and benefit them. For nearly 30 years my service has been spent almost entirely on work to do with the hill tribes. I have not, alas, been able to see them all, but I have attempted to study those I have seen and to read everything available on those I have not. I am therefore writing about my friends, whose welfare I seek before all else, and that extent I can fairly be called biased.

2. THE AVERAGE HILLMAN

It would perhaps be helpful to attempt a brief description of the average hillman whose future we are planning—what he is like, what he has now, and what he would like to have. To avoid undue distortion of the composite portrait I leave aside both the exceptional man who has virtually abandoned tribal life, and the Khasi, who is in general so different that he calls for special treatment. The exceptional man, largely because he is vocal and can speak English, is apt to thrust himself into the foreground, and since "the squeaking wheel gets the grease" he often receives an undue amount of attention. But it is the average man who really matters, for he constitutes the vast majority and it is by his happiness or unhappiness that the success or failure of all schemes must ultimately be judged.

(*i*) What is he like? He lives in a village, which may be very small or may contain 500 houses or more, according to the tribe. He and his fellow clansmen and villagers form a mutual co-operative society, helping each other to build their houses and cultivate their fields, and supporting each other in old age and times of sickness and need. He lives by agriculture, which usually yields a small surplus, and in a bad year he can always borrow grain, which he will repay in kind in better times. Very occasionally there is scarcity over a wide area, but the recent deaths from starvation in the Chang country are the first I have ever heard of personally. When he is too old to work his children or clansmen will feed him.

Villages within fairly easy distance of the plains grow a considerable quantity of cash crops, such as cotton or *pan*, but in those further in the hills there is normally little or no money in circulation, since they are practically self-supporting except for salt and iron, and most transactions are by barter. Self-sufficiency has produced a strong artistic sense, which is virtually dead in the plains. Lakher weaving, for instance, can hardly be surpassed anywhere in the world, buildings are often decorated with fine carvings, and the full dress of some of the tribe, can only be called superb.

Great pride and self-reliance are combined with a sense of humour so like our own that it forms one of the main ties between Europeans and hillmen. The great majority of hillmen are honest and truthful, for not only would it be a matter of shame to be otherwise, but in a small and closely knit community dishonesty quickly meets its reward. In a country where all journeys have to be performed on foot visits to the outside world are necessarily difficult and infrequent, and this inevitably means a narrow outlook. Little outside his village which does not affect his clan interests the average hillman and even the sense of tribal unity is often dim.

Clan feeling is strong and governs daily life. All fellow members of a clan are not only invariably addressed as, but are actually regarded as "fathers", "sisters", "brothers", and so on, however remote the relationship may be according to our ideas, and so close is the tie between members of the same clan that, to an extent it is difficult to realize till one has experienced it, a man often hardly seems to think of himself as an individual. It follows from this that an injury to one member of a clan is relationship, which naturally carries both privileges and responsibilities, has an important bearing on any political schemes.

This clan feeling is part of the all-important thing which is commonly called Custom. But this is too casual a word, just as "Law" is too rigid, and probably the closest translation one can get to the various tribal words is the "Way", using the term, not in the sense of a path which any man may make for himself in any direction, but in the New Testament sense of a pre-existing path which every man must follow if he is to win salvation. To illustrate this translation, Ao Naga Christians call themselves "Followers of the Way", using for the "Way" the old Animist word which means the whole body of tribal custom, religious and secular. But religion is only part of the tribal "Way" and after a short period of natural if rather irresponsible revolt converts almost invariably resume obedience to the old secular rules and regulations. The tribal "Way" is regarded not as manmade but something as eternal as the tribe itself; it is flexible enough to include both Animism and Christianity and can be greatly modified, but its essence must be preserved, for its destruction would mean social disintegration. It is extremely difficult to predict what will change quickly under pressure and what will present a hard core of resistance. For instance a Sema Naga chief will give up his beloved rice beer when converted by the Baptist Mission, but will retain his half dozen or so wives, while Lhota Naga converts abandon polygamy. Our policy has always been to suppress practices which are clearly evil, such as certain very cruel forms of sacrifice, but otherwise to confine ourselves to guiding to the best of our ability the tendencies which inevitably lead to modification of custom. Just as Hinduism covers both religious and secular life, so the "Way" of any tribe covers both the religion of its members, be it Christianity or Animism, and all else besides. Any legislation, therefore, aimed at the forcible alteration of any particular tribal "Way" would be as bitterly resented as an attack on Hinduism or Islam and it is important in any scheme to ensure that a tribal "Way" can be fundamentally altered only by the tribe itself, and not by a legislature on which its representatives would necessarily be in a minority.

(*ii*) What does the average hillman want? The answer might be summed up by saying that, like most people, he wants a Government which will leave him alone except when he requires help. He most certainly does not want union with or domination by either of the great Indian political parties. With the Muslim League he clearly has nothing in common and stories of Congress aid to the Japanese during the siege of Kohima have spread like ripples in a pond and created an impression it is impossible to exaggerate. The Congress flag was waved in the Japanese lines, Congress slogans were shouted, and Congressmen led Japanese foraging parties. To the Nagas who helped us so loyally Congress are therefore just enemies, and no dialectics on the meaning of the word "patriot" can alter that fact. Naturally this feelings is less strong in the partially excluded areas, which saw no fighting, but its existence among an important section of the tribes must most certainly be taken into account.

Nor does the hillman join in the cry for political freedom of which some hear distant echoes. This has been made clear on the few occasions when he has voiced his views (*vide* paragraph 11), the reason doubtless being that he already enjoys considerable freedom in all that matters most to him under the indigenous systems of local self-government referred to in paragraph 4.

Such direct administration too as there is in the hills is the reverse of autocratic, though critics more vocal than administrators are permitted to be frequently maintain the opposite. It is not difficult for a district officer in the hills, either through his staff of interpreters or otherwise, to sound public opinion, and if he knows his job he invariably does so, for he realises that if a reasonable order is first discussed with reasonable men its chances of ready acceptance are greatly increased. An outstanding example of the result of unwise peremptory orders is the Jaintia Rebellion of 1860–63.

The importance to a tribesman of his "Way" has already been touched upon, and preservation of it against unwise and unnecessary interference ranks high in his list of wants. In Assam we have—rightly, in my opinion—done our best to meet this wish by keeping hill officers as long as possible in the same district, on the ground that detailed knowledge of one district is more valuable to the governed than wider experience of several, and because the holder of the post of Political Officer means nothing as such to a tribesman, but a known and beloved officer means much. When the time does come for a trusted officer to be transferred a ferment of anxiety spreads in the district lest someone should be sent who will not understand and maintain the tribal "Ways", and a new comer is politely and silently placed on long probation.

In the way of material wants the tribesman probable puts medical attention first, for to a man dependent on the work of his hands disabling illness is a disaster. Towards education the attitude of the tribes varies greatly. None regard it as a gateway to a larger culture, of which they know nothing, and some look upon it merely as a way of wasting the time of little boys who ought to be out helping in the fields. But others regard it as useful, though only as a means of obtaining what they aptly call "sitting-and-eating jobs", which win for their lucky possessors considerable and certain wealth at the expense of the minimum of exertion. I may say here that I am myself very eager to alter this. It is difficult to call the present system education, in the true sense, at all. Literacy is, of course, important, but a knowledge of the world shared by whole communities is equally so from the point of view of political advance and I strongly favour something on the lines indicated in the Colonial Office White Paper on "Mass Education in African Society" or Sir Richard Livingstone's "The Future in Education".

A crying need of which all tribes not blinded by conservatism are aware is that of agricultural improvement. Pressure on the land is increasing and unless we can meet it with improved methods of agriculture fresh land will be sought, as it always has been in the past, and tribal migrations, slow but as irresistible as the advance of a glacier, will begin.

The question of financial assistance in general is referred to in paragraph 18. Here too tribes differ greatly. Some, which have been more spoon-fed than others are apt to apply to Government for everything they want. Others are inclined to feel that a dispensary, for instance, is more really their own if they have subscribed some of the money. In general, like most people, they want to see some return for their money.

3. THE KHASI

The Khasis are apt to attract more attention than other tribes because Shillong, the capital of the Province, is in their country, but it would be a great mistake to regard them as typical. Possibly partly owing to their different racial origin, but mainly owing to the particularly heavy impact on them of foreign culture they have reacted in a way different from that in which any other tribe has done. Sir Keith Cantlie, the greatest authority on them, considers that their culture has been completely smashed by money and the love of money, and finds it difficult to foresee any useful future even for the rural Khasi. What is left of their tribal "Way" is of little value, for though they plead Khasi custom when it suits them they break it without a blush when convenient, and public opinion is silent. An example is bribery. According to strict Khasi custom the taking of a bribe is *sang* (taboo), but every office in every State is bought. Land provides another example. By Khasi custom each generation holds clan land as trustees for the next, but in practice it is frequently either leased for a peppercorn rent and a large premium pocketed, or is even sold outright and the money spent on the luxuries civilization can provide. Most serious of all is the get-rich-quick practice of squeezing far more cash crops out of the ground that it can properly produce without a thought for future generations, with the result that erosion is ruining more and more land every year and competent observers such as the Director of Agriculture consider widespread disaster inevitable within a measurable time. In short, in everything he does the Khasi puts himself first and his clan and tribe a long way second. In contrast to the members of all other tribes he is a complete individualist, and this individualism has led to and been aggravated by his comparatively recent habit of living in scattered farms isolated from the influences of village life.

The fact that Shillong is several times larger than all the other hill stations in Assam put together has given rise to an urban class unique among our tribes, living in an environment completely distinct from the rest of the Khasi country, of which educated Khasis invariably refer as "the interior"—an uncomfortable, motorless land which they visit as rarely as possible. The distinction between the urban and rural Khasi is as sharp and definite as that between the tribe as a whole and other tribes, but the larger outlook one might have hoped for in the townsmen appears to be entirely absent. No educated Khasi will bestir himself to help his tribe, and the requests which we have made from time to time educated Khasis of good will to come forward with schemes of much needed reform have never evoked a response.

Since the tribe is matrilineal the child of a Khasi mother is automatically a member of a Khasi clan, quite regardless of who its father may have been, and Khasi women being notoriously free with their favours Shillong has long contained a large and increasing number of persons who, though calling themselves Khasis, would elsewhere be classed as Anglo-Indians or Indians of mixed descent. These have in turn intermarried with pure Khasis, persons of mixed blood, or foreigners till we have reached a position, which is not always realised, where few of the so-called Khasi families resident in Shillong are of pure blood, and for many of them the term "Khasi" is an entire misnomer. These and the pure Khasis who have taken to an urban life certainly have no need of protection. They could not possibly be described as primitive, they have nothing to contribute to the welfare of the tribal peoples as such, and I can see no possible justification for retaining them in that category. My suggestions for their future are contained in paragraph 13(*i*) below.

4. LOCAL SELF-GOVERNMENT AND ITS DEVELOPMENT

Human beings cannot exist in a state of anarchy and the hill tribes of Assam had their own systems of Government long before our arrival. It is an unforgettable experience to be the first European to enter a village of two or three thousand souls and to realise that they have managed their own affairs from time immemorial. Institutions which can control large numbers of by no means gentle savages clearly merit respect and we have been at pains to preserve the self-governing institutions we found. For example, an extract from the Rules for the Administration of the Lushai Hills reads "The administration of the district known as the Lushai Hills is vested in the Governor of Assam, the Commissioner and the Superintendent of the Lushai Hills and his Assistants, and in the chiefs and headmen of villages. The chiefs and headmen of villages are responsible for the behaviour of their people and the Superintendent and his Assistants will uphold the authority of the chiefs to the best of their ability". Similarly in other hill districts the indigenous village authorities are specifically recognized by rule as sharing with His Excellency and his officers responsibility for the administration. This is a very proper and very important recognition, which it is essential to preserve.

The Indian Penal Code and the Civil and Criminal Procedure Codes are not in force in the hills. There is no Bar except at

Shillong, and except there no pleader is ever allowed to appear except in murder cases and cases in which no hillman is involved.

Another point of importance is that, with few exceptions, the village authorities have not been created by Government. They were there before we ever entered Assam and have continued to function ever since. They vary greatly from tribe to tribe, but everywhere the village is the unit, save that a Konyak Naga "Ang" usually exercises control over a number of villages. To take some examples, a Lushai or Lakher chief is a chief by right of birth, and we recognize rather than appoint him. A chief is the protector and father of his people. He must help them in time of famine and other distress, and in return they must pay him certain dues, render him certain services, and come to his help when called upon to do so. He also represents his village in all dealings with Government. But he never acts alone; elders invariably assist him to allot the village lands year by year, to administer village affairs and to hear cases. In contrast the Ao Nagas provide an example of purely democratic Government. Among them once in a term of years the clans of each village elect a council of elders in which full power to allot land, settle cases and deal with all matters pertaining to the welfare of the village is vested. Their term of office lasts for a specified time, the length of which is fixed by tradition, and no re-election is permissible. Ao Naga villages are big and a village council is too unwieldy a body to represent a village in its dealings with Government, and we have therefore had to appoint "gaonburas" for the purpose. These are ordinarily members of their village councils, but they have no power to override the decisions of the councils, which are the only authority we recognize.

The judicial powers of village authorities are great, and appeals against their decisions are discouraged. In criminal matters they can take cognizance of all crimes except those defined as heinous, and in civil matters they can award compensation up to any amount. These extensive powers are in fact controlled by custom. In the eyes of the hillman there is no distinction between criminal and civil cases. In his view theft or grievous hurt are as properly dealt with by the payment of compensation as are trespass or an accidental injury, and since the amount of compensation payable for every conceivable offence is strictly prescribed by custom exorbitant claims for damages are impossible.

Village authorities are very far from being without financial experience, for from the earliest times communal ceremonies involved the collection and spending of communal funds, in which grain took the place of coin. Recently, certainly in the Baptist Mission areas and probably elsewhere, there has been a strong and successful movement to take over from European control the management of money collected in the tribe. Tribesmen like to watch the spending of their money, and are often surprisingly ready to subscribe in labour and money to any project on which they have set their heart. I have known for instance, several villages combine to make a bridle path they needed, and then ask Government to take it over and keep it up. This feeling of self-reliance and responsibility must clearly be fostered. Grants could advantageously be made to village authorities in part payment of schemes on the sole condition that the scheme is satisfactorily completed. Details can safely be left to the village authorities, who will levy their own share in labour, materials or money.

To fit the tribes to play their part in a larger world we must develop what we have preserved and the task before us is the formidable one of founding tribal councils on the basis of the existing village units. For a gathering of village elders to decide matters about which all those present have personal knowledge is one thing; it is quite another to consider and settle in debate questions on which personal knowledge is necessarily confined to a few. It will therefore probably be necessary to organize intermediate bodies, such as the Range Councils I have suggested elsewhere for the Ao Nagas, between the village and tribal councils to deal with matters of purely local importance and in particular to exercise judicial powers in cases in which the parties belong to different villages (*vide* paragraph 19 (*i*)].

Tribal committees are functioning in the Naga Hills, the North and South Lushai Hills have each a Council of Chiefs, and informal meetings of representative men have been held elsewhere. These tentative experiments must be encouraged and continued, and when any really suitable council emerges—for in no two tribes will the organization be identical—it must be put on a proper basis. Above all, any councils we set up must be given real work and responsibility. Sessions should not be frequent, for communications are slow and members cannot leave the work in their fields for long, but when meetings are held they must be busy ones. Nothing would be more fatal to the whole scheme than lack of real work.

It is from the tribal councils that representatives would have to be chosen for any general Assembly representing all the hill peoples, and here great difficulties of language and genuine representation would arise. The number of hillmen who can express themselves really fluently in English is very few, and those who can will almost certainly have spent so many impressionable years away in College that they are tribal in nothing but race and are entirely without first hand knowledge of the needs of their fellow tribesmen. Such men are far less representative of the ordinary hillman than a sympathetic European would be. To get over this difficulty there appear to be two alternatives. One would to put no obstacle in the way of the election to the general Assembly of men who speak their own language only and to provide adequate interpreters. The other would be to encourage the educated man, even if he is unrepresentative, but to assign to him really representative "observers" who would see that he speaks and votes for the tribe, or in other words to confine his functions strictly to those of a mouthpiece. This latter system is, I believe, in force in parts of West Africa which are under indirect rule, and where the same difficulty exists. Neither of these alternatives is at all satisfactory and any Council Chamber in which a general Assembly of tribal representatives was in session would inevitably resemble the Tower of Babel. It is partly this formidable difficulty which has led me to advocate only a small advisory Governor's Council in paragraphs 15 (I) (c) and 17.

One last point, but a fundamentally important one, remains. The Assam hillman is a true democrat in the sense that Government by counting heads is quite beyond his comprehension. To him a decision by a narrow majority would be no decision at all, for he would never regard a settlement opposed by a strong minority as a settlement in the true sense of the word. He will always strive for a compromise. Let me return for a moment to the unadministered village. Clearly it has to settle every question for itself somehow and finally, for there is no overriding authority to enforce a settlement, and an important discontented minority would be both a weakness and nuisance. Every question is therefore debated till it is settled, and this spirit of compromise survives in administered tribes. Many a time I have watched the process. Two parties have a dispute. Both sides turn up, strongly supported by clansmen. Everyone shouts at once, fists are shaken and chaos seems to reign. Meanwhile the elders sit listening and sipping drinks provided by the parties in lieu of court fees, occasionally intervening to ask questions. Order is gradually restored and in some miraculous, way a decision is arrived at to which both sides agree, even what we should call criminal cases being decided in this way. It is rarely that both sides cannot be got to agree, and when this happens the contest is regarded as a draw and the match has to be replayed before an officer. But I have known large villages from which no case has ever come into court for years on end, a record which speaks of itself. Clearly we shall have failed if we kill this spirit of compromise by a system of clear cut majority decisions instead of extending it to tribal Government and the larger field of politics.

5. THE HISTORICAL BACKGROUND

The future of the tribes cannot be considered apart from their immediate past. There have been three main periods of annexation, the first when the British first entered Assam, the second in the sixties and seventies, and the last, apart from minor additions, in the early nineties.

To the first period belong the annexation in 1832 of such areas of the North Cachar Hills as had formed part of the Kachari Kingdom, the surrender of his hill territory by the Raja of Jaintia in 1835, and the settlement of the Mikir Hills in 1838. To the second period belong the annexation of the Garo Hills in 1866 and of the Asalu area of the North Cachar Hills in 1867, and the conquest of the Angami Nagas in 1879. In the third period the Mokokchung Subdivision, of the Naga Hills was occupied in 1890, and the North Lushai Hills were taken over in the same year and the South Lushai Hills in the following year.

The whole of the hinterland North of the Brahmaputra and about half the Naga country are still independent and comprise the present Tribal Areas. Before the annexation of the Ahom and Kachari Kingdoms the only tribes under any sort of control were the feeble Mikirs who paid tribute to the Ahom Kings and the Kacharis of the North Cachar Hills who had been left behind during the tribal migration and continued to be subject to their own Raja. All the others were incorporated in Assam, not by the Assamese, but by the British, and not primarily with a view to benefiting the tribes, but to protect the plains against their depredations. The Ahom chronicles are full of accounts of expeditions against the hill tribes, but these never resulted in annexation, which only took place when the British were able to employ forces immeasurably better armed than the tribesmen. Such tribal territory as is attached to Assam is territory conquered by a third party, and of this the hillman is fully aware, as the representations quoted in paragraph 11 below show.

The Mongolians of the plains have been virtually submerged, but the resistance those of the hills were able to maintain till our advent has preserved intact the largest solid block of non-Indian people South of the Himalayas. Whether they will ever feel that they are part of the Indians nation remains to be seen. They certainly do not do so yet.

6. THE RACIAL AND CULTURAL BACKGROUND

I. As is suggested above the root of the matter is a racial conflict, not between two of the races which can truly be called Indian, but between Indian and Mongolians. There is no question of the tribes of the North Eastern Frontier being Indians whom other stronger Indians have ousted from the fertile plains and driven up into the hills. Racially they are no more Indians than are the Burmans to whom they are akin. Climate and vegetation proclaim Assam as truly a part of Indonesia as is Burma beyond the low ranges to the East, and the tribesmen are Indonesians with distant cousins in Formosa, Indo-China, the Philippines and elsewhere, but none in Indian proper. Their original home was somewhere far to the South East, and just as the Aryans entered the great peninsular from the North West, so the Mongolian Indonesians, pushing slowly up till they met the mountain barrier of the great Central Asian Plateau, swung West and South West, occupying first the hills and then the plains.

The parallel with Burma is striking. The fat plains of Burma and Assam with their indolent population have alike tempted India and she has invaded them both. The invasion of Burma has been economic, but so serious that it was largely in the hope of being able to halt it that she demanded separation. In Assam the invasion has been mainly one of priests, civil servants and peasants, and against far weaker opposition. For centuries, Koch, Kachari, and Ahom have followed each other down the valley of the Brahmaputra, only to meet coming up stream priests eager to teach Hinduism, literate Indians ready to offer their services and peasants hungry for land. Enervated by the climate each Mongolian Kingdom in turn sank under the flood, and the plains of Assam are now a great salient of India running up into the Western frontier of Indonesia. The Mongolians have lost the plains, and the problem with which this note deals is how they can be helped to save the hills till they are strong enough to make their contribution to India which has advanced to meet them.

II. The sharp cultural distinction between the hills and the plains is so clearly recognized that it needs little re-emphasis.

(1) The languages of the hills are all of the Tibeto-Burman group, except the Mon-Khmer language of the Khasis.

(2) While indigenous systems of self-government have disappeared from the plains they are vigorously alive in the hills.

(3) It is more accurate to describe the culture of the hills as different from that of the plains than as inferior to it. There are "black spots" in the hills, as there are in the plains, but on the other hand self-sufficiency is greater, artistic development is almost everywhere higher, squalor and misery are rare, the sense of social responsibility is high, democratic institutions are highly developed, and the deadening feelings of political frustration is entirely absent.

It is important too to note that all along the Northern Hills the tribesmen look to Tibet, and not to Assam, for their models. There, for instance, a man who gets on in the world does not buy a coat and a *dhoti*, but a Tibetan cloak and ornaments and a piece of Chinese silk.

7. RELIGIOUS BACKGROUND

The great religions of India proper, Hinduism and Islam, are alien religions in the hills, where Animism in various forms is the original faith of every tribe. But Animism has not hardened into a communal creed and is giving way before the impact of Buddhism in parts of the Northern Hills and of Christianity elsewhere. The number of Buddhists South of the frontier of Tibet must be very considerable, but most of them inhabit areas of which we as yet know little or nothing. The Christian block is therefore of more immediate importance. This can be said to cover the Lushai Hills, Garo Hills, Khasi and Jaintia Hills, and the Ao, Sema and Lhota tribes in the Naga Hills and is therefore probably the largest solid Christian block in India. It will certainly increase in size, and since Christianity is rapidly assuming a communal tinge the existence of this expanding block must be taken into account.

8. INCREASING DIVERGENCIES

However attractive in theory an immediate union of the hills and the plains may be the fact must be faced that any attempt to bring this about would involve, not the hastening of the union of two groups of peoples already approaching one another, but the forcible bringing together of two groups which have been moving away from each other for a hundred years. It is certain that the plains and the hills were much more alike in the days of the Ahom Kings than they are now, and it is at least reasonable to argue that if no voluntary union took place then no union now would be voluntary. From the earliest days of the British occupation of Assam education has spread in the plains at a far greater speed than in the hills, and it is in the plains that an elaborate administrative machine has been set up. The plains too are being increasingly occupied by a Bengali Muslim population with no connection either cultural or ancestral with the hills, and are thereby being rapidly altered in character and outlook. The war has brought money into much of the hills and plains alike, but the industrialisation which bids fair to change the social structure of India proper is represented in the hills only by a handful of trained mechanics. Though many hillmen have now been educated up to a point, it will take time to bridge the gap and the tribesman of to-day looks down from the hills upon a far more alien Assam than his great-grandfather did.

9. THE GEOGRAPHICAL FACTOR

The map, in that it represents space only, is apt to be misleading. From it might at first sight appear that any separation of the hills from the plains they encircle means the setting up of an artificial barrier between two areas closely united geographically. This is not so. The barrier is there already, and if some scientist could devise a time-map based on present speed of communication it would present a very different picture. For instance on such a map Calcutta would be nearer Charduar than the closest hill village; Mokokchung and Bombay would be roughly equidistant from Jorhat, and the McMahon Line would be further from Sadiya than is America.

It is true that a journey from one hill area to another usually entails descending to the plains and climbing into the hills again, and that the geographical formation of the mountains North of the Brahmaputra would render it extremely difficult to remedy matters there. But South of the Brahmaputra conditions are entirely different, since ranges tend to run parallel with the plains, making lateral communication comparatively easy. Even now it is possible to travel from the extreme North-East of the Naga Hills to the extreme South-West of the North Cachar Hills by a bridle path which only crosses two rivers of any size and encounters no serious climbs. Similar conditions obtain in the Lushai Hills and elsewhere, and the building of a network of communications knitting the whole Southern frontier together would entail no engineering difficulties comparable to those likely to be met with in connecting this network with the plains. This point is illustrated by the fact that for fifty years we never seriously attempted to make anything better than a bridle path from the plains to Aijal in the Lushai Hills and that when the attempt was at last made under the pressure of military necessity the result has proved far from satisfactory.

The geographical separation of the hills from the plains therefore appears to be a fact which must be recognized politically and can only be altered by greatly improved means of communication.

Nor is there any reason, in my opinion, to fear that political recognition of geographical conditions will have an adverse affect on trade and intercourse. I have never heard it claimed that trade between the Garo Hills and Goalpara is any easier than trade between the Garo Hills and Mymensingh, and for hundreds of miles from the frontier of Bhutan right round to Sibsagar and along the borders of the Khasi States the plains of Assam march with hills which are not part of the Province, but money, labour, oranges, potatoes, cloth, salt, rice, iron and other goods pass freely across the frontier.

10. THE ANALOGY OF BURMA

The historical analogy between Assam and Burma has been referred to in paragraph 6 (I) above. She also provides within herself a close geographical and ethnographical parallel, for, as in Assam, great alluvial valleys run deep into hills inhabited by tribes of Indonesian stock in general more primitive than the plainsmen. In the "Blue Print" it was recommended and in the White Paper laid down that these hill tracts, including even the advanced Shan States, should not be united with the plains of Burma till their people expressed their desire for union. It is important to note here that every argument against separation which could be used with regard to Assam applies with equal force to Burma, but has been overruled by more cogent considerations, and, further, that the Government of Burma has decided against any imposed union of the hills and the plains though the racial and cultural dissimilarity is far less than in Assam and many of the hillmen are adherents of the Buddhism of the plains.

All Burma officials of whose opinions I am aware stress the identity of the problem of the Burma and Assam Hill tracts, and Professor Coupland takes the same view. I would therefore venture to say that the burden of proving that the hill tracts of Assam and Burma should be accorded fundamentally different treatment would seem to lie on anyone advocating this course. I have myself proposed considerable divergence from the Burma scheme in the matter of a separate Governor for the hills (paragraph 21) and the establishment of a protectorate (paragraph 25) but I consider this is fully justified, for far less understanding of and sympathy with the tribes of the remote North-East Frontier can be expected in Delhi than of the hill tribes of Burma by their kinsmen in the plains.

11. THE VIEWS OF THE HILLMEN

There are still many areas in the hill tracts of Assam where the existence of the teeming plains of Assam is either unknown or known only as a travellers' tale. Even in the less remote areas the vast majority of the people have no conception of Indian politics and have expressed no views on their future because they do not know that it is under discussion. But where views have been expressed they demand careful consideration if we are to adhere to our declared policy that Government must be with the consent of the governed, and to leave the hillmen, as we propose to leave the Japanese, free to decide their ultimate form of Government. I know of no case where a desire for union has been expressed by representative hillmen themselves, and since April 1937, no request has ever been received from an excluded area for partial exclusion, or from a partially excluded area for full inclusion. On the other hand, the request for special treatment voiced before the Simon Commission has been more than once repeated.

It can be taken as certain than any published proposal for the separation of the hills from the plains would meet with opposition as vocal as that of the silversmiths of Ephesus and based on the same motives, for the Members of Legislative Assembly from the partially excluded areas undoubtedly find in their salaries, quite apart from other sources of income, a very profitable and easy means of livelihood. Even now, with only rumours in the air, one sees from time to time accounts in the Press of meetings of unspecified hillmen, vaguely described as "from all over Assam", at which resolutions are passed advocating continued union with the Province, but it is significant that such meetings are never held in the homelands of the tribes, where public opinions is most easily accessible. No tribes have ever sent any accredited representatives to Shillong to attend political meetings, and it can be safely assumed that the reported resolutions are moved by urban Khasis with axes to grind and carried by schoolboys who do not understand them.

But two more genuinely representative meetings have recently been held in Manipur and the Naga Hills. In a representation dated February 27th, 1945 it is stated on behalf of the hill tribes of Manipur that "should the time come to fulfill the Cripps award it should be understood that we the Nagas and Kukis are not ready to take our place in a democratic constitution or to compete with the sophisticated so-called Indian politicians............ The so-called clamouring for the independence of India was formulated by political leaders of India who called themselves Indians and the British an alien race to India. History teaches us that these same politicians were no other than invaders of India themselves. Whereas, as stated above, we the Nagas became dependent only to the British; therefore, it is immaterial to us who rules Hindustan or Pakistan as long as we are the subjects of the British under the Great King of Great Britain and his British representatives".

At Kohima on April 10th, 1945 Tribal representatives of the Naga Hills passed the following resolutions:—

"1. An administrative unit comprising the hill districts of Assam and the neighbouring hill tracts should be formed under the British Crown.
2. The Hill Province so formed should have a Legislative Council consisting of the people's representatives with powers:—

   (*a*) To take full autonomous control when such Council so decides.
   (*b*) To decide to be included in a Federal India (if such is formed) when the hills reach a sufficient stage of advancement to be so included."

Language could hardly be plainer.

It so happens that while I was drafting this note I received a visit from an educated Lushai pastor who, with a considerable body of adherents, has settled in Cachar district just outside the Lushai Hills. He came to ask that the "privileges" (to quote his own word) of exclusion might be extended to him and his followers, thereby showing both his dislike of plains administration and his ignorance, educated though he is, of the Constitution.

12. THE VIEWS OF SIR ROBERT REID AND OTHERS

The problem is fully treated in Sir Robert Reid's Note, which contains a valuable historical survey of the question. In advocating separation he is followed by Professor Coupland at pages 164 and 165 of Volume III of his Survey. The few Indian writers who have seriously considered the future of the aboriginals tend to advocate the full inclusion in any new constitution of the tribes of the Central Provinces, etc., whom they regard as genuinely Indian, but no one, as far as I am aware has ever even contemplated the inclusion of the Mongolian block of North-East India.

13. THE AREA UNDER CONSIDERATION

This note deals primarily with the excluded and partially excluded areas of Assam, the tribal areas under the control of the Governor as Agent of the Governor General and the Khasi States and Manipur. But to round off the area requiring special treatment certain exclusions and additions appear to be desirable.

(*i*) Part of Shillong is in British India, but the greater portion is in Mylliem State. As I have indicated in paragraph 3 above I can see no justification whatever for treating the urban Khasi as a "hillman" in the sense in which the word is used in this note. Many of the urban Khasis, as I have pointed out, are only so called because their mothers happened to be wholly or partly Khasi, and all of them are as able as many plainsmen to hold their own in politics. To include the urban area of Mylliem State with the rest of the hills would not only upset the whole balance, but would be extremely unfair to the very large cosmopolitan population. Nor would the retention of the urban Khasi, with his entirely different outlook, in the "hillman" class in any way assist the progress of the true tribesmen. In my view the present small "island" of British territory should, by purchase, perpetual lease, or otherwise, be enlarged to include the whole of Shillong and its suburbs, and should continue to elect a member to the Assam Assembly. I would go further and would make a "corridor" through the hills for the Gauhati-Shillong-Sylhet road. At present parts of the road run through State territory, and awkward question of jurisdiction arise. The Government of Assam pay the entire cost of the road, which is an important artery of traffic from the Assam Valley to the Surma Valley, and by taking over a strip of roadside land where necessary they should be given undisturbed jurisdiction.

(*ii*) Along the edges of hill districts, *e.g.*, near Dimapur there are stretches of country inhabited by plainsmen which ought to be excluded from the special area.

(*iii*) Similarly, e.g., along the Northern fringe of the Khasi and Jaintia Hills, there are considerable strips of submontane country, inhabited by genuinely tribal people, which ought to be included. In a similar category, I would place the Miri country which fringes the hills North of the Brahmaputra.

These small adjustments of boundary will require detailed examination, in the course of which the question of forests could be taken up. For reasons which were sound at the time submontane forests have almost everywhere been included in plains districts, though they belong geographically to the hills behind them. This, on any separation of the hills from the plains, would give the plains an unfair financial advantage which appears to merit reconsideration. The Digboi oilfield and the Ledo and Margherita coalfields also belong geographically to the hills, but Assam could hardly be expected to relinquish these valuable assets and there is nothing tribal about the industrial population they employ.

(*iv*)(*a*) On geographical and cultural grounds there is clearly a case for the inclusion of Tripura State and the district of the Chittagong Hill Tracts. They both lie in the mountainous massif which divides India from Burma and their inhabitants form part of the North-East India Mongolian block.

I can claim no first-hand knowledge of the administration of Tripura, but unless consistent rumour lies the treatment of its hill tribes leaves much to be desired. If it were included the relationship of the Ruler with his State would have to be modified, as will that of the Maharaja of Manipur. Indeed these two States so closely resemble each other, and are so different from any other of the Indian States that *prima facie* arguments in favour of similar treatment appear overwhelmingly strong. I have toured over a good deal of the Chittagong Hill Tracts and a report on the position of the Chiefs which I wrote for the Government of Bengal in January 1927 is available for reference. Part of the district ought, in my view, to be included in Burma and there should be no difficulty in developing indirect rule in the rest of the district, which is already, except for the Reserved Forests, divided up between the Chakma Raja, the Mong Raja and the Bohmong, the boundaries of whose jurisdictions would require adjustment to accord with tribal divisions more closely.

(*b*) Corresponding to Tripura State and the Chittagong Hill Tracts at one extremity of the great Mongolian horseshoe are Sikkim and Bhutan at the other, the only States South of the Himalayas where Mahayana Buddhism is the recognized religion. Their status is, of course, different but they will be alike in their isolation in a predominantly Hindu and Muslim India. Their immediate future therefore appears to lie in union of some kind either with Tibet to the North, or with the areas to the East with which they have at least some kinship, and of these two courses the latter is clearly greatly preferable. In paragraph 15 below I give an outline of the union of States which I visualise for Assam, and I can see no insuperable difficulty in including Sikkim and Bhutan in it. The former is, from all accounts, admirably ruled, and the latter is bound to emerge in time from its present somewhat primitive condition.

(*c*) In commenting on the future of areas not within the jurisdiction of the Governor of Assam I am going beyond my terms of reference. I therefore do so with diffidence, and only because the immediate problem is not one which can be properly confined within artificial administrative boundaries. There is, of course, no suggestion that these exterior areas should eventually join Assam. Their future clearly lies in union with Bengal, and their temporary inclusion in the North-East States is designed only to provide them with a refuge, as it were, while they prepare for the future.

14. THE RELATIONSHIP OF THE HILLS WITH THE PLAINS OF ASSAM

There appear to be three possible alternatives:—

(1) Inclusion of all the hills in Assam,
(2) Inclusion of some of the hills in Assam, and
(3) Exclusion of all the hills from Assam.

1. The first alternative is clearly impossible. The words "Unknown Tribes" still have to be written across parts of the map, and it will be many years before many even of the tribes we know well will be capable of contributing anything to a Ministerial Government. There is in addition the financial difficulty. Popular Ministeries have undoubtedly tended to show considerable timidity over taxation, and should Assam in the future find herself short of funds the politically unimportant hills are likely to suffer first.

2. Under the second alternative the choice appears to lie, broadly speaking, between the two extremes of excluding only some of the present tribal areas and of including only the present partially excluded areas.

An argument in favour of including in the Province the present partially excluded areas is that it might appear a retrograde step to debar from Provincial political life communities which have sent members to the Assembly in the past. But against this it can be held that the members representing the present partially excluded areas have rarely themselves been in touch with tribal life and have in some cases played an inglorious part as Members valued merely for their votes rather than for any contribution to policy. This may have been advantageous to themselves, but has brought little gain to their constituents. Nor is it proposed to debar them from political life. In the scheme outlined later in this note full scope is, it is hoped, provided for really representative men not only from these areas, but from a far wider field. It would be a mistake to suppose that the three categories of tribal, excluded and partially excluded areas represent three grades of political progress, for cultural and political advancement was not the only factor considered when the tribes, without reference to their own wishes, were divided into three categories under the Government of India Act. Indeed the partially excluded Mikirs are in many ways as primitive as any tribe in Assam. In preparing the scheme contained in this note the categories under the Government of India Act have therefore been ignored and equal opportunity offered to any community capable of taking advantage of it.

It is this absolute necessity, as I see it, of giving an equal chance to all that rules out the possibility of including in the Province all but the present Tribal Areas. Admittedly the Tribal Areas are less advanced than the administered districts, but the difference is one of degree and not of kind. In my view therefore the present distinction between areas for which the Centre is responsible and those which form any sound scheme applied to the rest of the hills would, in my opinion, be detrimental to their interests. No one expects the pace of all the runners to be the same, but no tribe should be scratched and all, from Khasis to Abors, should come under the starter's orders.

If any tribes, whether few or many, were included in the ministerial Province certain difficulties would arise. A serious one is that of safeguards. Even if the framers of the future Constitution were to agree to safeguards, irritating as they have always proved, I greatly doubt whether they would be effective. Governorships under the new Constitution will almost inevitably soon go to party men even if Europeans are accepted by India for a few years at first, and holders of the office would find it virtually impossible to exercise their "individual judgment" in opposition to their Ministers, while the Ministers themselves would be unable to withstand pressure to bring in legislation detrimental to the hill tribes. A typical and inevitable demand would be for the extension of the jurisdiction of the High Court, which, while providing a means of livelihood for a horde of needy pleaders and muktears at the expense of the hillmen, would foment litigation, retard the speed of justice, deprive the indigenous Village Councils of their main function, and add greatly to the cost of administration. The financial position is likely to be equally unsatisfactory, for power to "charge" can hardly be given and Ministers are not likely voluntarily to allot large funds to the unimportant hills or Governors to be able to insist on their doing so.

It is hoped that all tribes will eventually join Assam and be united under one Government, and it may be argued that to postpone the union of any now is to make the ultimate union of all more difficult. Even if this were true, which I hold it is not, to include a few tribes now while leaving the rest outside would be no real solution. I rather hold to include any tribes forthwith would be to delay the union of the remainder. A sense of unity is very slowly, but surely, growing among the tribes, and if the more advanced be omitted from the community the rest will be deprived of their assistance and example, and will suffer. There is also a very real risk that if tribes insufficiently advanced are included in the Province from the beginning they will suffer from neglect or even harmful treatment, for, as suggested above, no safeguard are likely to be effective. This would certainly not escape the notice of the tribes still separate from the Province and would discourage them for an indefinite period from joining voluntarily.

3. There remains therefore the third alternative, that of temporarily excluding all the hills from Assam and according them special treatment designed, on the lines of indirect rule, to develop those indigenous institutions which so happily survive and to fit the tribes for eventual union with the Province. The problem of the hill tribes is essentially one. Some areas, it is true, will need more attention than others, and detailed treatment suitable for

one tribe will by no means necessarily be suitable for another. But the broad lines of treatment should be the same for all and they should come under a single general scheme, of which an essential element is separation from the very different Province. This, I am convinced, is in accordance with the wishes of the tribes themselves and the course most likely to result in their ultimate good and that of India, for they have many excellent qualities and a real culture of their own which, if not flattened by the steam roller of unsympathetic administration, can be of benefit to others. India too is now, and for some time will be, torn by Hindu-Muslim rivalry, and the tribes whether Christian, Animist or Buddhist, must not be forced into the arena to be buffetted by both sides, for their final contribution to India will be valuable only if they are given the chance of developing in peace.

I am convinced too that temporary separation of all the hills would be in no way harm Assam. It has been suggested that unless some at least of the hill districts are included in the Province it will be inconveniently small and, in particular, that if the Garo and Khasi and Jaintia Hills are not included the Assam Valley will be cut off from the Surma Valley and Bengal. To take the second point first, I would suggest that this will not be the case, for neither the railways nor the Gauhati-Shillong-Sylhet road will be affected, and a journey by any other route would be equally arduous whatever be the jurisdiction over the hills and gorges the traveller had to traverse. With regard to the other point, inclusion of some of the hills forthwith would add nothing to the wealth of the Province and would give it no increase of territory easily and naturally accessible. Moreover the suggestion is freely made that the Surma Valley should be taken away from Assam and added to Bengal, though the differences between the Surma and Assam Valleys, considerable though they are, are far less than those between the hills and the plains, and are rapidly diminishing. Compared with the camel of the exclusion of the Surma Valley the exclusion of the hills is surely a mere gnat. If Assam is too small to exist alone the proper course would appear to be to retain the more kindred Surma Valley.

15. THE NORTH EAST STATES

If the hills are to be treated in separation from the plains the two alternative appear to be to form a Province composed of Districts, Frontier Tracts, Agencies and States, or to form a union of States From the outset. I strongly favour the latter alternative under the conditions and for reasons, which will, I trust, not only make the proposal appear less fantastic than it may seem at first sight but commend it to serious consideration.

I. The first condition, and one that cannot be too strongly stressed, is that States in the ordinary Indian sense of the word are not visualised, the term being used more in the sense in which it is used of the Shan States, which are British territory and part of Burma. Objection may be raised to the use of the word at all, in view of its usual implications, but it has certain advantages which I have indicated below, and there is no other word to describe a unit enjoying the greatest possible measure of self-government. "Canton" is not far from my meaning, but it lacks the advantages of "State" and would be unfamiliar to Indian users. The second condition is that though I would recognize and employ existing tribal chiefs where they exist, I would create no new Rulers, and would indeed abolish most of the Khasi Siems and greatly curtail the powers of the Maharaja of Manipur, and of the Maharaja of Tripura if his State be included. There is a humble precedent in the Shella Confederacy, one of the small Khasi States, for a democratic, rulerless State and that precedent I would follow.

The scheme I desire to put forward is in outline as follows:—

(a) Reasonably homogenous areas would be termed "States". For instance there would be an Abor State, covering all the tribes included under the term, a Lushai State, a Khasi State, which could include the Garos and Syntengs, and so on. A very rough indication of the probable States is given in paragraph 17(II) below.

(b) A State would be composed of "Sub-states"—another useful term borrowed from Burma. Small or intermingled tribes would have to be combined in a single Sub-state, but normally each tribe of reasonable size would form a Sub-state.

(c) The Tribal Council would thus ordinarily be identical with the Sub-state Council and would send representatives to the State Council, which would in turn send representatives to the Governor's Council, except in the case of the Unrepresented States, to which I refer in paragraph 16 below.

(d) I would make full use of existing customs and institutions by keeping power in ordinary affairs as local as possible, for it is local affairs that arouse the greatest interest of the greatest number, and where the interest is the energy and application will be. I would therefore in no way diminish the responsibility and authority of Village Councils, though in certain matters there would be overriding power in the Sub-state Councils, possibly through intermediate councils, and overriding power yet again in the State Councils and Governor's Council. All these powers would require very careful definition.

(e) The existing States would present difficulties in varying degrees. It is clear that the tiny Khasi States, some with a total income of couple of hundred rupees or so a year, cannot possibly continue to exist, but will have to be merged in larger units, which would in turn form a Sub-state. No *Sanad* gives any guarantee of the continuance of a Siemship and there should be no great difficulty about this. A State such as Manipur represents more difficulty, but curtailment of the Ruler's powers is not only necessary, but logical, though unlikely to be more acceptable to the Maharaja on that account. The principle of primogeniture is a useful device for avoiding disputed successions, but the conclusion has always appeared to me to be irresistible that, if it is accepted that the eldest son must always rule however vicious or incompetent he may happen to be, very great care must be taken to see that powers available for misuse are as limited as possible. A Ruler who wishes to devote himself to the good of his State needs no wide constitutional powers to enable him to do so. I would therefore divide Manipur into a Sub-state for the valley in which alone His Highness now exercises effective power, and one or more Sub-states for the hills. The very considerable powers of control we possess could be used to transfer as many as possible of the Maharaja's powers to the Darbar, while seeing that he did not suffer unduly in income and dignity. If Tripura and Sikkim were included the desirability of treating them on similar lines would demand consideration. In Bhutan much of the power is in the hands of local Chieftains and her special position as an independent State would seem to preclude any immediate interference.

In general, speaking as one with little knowledge of politics, I feel that there will be a tendency under the new Constitution, with the present distinction between British and non-British territory abolished by the disappearance of the former, for Provinces and States to draw nearer together in their characters, with the former enjoying more independence and the latter less. I would also submit that the scheme of a union of States, as opposed to a Province, is likely to facilitate the inclusion of existing States, which could hardly, in a Province either be reduced to the status of districts or permitted to continue as States in the ordinary sense.

(f) With regard to staff, as far as can be foreseen in the absence of a detailed plan each State will require a Political Officer, with an Additional Political Officer in the larger States. It might also be found necessary to have two officers of the status of Commissioner for the charges North and South of the Brahmaputra. With a few Assistant Political Officers there ought to be enough posts for a small cadre, but I return to this point in paragraph 22 below.

Our object being to guide rather than to govern the administrative staff should be as small as possible, but we shall have to give all the technical assistance we can.

The question of the extent to which the States and Assam can conveniently share a technical staff is dealt with in paragraph 23 below.

(g) Finance is also dealt with separately in paragraph 18 below.

II. The reason why a union of States, rather than a Province, is advocated may be summarised as follows:—

(a) The term "Province" implies at least considerable uniformity in forms of government and level of culture throughout its component districts. But this by no means obtains in the hills of Assam, which contain, on the one hand, the only completely uncivilized tribes and unexplored country in India, and on the other, tribes such as the Khasis and Syntengs with a level of education considerably above the Indian average, while forms of government range from the Maharaja of Manipur or the hereditary sacred chiefs of the Konyaks to the elaborate elected councils of the Ao Nagas or the tiny village gathering of the Mikirs. Even if the Tribal Areas were excluded we should still be left with "districts" differing so widely in character that the term "Province" would hardly be applicable. On the other hand a union of States carries no implication that all are even approximately the same stage of progress or require the same treatment.

(b) As has been suggested above, it would be difficult to incorporate the existing States in a Province either as States, in the Indian sense of the word, or as districts. This incorporation would not be so difficult in a union of States of the type I visualise.

(c) We have in parts of the tribal areas, such as the Aka and Konyak areas, forms of government which can only be described as States. It would, in my view, be equally fatal either to recognize these as Indian States in the ordinary sense of the word, or to attempt to abolish their rulers.

> In the scheme I venture to suggest their recognition as Sub-states would be simple.
>
> (d) The word "district" is apt to attach to itself the word "administration", and I cannot too strongly stress my view that our aim ought to be indirect rule rather than administration. No word but "State" fits units under guidance of this kind, and the term itself may well help to engender a feeling of responsibility and cohesion in the people.

It may be argued on the other hand that the use of the word is itself a retrograde step and that by its use we are in fact dividing what we hope to unite. To this I would say that the tribes in the hills are not broken and scattered as they are in the plains, but are individuals, each, with few exceptions, with its own homeland, customs and language. They will doubtless grow to resemble each other more as they tend to reach the same level of progress, but there is no reason to suppose that the tribes as such will ever disappear and the population of the hills become a uniform mixture of mere human beings. The distinctive localised tribe is something which has to be reckoned with, and to attempt to unite them into States now, and to combine the States in a union is surely the first step towards the ultimate union of the tribes, and not merely of tribesmen, with Assam. I would go further and claim that no other scheme is so likely to achieve the twin objects of internal progress now and union with Assam later. District boundaries, however convenient administratively, tend to divide and weaken, since they pay little heed to racial boundaries. For example, the Zemi Nagas can hardly be expected to advance divided as they are between the Naga Hills, Manipur and the North Cachar Hills, and even if they did advance how could one section of the tribe be expected to federate with Assam leaving the other two sections behind? Their feelings would be very different if they formed a Zemi Sub-state, and the same applies to other tribes. But even a tribal Sub-state is an inconveniently small unit of federation and it is for this reason that I propose the formation of States, roughly the size of districts, but far more homogenous. Such units and such units alone can, I feel, be expected to foster within themselves the pride and ambition without which progress is impossible and finally to take the decision of federation with Assam. (As an example of the psychological effect I have in mind, the very definite recent growth of tribal feeling among the Lushais has caused the educated among them to begin to speak of their districts as "Lushai" or "Lushailand" with such persistency that the term is beginning to creep into official correspondence.)

16. THE TRIBAL AREAS

No reference has so far been made above to the present Tribal Areas as such, but as they will require special treatment a brief description is necessary.

They consist of the hills of the Balipara and Sadiya Frontier Tracts, which form the present North-East Frontier Agency, almost the whole of the Tirap Frontier Tract, and the unadministered Naga country. In the Se La Sub-agency, between the Eastern frontier of Bhutan and the Bhorelli river, there is little country that is not fairly well known up to the Southern limit of Tibetan control. But between the Bhorelli and the Subansiri, including a large area East of the upper waters of the latter, our knowledge extends to little more than a strip near the plains. The Siang Valley Sub-agency is again fairly well known, but the Western Mishmis to the East are a tribe with which we have had few dealings, though the country has been surveyed. Further East again, round the head of the Assam Valley, the country is well known as far as the North-East border of the Konyak country which forms a block of thickly populated country, extending to the northern extremity of the Naga Hills district, of which we have only entered the fringes since it was visited for the first time and surveyed some 70 years ago. The country to the East of the Naga Hills again is fairly well known, the tribes tending to become weaker as one goes South.

The Tribal Areas therefore consist of a large tract of country, some of which is entirely, and much of which is virtually, unexplored, inhabited by tribes of which we know little. A fact of importance from the administrative point of view, is that much of the Tribal Area is so completely cut off from civilization that money is unknown and is refused as unless if offered.

Some of the tribes with which we are in touch would welcome our control, but they are in a very small minority. Of the rest some have never heard of Government and the others, who have heard of it, desire only to be left in peace to enjoy their age-long freedom. Annexation is apt to be viewed in a different light by the annexers and the annexed, but it is inevitable sooner or later, and what is of importance is to ensure that it is carried out without bloodshed if possible. The independent tribesman is apt to be 'jumpy", and if he thinks that his country is being invaded he delivers what we call an attack, and he would call a counter-attack, on our column. Clearly, therefore, not only will it be patently impossible for tribes of which we know little or nothing to send representatives to the Governor's Council, but the preliminary annexation will be a very delicate business. Merely to invade is to invite either hopeless armed resistance or sullen non-co-operation. We must seek a welcome as friends with something to offer, and plans with this in view will demand the most detailed and constant attention of the Governor and his officers.

17. COUNCILS AND THEIR POWERS

I. The chain visualised in this note is:—

(1) A Governor's Council.
(2) State Councils.
(3) Sub-state Councils, which would as far as possible be identical with tribal councils.
(4) Regional Councils where necessary.
(5) Village Councils.

The precise powers which each grade of Council should possess is a matter for detailed examination and only an indication of policy can be given here.

All we have now are Village Councils varying greatly in structure but on the whole functioning vigorously and well. Above them there are as yet only the somewhat nebulous beginnings of tribal councils. The base of the pyramid is therefore the Village Council and it is on this, and not on its apex, that it must rest. In other words it is not, in my opinion, a question of what powers should be delegated by the Governor's Council to the Councils below it, but what powers should be reserved from the Village Councils for the Councils above them.

Though it is to be hoped that a convention will develop by which the advice of a Council is normally accepted all Councils must, I feel, be advisory only till more experience has been gained. Normally each grade of Council should be empowered to advise on any matter affecting only its own jurisdiction and to recommended to the Council next above if action which would affect a larger field. To Village and Sub-state Councils it might be possible to give considerable powers of taxation, but the inevitable lack of complete uniformity in the States might tempt their Councils to treat weak Sub-states unfairly and their proposals for taxation ought to require the approval of the Governor. (This is virtually the position with regard to Manipur now).

Regional Councils are suggested because the gap between Village Councils and large Sub-state Councils may prove too great. A Sub-state Council composed of one or more representatives from every village of a large tribe would be of considerable size, and purely local questions concerning one part of the tribal territory might be of little interest to members from other parts. It is therefore likely to prove desirable to provide in some cases for authorities with jurisdiction, particularly in judicial matters larger than that of the village but smaller than that of the Sub-state [*vide* paragraph 19(1)].

Any matter involving a question of tribal rights or customs should be reserved for the Governor. Under the existing Rules for Administration the Commissioner is given special powers in this respect, and these powers cannot for some time safely be abandoned. There is always the danger otherwise that some Sub-state or State Council might follow an *ad hoc* or short sighted policy without considering its full implications, or that a State Council might attempt to abolish a custom innocuous in itself and valued by a section of the community, just as not long ago the Maharaja of Manipur attempted to abolish the killing of cattle throughout the hills of his State, though beef is an important article of diet for Christians and Animists alike and cattle sacrifice is incumbent on the latter.

II. The Governor's Council would be composed of representatives from the States. The boundaries of the States would be a matter of detailed examination, but a very rough estimate of their number gives the following result:—

(1) A Monba State, to include the Monbas, Akas, Mijis, etc.
(2) A Dafla State.
(3) An Abor State.
(4) A Mishmi State.
(5) A Konyak State, to include as Sub-states the jurisdictions of the various Konyak Angs, the small Naga tribes South of Margherita, the Kachins, etc.
(6) A Naga State, probably to include some of the present Tribal Area to the East of the district boundary.
(7) A Mikir or Kachari State, to include the various tribes of the North Cachar Hills and the Kukis and mixed Mikris and Lalungs of the Khasi and Jaintia Hills.
(8) A Khasi State, to include the Garos as a Sub-state.
(9) A Lushai State.
(10) Manipur State, with boundaries adjusted to follow tribal boundaries.

This list makes no pretence of being final, for numerous variations are possible, but it is probably within 2 or 3 either way of the total any reasonable division would give. If we add Sikkim, Bhutan, Tripura and the Chittagong Hill Tracts we get a total of 14 (or 13 if the Chittagong Hill Tracts are made a Sub-state of Tripura). From this total the first 5 on the list, and probably Bhutan, must be deducted as unable to send representative, leaving a total of eight.

This is a very convenient number for an Advisory Council. The question is whether there should be in addition something in the nature of a Central Assembly. I think there should not, for it would serve no useful purpose and would probably not attract the right type of man. It would almost inevitably have to be composed of a representative from each Sub-state, but this is the only possible composition of the State Councils. There would be no advantage in a large number of individuals playing this double role and work on the State Councils is more likely to attract really representative men, as opposed to men of the professional politician type, than a Central Assembly which would inevitably spend much of its time debating matters of no immediate interest to most of the members. I prefer to visualise a small Governor's Council guiding the State Councils rather than a large Assembly attempting to dominate them.

The above agreement emphasises what I regard as important aspect of the whole scheme. If Sub-states (*i.e.*, tribes) are looked at as constituencies the wide and important difference between them and plains constituencies becomes immediately apparent. Though communal demands have been recognized Indian constituencies are in essence territorial, with the result that from the widely separated constituencies Caste Hindus identical in race and views, Muslims identical in race and views, and so on are elected. The Sub-states, or hill constituencies, on the other hand would be both territorial and racial. That is to say a Garo Sub-state, for instance, would necessarily send a Garo to the State Council and it would be virtually inconceivable that any other Sub-state would do so; with the result that a State Council would not, as a Provincial Assembly does, consist of groups of individuals indistinguishable for all practical purposes, but of members differing in varying degrees in race and each representing a localised tribe. While therefore the Ministers of a Provincial Cabinet, since each speaks for a group, tend genuinely to represent the whole of the majority in the Assembly, a State representative, since he inevitably belonged to a particular Sub-state unique in some degree, would primarily represent his Sub-state only. The Governor's Council could never therefore be truly representative, and this criticism would apply with equal force to a Cabinet selected from an Assembly composed of the representatives of all Sub-states. This consideration is an additional argument in favour of confining the power of the Governor's Council to advice till tribal differences and rivalries become more blurred.

With regard to meetings of the Council, I think one a year would be sufficient. The work will be light, and I understand one annual meeting of representatives of the Shan States was found to be sufficient.

III. There remains the question of the Unrepresented States, a term I prefer to anything implying any form of exclusion. These will consist of the Tribal Areas and till they are sufficiently advanced to send representatives to the Governor's Council there will no course open to the Governor other than to control them "in his discretion" through his officers, who would put forward their needs and views.

18. FINANCE AND INDIRECT RULE

Like the old lady who proudly feels that she owns a plate of a battleship because her taxes have paid for it the hillman likes to see how his money is spent. Receipts from minerals, forests, income-tax, excise, etc. clearly ought to go into the common fund of the North-East States. But there is much to be said for leaving the raising and spending of house (or poll) tax, which is *the* tax *par excellence* in the hillman's eyes, to the Sub-state Councils. This tax is paid willingly enough now, for the payers know that they get a great deal in return for very little. But, far from agreeing that the benefits obtained from Government would justify heavier taxation, any proposal to increase this one universal direct tax would meet with strong—almost unreasonably strong—opposition if the money went to a general fund. Yet there is certainly a case in many areas for increasing the rate of taxation, and I consider it probable that opposition to an increase would be very greatly lessened, and might disappear altogether, if the whole of the house (or poll) tax raised in a Sub-state were allotted to that Sub-state. In return the Sub-state should be required to take over certain items of expenditure, dispensaries and schools being obvious possibilities, somewhat after the manner of Local Board institutions in the plains, while Village Councils would continue to raise and spend money on purely local needs. In general what Sub-states raise must be related to their capacity, and what they get must be related to what they raise. We must not repeat the mistake we have made in the case of the Khasi States, the comparatively prosperous inhabitants of which pay no direct taxes at all and yet have obtained no mean share of amenities such as schools, dispensaries, etc.

Special arrangements will have to be made in Manipur and any other existing State included in the union for the support of the Ruler, and in Manipur the rich valley should continue to contribute something to the poorer hills. But in general the Central expenses of a State ought to be very light if Village Councils continue largely to take the place of stipendiary magistrates and village authorities.

The principle suggested above of, as far as possible, spending direct taxation where it is raised will greatly ease the undoubted difficulty of demanding tribute from, or raising taxes in, areas which have hitherto been proudly independent. Added to our uninvited presence taxation for no immediately discernible object might well lead to serious opposition and trouble. Did not Tuensang, the leading Chang Naga village, once reply to a demand for a fine with the message. "We understand the Sirkar makes rupees. If the Sirkar is short of rupees let it make some more. We have none"?—and it took an expensive column to explain the position. This opposition will be considerably lessened, I feel, if we begin by imposing no taxation in parts of the Tribal Areas where it would be resented till we have brought some benefits; then we can justifiably ask the local people to raise money for further benefits and make it quite clear to them that it is spent on specific objects. It will be some time before any central State organisation can be set up in these very primitive areas and till it is no question of contributions by Sub-states funds will arise.

Overhead charges and the maintenance of the Governor and his administrative and technical staff will undoubtedly involve an over-all deficit. How much it will be will depend on policy, and it is likely to fluctuate considerably, rising while we put money into the development of resources, falling again when the resources bring in income, and rising again when we further extend our control without a concomitant increase in resources. But I take leave to think that the deficit will not be very great, provided we maintain a small, but really good, staff and foster self-support in the Sub-states and States. The resources on the credit side are undoubtedly considerable. There are accessible supplies of coal and limestone, and the source of the gold in the river sands may yet be found; the forests should provide a steady income; and Assam will have to rely on rivers in the hills for her electric power. In any case the money must be found if the hills are not to slip back to what they were a hundred years ago, and it can justifiably be regarded as an insurance premium, for if we do not offer the hills our friendship and help not only will any slackening of control be the signal for raids on the plains in the traditional style, but should the North-East Frontier ever again be attacked from outside we shall find ourselves without the loyalty and assistance which proved so invaluable against the Japanese. If H.M.G. does not take over the States the money will have to be found by the diversion of some or all of the present subsidy paid to Assam, and by a contribution from the Province justified by the fact that control of hills is necessary for the safety of the plains.

19. JUDICIAL POWERS

I. In the eyes of the hillman the judicial powers of the District or Political Officer loom large. He is above all the man to whom intractable disputes can be brought for settlement, and his decision are almost always regarded as final, appeals being very rare indeed, except in the Khasi and Jaintia Hills, where there is a Bar, and in the Garo Hills, where the Gauhati Bar maintain touts to encourage appeals to the Commissioner. In fact public opinion in the hills definitely regards it as rather rude to appeal against the decision of a trusted officer! To the hillman any distinction between judicial and executive functions is unthinkable, and an administrator who did not settle disputes would not be regarded as an administrator at all. With what is regarded as a Court of final jurisdiction always readily available there is a tendency to appeal against the decisions of village authorities and try one's luck in it. But discouragement of this has the approval of the sounder sections of the community everywhere, and there would be no serious opposition to measures designed to allot more and more of the judicial work to what may be called People's Courts.

The very great majority of cases, especially in tribes where the villages are large are between inhabitants of the same village, and the present judicial powers of Village Councils should undoubtedly be maintained. But, apart from the comparatively few cases of heinous crime, a very considerable number are beyond the jurisdiction of individual Village Councils in that they involve parties living in different villages. For these there is no adequate indigenous machinery. In the Tribal Areas they are apt to result in a long chain of acts of revenge and counter-revenge, and in administered territory they come before the regular Courts. It is desirable, if our control is not to be too like close administration, to set up more "popular" courts, while being careful to maintain the union of judicial and executive power which the hillman regards as right and natural. Though the Sub-state, or tribal, Councils might hear appeals on particularly knotty points of customary law, etc., but they could not undertake constant judicial work, for the distances to be travelled on foot by members drawn from a large area would make it impossible for men dependent on agriculture to be absent from their cultivation for frequent and prolonged sessions. The jurisdiction, therefore, in cases where the parties belong to different villages should belong to the Regional Councils, members of which would normally live within a day of two's journey of one another and could meet fairly frequently without inconvenience.

Heinous crimes, such as murder, should be tried by the Political Officers, with a right of appeal to the Governor and provision that a death sentence requires his confirmation.

II. There is always a tendency among inexperienced or subordinate officers to be over-ready to admit and hear appeals against the decisions of indigenous Courts. This, in a community where judicial power is regarded as the chief outward sign of Government, seriously undermines local self-government and must be restrained. Village and Regional Councils should therefore be regarded as foreign courts, as Siems' Courts are now, and their decisions should be final subject to the provisions of Section 13 of the Code of Civil Procedure, or rather to its spirit. This would permit review by the Governor or his Political Officer in certain cases, but would effectively prevent frivolous appeals. Nor should there be any right of appeal to a Regional Council from a decision of a Village Council. I visualise them rather as Courts with equal jurisdiction, one over parties belonging to different villages, and the other over parties belonging to the same village. There should be provision by which a Sub-state Council can hear and determine a point of customary law arising in either class of Court, but only by special permission of the Political Officer granted on review.

III. A specific and serious legal abuse can conveniently be mentioned here. Justice in the hills is at least prompt, whereas the law's delays in the plains are notorious. Very large numbers of hillmen come down every year to work under plains contractors at cane cutting, jungle clearing and similar work at which they are unrivalled. This labour benefits both the hillman and the plainsman, but, as I know from my own experience, the hillman is only too often cheated of his wages by deliberate use of the law's delays as a weapon. If he files a case in the plains Court the defendant's pleader obtains adjournment after adjournment on one pretext or another. But the hillman can neither wait in the plains with no money and nothing on which to live, or go backwards and forwards to his home, which may be several days' journey away. His only alternative is therefore to abandon his case and lose his money. So serious is this abuse that I have often been told that it is not worth attempting to get justice in the plains, an attitude of mind not conductive to eagerness to come under ordinary Provincial administration. But a remedy is not easy to find, for the immense influence of the Bar is unfortunately against any speeding up of legal processes. Perhaps a convention could be arrived at by which all cases in which inhabitants of the States were concerned went to specified magistrates, on the speed of whose work the Session Judge could keep an eye during his inspections.

20. THE OFFICE OF GOVERNOR

Two questions appear to arise, the first whether it is physically possible for a single person to combine the offices of Governor of Assam and Governor of the North-East States, and the second whether such a combination of offices is desirable.

The States, as we have seen, are likely to number between 10 and 14, and will cover a vast area very badly served by communications. No one pretends that a Governor, or anyone else, can be expected to travel over the whole of this area, but it is desirable that a certain proportion of the States should be visited by the Governor each year, and if Sub-states are visited much of the touring must necessarily be on foot over bad country and confined to the cold weather. This would appear to mean that touring in the States will leave little time for touring elsewhere.

Apart from the touring the office work will be heavy. The first Governor to assume office will not take over a "going concern" but one which he will have to build up almost from nothing, and it will be many years before constructive work is finished, every State is functioning, and there is little left to do but watch their progress. Even now, as a result of the beginning we have made in the North-East Frontier Agency, the Governor spends several times more hours per month on its problems than his predecessors did in the days when we just "sat back", and this increase of work will grow as we extend our activities elsewhere. In this connection it is worth stressing an important difference between the work of an ordinary Provincial Governor and that of the Governor of the North-East States. In a Province policy is initiated by the Ministry and the functions of a Governor are primarily those of a guide. In the North-East States, on the other hand, while guidance in matters within the comprehension of the tribes will always be an important part of the Governor's duties, the main task of initiating policy on broader questions will inevitably fall upon him for a considerable time, and in technical matters perhaps for an indefinite period.

It would therefore appear that, whatever the advantages, the volume of work in itself would render the combination of the offices extremely difficult, or even impossible. That there are certain advantages is clear. Firstly there is a natural alliance between the plains and the hills, whatever their differences, and there is much to be said for symbolising this alliance by a single Governor for Assam and the North-East States, especially as this union of offices might facilitate the adherence to Assam of a State which would otherwise hesitate to transfer its allegiance to a king which knew not Joseph. Secondly the combination of the two offices in the same person would facilitate the borrowing and interchange of staff. Thirdly it would reduce expense, but not, I think, very greatly, for a Governor of Assam who was also in charge of the States would certainly require an Adviser to assist him in his duties, whereas not only would a Governor in charge solely of the States not necessarily require an Adviser, but he might well receive emoluments on a lower scale than those of a Provincial Governor, say on the scale of a First Class Resident. (There is even something to be said for using the term "Resident", rather than "Governor" for the Head of the union of States, but on the whole I prefer the latter term as tending to stress the fundamental difference between the North-East States and ordinary Indian States).

But, I would venture to submit, there are two serious difficulties which merge into one another but are to some degree distinguishable as arising the one from the nature of the work and the other from the type of man who is likely to be called upon to undertake it. The ordinary way of stating the problem would be "Is it advisable that the man selected as suitable for the Governorship of Assam should also be placed in charge of the North-East States?" Logically it can also be stated in the form "Is it advisable that the man selected as suitable for the Governorship of the North-East States should also be placed in charge of the Province of Assam?", and the very emphasis with which this form would usually be repudiated as showing lack of a sense of proportion is a criterion of the danger that a Governor holding both charges might regard the States almost as a sideline. Not only cannot one man serve two masters, but one man cannot normally undertake two heavy and very different tasks without neglecting one of them. From several points of view the Governorship of Assam is the more important of the two, but it does not follow from that that even the risk of neglect of the States can be justified. In my opinion the task of the Governor of the States, with so much still to be done, will more than fully occupy anyone.

The second question is whether, even assuming time could be found to perform both tasks thoroughly, the type of man likely, in an independent India, to be selected for the office of Governor of Assam is one also likely to be suitable for the Governorship of the States. Advantageous though the appointment of neutral British Governors would be till communal equilibrium is reached I see no likelihood of this, since no Indian politician can be expected to jeopardise his future by advocating such a course, and in no event would it be adopted for more than a very short time. We must therefore, I feel, expect appointments to Governorships under the new Constitution to be political and likely to come to their recipients rather late in life. It can hardly be expected that an Indian Governor, no longer young and with experience only of party politics, will have either knowledge of the problems of the hills and sympathy with their people or the physical strength required for very strenuous touring in the States. The Governorship of the States should therefore be a separate charge and the post should go to an official with either knowledge of them or special aptitude for work of this type.

21. INDIANISATION AND THE FUTURE

Before considering the difficult question of staff a paragraph on Indianisation can be conveniently interposed, and at the outset I wish to say that I consider a greater or less degree of Indianisation both natural and inevitable. But this inevitability does not lessen the difficulties or make it less important to visualize them as clearly as possible.

Certain misconceptions are current on the subject. I have frequently heard statements made which seem to imply a belief firstly that all European officers like and are fit for service among the backward tribes of the North-East Frontier, and secondly that there is a tendency deliberately to keep Indians out of the hills. This is very far from being in accordance with my own experience. By no means all Europeans even imagine they would like work in the hills, and of those who do comparatively few prove really fitted for it. Hill administration is not, as is sometimes thought, work which any normally capable European can do "on his head", and in practice really suitable officers are by no means easy to find. I would sum the matter up by saying that the good hill officer is born, not made, and that once such a man find himself in the North-East hills he never wants to leave them. With regard to Indians the question has not been so much one of keeping them out of the hills as getting them into the hills when they are wanted. Service among hill tribes without the companionship of his kind is Siberian exile to a member of the intensely sociable urban classes of Eastern Bengal and Assam from which our staffs are necessarily drawn. The Assamese looking up into the hills does not long to serve in them any more than the Bengali graduate watching the shipping on the Hooghly yearns for a life on the ocean wave. It is not a matter of praise or blame, but of national temperament, which has to be faced.

Just as the plainsman, be he Hindu or Muslim, find himself out of sympathy with the beef and pork eating Mongolian of the hills, so the latter is apt to dislike the former. This undoubted mutual antipathy would be a serious handicap even under a system which at the lower levels involved little more than the application of the right section of the right Code, but it creates infinitely more serious difficulties in a scheme of indirect rule, where persuasion must as far as possible take the place of orders and sympathetic understanding on the one side and liking on the other are of supreme importance not only for the welfare of the people but to control them and ensure that the desire to raid, still latent over a wide area, is not revived, for scratch a Naga or Lushai Christian and you will still find a head hunter.

This being so I am driven to the conclusion that little or no progress, especially in the Tribal Areas, can be expected under an entirely Indian administration staffed by local officers. A remedy might lie on the recruitment of Indians from other parts of India, but provincialism may well make this difficult and we do not know where to look for the right men a long series of experiments with Punjabis, Madrasis, Sikhs, Parsis and so on being both impossible and undesirable. All we know for certain is that European officers of the right type can manage the tribes reasonably well, but whether it would be possible to find them and keep them remains to be seen, and in any case all posts cannot go to them.

22. POLITICAL STAFF

It is hoped that ultimately States will be evolved as self-sufficient in staff as on ordinary Indian State in now. But during the long period which must elapse before this process can be completed the Governor will require a supervising staff which, even though kept to the minimum to encourage self-reliance, is bound to be considerable.

There should be no great difficulty in recruiting the necessary subordinate staff from the States, but the problem of obtaining superior officers of the right type is both extremely difficult and supremely important, for it is axiomatic that the whole success of the scheme will depend on the quality of the staff employed. No guidance is obtainable from All-India recruitment schemes, for they naturally stop short at the granting of complete independence and it will be for the Indian Government to make their own arrangements for subsequent administration. On the general position a reference may be made to the Foreword by the Secretary of State to the pamphlet on Civil Appointments issued by the Federal Public Service Commission. Briefly all appointments will be terminable on 12 months' notice and it will for the Indian Government to decide whether to re-engage any of the officers or not. There is therefore at least a possibility that every superior administrative officer working in the hills of Assam will be dismissed or will resign immediately prior to the coming into force of the scheme I have set out or any other scheme which may be devised.

This would create so serious a situation that the probabilities merit further brief examination. Up to the time when the new Constitution comes into force the hills will presumably be staffed, very much as they are now, by officers, predominantly European, from the I.C.S., Indian Political Service, and possibly the Indian Police, and the problem in a nutshell is whether any means can be devised to retain at least a good proportion of these officers and to recruit others as the need arises. The first question is whether these officers are likely to resign if they see changes coming, and my answer is that they will almost certainly do so unless they can obtain a promise of permanent employment in the North-East States, since they will not agree to remain on under the liability of transfer to posts where the work is not likely to be congenial. This may be very inconvenient to the administration, but the utterances of Indian politicians have not been such as to induce the average European officer to place his convenience above theirs. But hill service gets into the blood, and a keen man would very likely agree to go on serving on the understanding that he would not be required to do so outside the States. Nor do I consider it improbable that an Indian Government would re-engage them on these terms, since the posts they hold are by no means popular with the general run of Indians.

Since a guarantee of service in a particular area is incompatible with membership of an All-India Service, assuming that such Services continue to exist, the formation appears inevitable of a special North-East Frontier Service to which serving officers would transfer and recruitment would be made. To this the objection may be raised that, consisting as it would of some 15 or 20 senior posts with a proportionate number of junior posts, it is too small for an orthodox cadre. But the objection to small cadres is based primarily on the arguments that the ambitions of their members are frustrated, and if the officers of the North-East Frontier Service attain their goal of happiness in congenial work this objection largely disappears. The days too of cadres, for Europeans at any rate, appear to be passing. Officers being recruited to the All-India Services now can hardly be said to be joining a cadre in the ordinary sense of the word, seeing that their appointments are terminable at 12 months' notice. It would be more correct to view them as working on contract, and I do not see why both they and officers who ante-date them should not do so in the North-East Frontier Service, the terms of contract being embodied in the offer of re-employment and made applicable to future recruits.

Seeing that work in the North-East States would have more affinity with work in the Burma Hills than with work elsewhere in India and in view of the long common frontier it might be found desirable so to correlate the terms offered by an independent Burma and an independent India that officers could be interchanged if so desired.

23. TECHNICAL STAFF

It is clearly desirable, on the grounds of economy if nothing else, that the States and Assam should as far as possible share the services of Heads of technical Departments. Medical personnel has always been a great difficulty in the hills as the class from which it is chiefly recruited loathes service there and an application for long leave is a common response to an order of transfer thither, bad work with a view to a transfer back to the plains being the next card. The States should therefore have their own medical staff but the services of the Inspector General of Civil Hospital and all other Heads of Departments could, I would suggest, be conveniently shared, with the exception of the following—

  (*i*)   *Director of Agriculture*—Agriculture in the hills differs so entirely from that in the plains that it cannot conveniently be under the same directive. This has to some extent been recognized and arrangements are being made now to appoint a special Agricultural Officer for the hills.

  (*ii*)   *Director of Industries*—Hitherto exports from the hills have consisted entirely of labour, foodstuffs and a small quantity of raw material. But finished articles from the hills will differ greatly from those made in the plains, since the raw materials differ, and the States will require their own Director of Industries. His work will probably not be heavy and might be combined with other duties.

  (*iii*)   *Conservator of Forests*—Though the States will in general produce their own types of timber there is some likelihood of trade rivalry with Assam. This will be a by no means unhealthy symptom, but it is desirable that the forests in the States should be under a Conservator who can give his whole attention to them.

  (*iv*)   *Inspector General of Assam Rifles*—The Assam Rifles, or their equivalent, will be stationed entirely in the States and could not conveniently be left under the control of the Inspector General of Police, Assam. I visualise a very small force of Civil Police in the States, and they could conveniently be placed under the control of the Inspector General of Assam Rifles.

(*v*)   *Director of Public Instruction*—As the medium of instruction in the States at the lower primary stage must necessarily be tribal languages and as the nature of education is likely to be modified in accordance with the environment for which it is intended the work is likely to differ greatly from that in Assam and on the whole I consider a separate Director of Public Instruction is advisable.

(*vi*)   *Chief Engineer*—The work in Assam has increased so greatly in recent years that it has for some time been found necessary to divide it between two Chief Engineers, and it is unlikely that either of them could find time to supervise work in the States, especially as it would involve long and slow touring. The States should therefore have their own Chief Engineer.

(*vii*) *Public Service Commission*—The Assam Public Service Commission could not be expected to have intimate knowledge of the qualifications desirable in candidates for appointments in the States and there would be no advantage in sharing their services. I doubt whether, with his Council acting only as an advisory capacity, the Governor would require a Commission at all.

24. THE SITE OF CAPITAL

Though the necessity of sharing the services of several Heads of Department would seem to indicate Shillong as the site of the capital of the States there are disadvantages in this, unless, of course, the Governorships of the Province and of the union of States were held by the same person. The availability of Heads of Departments for personal consultation is clearly desirable, but few matters are likely to arise which could not be settled by correspondence with those whose services it is suggested should be shared. On the other hand the absence of air facilities near Shillong is a very grave drawback indeed. Clearly the existing capital cannot be moved on that account, but equally a site suffering from this disability should not be selected for a new capital unless there are overwhelmingly strong reasons for doing so. Another disadvantage is that building sites are very hard to find in Shillong and land is extremely expensive. Yet a third disadvantage is that if the town of Shillong is included in the Province a Governor of the union of States living there would reside outside his own jurisdiction.

Were the capital to be at Smit in one direction or near Burra Pani in the other consultation with the shared Heads of Departments would be possible at the cost of some inconvenience, and it is just possible, though extremely doubtful, that a landing strip could be constructed. But this is very problematical and Imphal appears to offer greater advantages. From there it is a short flight to Sadiya in one direction or Cachar, whence the Lushai Hills can be reached, in the other, and if Tripura, Sikkim, etc. were included in the union access to them would be equally easy. In addition the Governor would be in one of his most important States, the Naga State would be within close reach, and communication with Burma, with which relations are likely to become closer, would be easy.

25. THE CONTROLLING AUTHORITY

The union of States must be under the control either of H.M.G. or the Government of India, or, as a possible compromise, the Indian Government might be given a form of mandate. I fully realise that H.M.G. might well decline either to find the money or to face the political outcry which would inevitably arise, though the North-East States on cultural, religious and racial grounds are as fully entitled to separation as is Burma, and the pill of temporary separation would be sugared by immediate financial relief and the assurance of eventual re-union. But I feel that the practical advantages of treating the union of States as a Colony till such time as they are sufficiently advanced to unite with India are so great that the idea should not be rejected out of hand. In this connection it is interesting (though perhaps nothing more) to note that, assuming the correctness of a reference I have been unable to verify, the present States and Tribal Areas are in fact legally colonies since a "colony" is defined in the Interpretation Act of 1889 as "any part of His Majestys' dominions exclusive of the British Islands and British India".

I. I would therefore urge serious consideration of the possibility of forming a Protectorate after the precedent of those of Basutoland, Bechuanaland and Swaziland, which provide a remarkably close parallel in many ways and have on the whole succeeded in both protecting the inhabitants against exploitation and in furthering their progress. Under a scheme on these lines the Governor of the North-East States would be responsible to the British High Commissioner who will presumably be assigned to the Indian Government.

The grounds for and advantages of the proposal may be summarised as follows:—

(*i*)   While in no way hampering progress it would give effective protection while the Stated fitted themselves for union with India.

(*ii*)   It would be suited to the average general cultural level of the States, which far more closely resembles that of a backward colony than that of any other part of India.

(*iii*)   While Indians would in no way be debarred from serving the provision of a suitable European staff would be greatly facilitated.

(*iv*)   The Colonial Office are now engaged, especially in Africa, in fitting primitive communities to play their part in the modern world, and their experience, to which there is no equivalent in India, would be invaluable.

(*v*)   The Colonial Office tend to insist on a far higher standard of qualifications in all technical services than Indian opinion on the whole considers necessary, and are in addition in touch with experts in agriculture, specialised education and other "nation building" activities.

(*vi*) No valid argument can be based on an assumption that to place the States under a Protectorate would delay their union with Assam. That union must be voluntary and Assam must play her part, for the sooner conditions within Assam become more attractive than those outside the sooner the States will join her. If, as I think is the case, existence under a Protectorate is likely to be happier than that under the Central Government there is all more reason for choosing the former; the States cannot be given a second-best organisation in order to make them readier to leave it and join Assam.

II. Throughout this note the alternative of control by the Central Indian Government has been borne in mind and its implications have necessarily had to be considered, especially in the matters of staff and finance. If it be decided that control must lie with the Central Government it should be as light as possible. Members of the Central Government will undoubtedly be without any knowledge of areas entirely unlike any others in India, while the unique character of his charge will relieve the Governor of the necessity of maintaining that close and constant touch with the Centre which the need for a reasonably uniform policy in not wholly dissimilar Provinces throughout India makes it incumbent on present Governors to maintain. Assistance from the Central Government will be necessary at times, but any attempt by them to control day to day administration would undoubtedly hamper progress. The Governor will be the man on the spot and the possessor of local knowledge, and subject to the inherent power of the Central Government to issue directives on major questions of policy his hands should be left as free as possible, the Central Government if they wish, maintaining an Agent at his headquarters to keep them in touch with events.

III. There is little or nothing, I feel, to be said in favour of a mandate as a compromise between the above two alternatives.

On the one hand the control of H.M.G. would be too remote to be effective, and on the other hand a political grievance would be made out of the absence of complete theoretical control. If there is to be a grievance let it at least be over a system which will bring real benefit to the States.

26. SUMMARY

If he is to play his part in the future the hillman needs protection, not from change, which is inevitable, but from change, so swift as to be destructive (para. 1). This point can best be made clear by a survey of his attitude towards life (para. 2), but care must be taken not to regard Khasis, to whom their geographical position is apt to give undue prominence as typical of the tribes with whose future we are concerned (para. 3). Nothing is more distinctive of the tribes than the vigorous life of their self-governing institutions and one of our most important tasks will be to preserve and develop them (para. 4). In deciding on our line of policy note must be taken of the historical, racial, cultural and religious background of the tribes (paras. 5, 6, 7) and of the increasing divergence of the plains from the hills accelerated by the recent mass immigration of Bengali Muslims (para. 8). Geographical features too tend rather to divide the hills from the plains than to unite them (para. 9). In planning for the future due weight must be given to the analogy of Burma and to the views of the hillmen themselves and of authorities who have studied the subject (paras. 10, 11 and 12).

The present boundaries of hill districts are based on administrative convenience rather than racial divisions and will require adjustment. In particular steps should be taken to include the whole of Shillong and its suburbs in the Province of Assam. The advisability should also be considered of granting a temporary refuge under the scheme to certain areas which are not now under the control of the Governor of Assam (para. 13). Of three possible alternatives the exclusion of all the hills from Assam is the best (para. 14), and from them a union of North-East States should be formed, details of which are given and which is put forward as the best solution of the problem (para. 15). This union should include the Tribal Areas, though these will not for some time be able to send representatives to the Governor's Council (para. 16). Indirect rule, rather than close administration, being our object a chain of indigenous Councils is necessary to which certain financial and judicial powers should be granted (paras. 17, 18 and 19).

The combination of the Governorships of Assam and the North-East States appears to be impracticable (para. 20). Indianisation of the Services through inevitable, presents grave difficulties owing to the reluctance of Indians to serve in lonely stations in the hills (para. 21). Equally grave are the difficulties arising from the increasing reluctance of European officers of the type required to serve elsewhere than in the hills and the uncertainty of the future of the All-India Services. The solution suggested is the formation of small North-East Frontier Service (para. 22). The services of certain Heads of Departments should be shared by the union of States and the Province (para. 23). Imphal is preferable to Shillong as a site for the capital since air facilities can be easily arranged there and there is less congestion (para. 24). Of the alternatives of control by H.M.G. or control by the Central Government the former is greatly preferable, the South African Protectorates providing a precedent. If this alternative be rejected control by the Central should be light as possible (para. 25).

The Future Government of the Assam Tribal Peoples

Sir Andrew G. Clow

REFERENCES

Citation of the views of Dr. Hutton, Sir Robert Reid and Mr. Mills and quotations from them refer, unless contrary is stated, to the following papers:—

1928—A note on the case for the withdrawal of the Hill Districts of Assam from the operation of the Reforms; by Dr. J. H. Hutton, C.I.E., I.C.S. [Printed in the memorandum presented by the Government of Assam to the Indian Statutory Commission, pages 111–118.]

1941—A note on the future of the Present Excluded, Partially Excluded and Tribal Areas of Assam; by Sir Robert Reid, K.C.S.I., K.C.I.E., I.C.S., Governor of Assam.

1945—A note on the future administration and constitutional position of the present Excluded, Partially Excluded and Tribal Areas of Assam; by J. P. Mills, C.I.E., I.C.S., Adviser to the Governor of Assam for Tribal Areas and States.

PREFACE

The question here considered is—Assuming complete Indian self-government, what arrangements are feasible and appropriate for the tribesman of Assam? The discussion is based on the assumption of the advent of self-government at a very early date. The aim throughout has been to analyse a very complicated situation and the possibilities it offers, rather than to present a cut-and-dried case for any particular solution of the difficulties.

I am indebted to the three papers cited opposite and to numerous discussions with Mr. Mills and other officers who have served in Assam and especially in the hill areas.

Andrew G. Clow
Shillong
29 October 1945

TABLE GIVING DISTRIBUTION OF POPULATION BY DISTRICTS, ETC.

(in thousands)

		Total population	Tribal population
Hills (excluding Mikir Hills):-			
British India:			
Garo Hills	...	224	198
Khasi and Jaintia Hills	...	119	104
Lushai Hills	...	153	147
North Cachar Hills	...	37	37
Naga Hills	...	189	185
		------	------
		722	671
States:			
Khasi States	...	214	186
Manipur	...	512	152
		-----	-----
		726	338
Plains (& Mikir Hills):-			
Goalpara	...	1,014	238
Kamrup	...	1,264	198
Darrang	...	737	261
Nowgong	...	711	167
Sibsagar	...	1,075	361
Lakhimpur	...	895	335
Sylhet	...	3,116	70
Cachar (excluding Hills)	...	604	141
Frontier Tracts	...	66	44
		------	------
		9,482	1,815
		--------	--------
		10,930	2,824

NOTE 1—*Mikir Hills*—The Mikirs are about 150,000. Some are in the plains and other hill areas, but there are a few Nagas in the Mikir Hills. A deduction of 140,000 from the plains total and a corresponding addition to the hills would give a reasonably fair comparison.

NOTE 2—*Manipur*—In Manipur, the second column includes only the hill tribes and thus excludes the bulk of the population, although that belongs ethnologically to the same stocks as the hill tribes. Of the excluded population of 360,000, nearly all are Manipuris. About 30,000 are Muslims, the only appreciable body of this community to be found anywhere in the hills.

NOTE 3—*Tribal areas*—The above table omits the Naga Tribal Area and the Northern Hills, where there has never been a census. The population of the former is estimated (see paragraph 194) at 160,000. That of the latter cannot be estimated with any approach to accuracy; but see paragraph 189.

CHAPTER I—DESCRIPTIVE

A. Assam and Its Tribes

1. Assam and the territories associated with it have an area of roughly 100,000 sq. miles. The plains consist of two entirely separated areas, the Assam Valley, which is the Valley of the Brahmaputra, and the Surma Valley.

2. The mountain areas may be divided into:

(a) *the Northern Hills.*—This consists of a large Himalayan area to the north with a flank to the East ending near the Pangsau Pass, and lying between the MacMahon Line or Tibetan Frontier and the Assam Valley.

(b) the Southern Hills.—This consists of the long series of ranges which lie against the Burma border and separate it from both the Valleys.

(c) the Central Hills.—This consists of the broad east and west Peninsula which completely separates the two Valleys, together with an outlying area on the North-East, the Mikir Hills, which almost bisects the Assam Valley.

3. Very roughly, the total area of the Valleys is 30,000 square miles, that of the Northern Hills is about the same, while the Southern and Central Hills cover about 40,000 square miles. The population of the plains is about 9½ millions; that of the Southern and Central hills is about 1¾ millions, of whom about half live in British India. That of the Northern Hills has never been counted, but is perhaps about 400,000. (See para. 189.) Almost everywhere the country changes abruptly from the plains to the hills and historically the two regions have had little contract until recent times.

4. The province is unique in the proportion and variety of the tribal peoples. The distribution by districts, States, etc., is given in the table opposite which shows that in the hills nearly the whole population is tribal and that in the plains districts, with the exception of Sylhet, they form a very substantial minority.

B. The Hill Tribes

5. The hill tribes exhibit marked differences from the people of the plains. These have been vigorously set out by Dr. Hutton and are also stressed by Mr. Mills. A brief summary of the main points will suffice at this stage: some other points of difference are indicated later. Ethnologically the hillmen are composed of entirely different stock from most of the plainsmen. In the northern hills, where the population is probably indigenous, they are

Mongolians akin to the Tibetan and Bhutanese. Elsewhere they represent waves of invasion which came from the South, but are nearly all Mongoloid also. Their many languages belong to the Tibeto-Burman group, with the exception of Khasi which is one of the Mon-Khmer group.

6. Culturally the outlook of the hills differs entirely from that of the plains and social customs are radically different. The social organization is that of the clan, the village, and the tribes, and in the Southern and Central Hills the outlook and structure are usually democratic. This appears to be generally true in the northern hills also. But slavery continues in some places to which our administration does not penetrate. The economic system is in many ways different: in particular agriculture is everywhere carried on largely by "jhuming" which involves cutting down the forest or jungle periodically to secure crops for a few years from constantly changing areas.

7. The religion of the hills is generally described as Animism; it has elements of theism and ancestor-worship and is largely concerned with the propitiation of spirits. It is yielding in many places and with considerable speed to Christianity. Neither Hinduism nor Islam has any hold except in the Hinduised Imphal plain of Manipur State. The northern hills are scarcely touched by any of these religions, but Buddhism has an influence in some areas.

8. While the hillmen are separated from the plainsmen by these and other differences, it would be a mistake to think of the hill peoples as having much homogeneity, for there are very important differences between them. The broadest line of demarcation is that between those in the northern hills and the others. The former, who have affinities and some contracts with Tibet are, except in the very limited areas to which Buddhist influence has permeated, in an almost virgin state. One officer familiar with both areas said "The Nagas are 100 years ahead of the Abors" and this, through an exaggeration, has a considerable element of truth.

9. For practical purposes, they have never come under official administration. Until the last few years contacts were limited to the maintenance of a few posts near the foot of some of the bigger

valleys, occasional 'tip-and-run' visits by officers with escorts and some unfortunate expeditions rendered necessary by earlier mistakes. In 1939–40 cold weather posts were established in one or two places and in 1943 a forward policy was initiated. Large areas have never been surveyed or even visited, and the whole is the largest *terra incognita* in the Indian Empire. The most important of many tribes of the northern hills are, from West to East, the Mombas, Akas, Daflas (or Nisus) including the so-called Hill Miris, the Apa Tanis, Abors, Mishmis and Singphos. Several of these are groups of tribes rather than individual tribes.

10. The remaining tribes are at varying stages of development and organization. Taking the southern hills and starting at the northern end, the Nagas stretch roughly from the Pangsau pass to the northern half of Manipur and cover a considerable adjoining area of Burma. They are not a people but a collection of peoples. Nagas (= naked) is a collective nickname bestowed by plainsmen on a dozen or more tribe who look much alike to strangers but whose languages are so distinct that most of them are unintelligible to any other tribes, and whose customs and methods of social organization also differ considerably. Furthest back are the Nagas of the unadministered area, of whom the most important are the Konyak group. In much of this area the primæval way of life has been undisturbed. Furthest forward are the Aos, Angamis, Lothas and Semas; here better communications (the Angamis are astride the Manipur Road) have been followed by Christianity and education, and the desire for the latter has been given a tremendous impetus by the war. The Nagas in Assam and Manipur number about 226,000. The population of the tribal area has been estimated at 160,000*.

11. The Kukis live for the most part in the southern half of the hills of Manipur, and are also found in Burma. They have a traditional hostility to the Nagas, and the serious Kuki rebellion of 1917–18 was partly due to this. They were used at one time by Manipur to police the Nagas, and in another area were called in by one tribe of Nagas to protect them from another. Thus their

---

* See paragraph 194.

villages do not form a compact block but are interspersed in places with those of the Southern Nagas. Those in Assam number about 93,000. The Imphal plain, which occupies the centre of Manipur and has the bulk of its population, is inhabited by Manipuris (about 350,000). They are almost certainly of the same racial stock as the hillmen round them, but they have been Hinduised and have lost much of their tribal character through the spread of Hindu culture and life in a plain.

12. The Lushais, in the Lushai Hills, which has always had poor communications with any other area, number about 142,000. They are akin to the Kukis (and to the Chins of Burma). They have taken rapidly and eagerly to Christianity, which the great majority now profess, and are anxious for education and advance. No people in Assam have done better in recruiting for the Army. They are organized under Chiefs who have still considerable power. The Southern tip of the Lushai Hills is peopled by Lakhers, an allied tribe, found in larger numbers in the adjoining parts of Burma.

13. Passing to the Central Hills, the Khasis number about 192,000. Owing to the presence of the provincial capital, to the long work of a Christian Mission and to fairly good communications, they are the most advanced of the hill peoples, although away from the main roads their life has still much that is primitive. Their matriarchal system has encouraged female education, and their division among a lot of petty States has not prevented a certain cohesion, a rather democratic outlook and an interest in politics. The allied Syntengs (or Pnars) to the east in the Jaintia Hills are less sophisticated on the whole. They number about 64,000.

14. The Garos on the west, who are also matriarchal, are a section of the Bodo races, which include the Kacharis found in different parts of Assam, the Chutiyas (mainly in the Sibsagar district) and the Tipperas. They are in a more primitive state than the Khasis and have less initiative. They also have tended to suffer somewhat from neglect. They are a peaceable people and the growth of their population, which has encouraged emigration to

the adjoining plains of Goalpara and Mymensingh, is leading to fairly rapid denudation of their soil. This is a problem in many hill areas, but nowhere more than in the Garo Hills. The number of Garos in Assam is about 226,000.

15. East of the Khasi and Jaintia Hills and connecting them with the Naga Hills lie the North Cachar Hill with a medley of tribes, including Nagas, Khasis, Mikirs and a number of Kacharis, a tribe which formerly had a kingdom here and derive their name from Cachar. The area is somewhat neglected, but less so than the Mikir Hills, between this area and the Brahmaputra. Although these hills lie across the middle of the Assam plain, few penetrate their jungles and it is an almost forgotten land. The Mikirs, who number about 150,000, are a law-abiding but rather opium-ridden people who are not unwilling to spread into the plains. Alone of the hill peoples, they have been given the Assamese and not the Roman script. A few Nagas also live in this area.

C. The Plains Tribes

16. Dr. Hutton wrote "The hill-man of Assam differs as greatly in race, language, religion and culture from the Bengali of the plains as the Englishman does from the Turk. This is no exaggeration." Literally taken, it is not; but as an indication of the differences between the hills and the plains it is misleading. Only a minority of the plainsmen are Bengalis and like most of those who have discussed the future of the hill-tribes, he ignores the existence of a large tribal population in the plains.

17. This population falls into three groups. The first consists of the older plains tribes. These comprise a number of peoples who can claim, if any one can, to be the original peoples of Assam. They are found mainly in the lower districts of the Assam Valley and there principally, though by no means entirely, in the less developed submontane areas. The most important group are the Kacharis (429,000) who are predominant in the belt which

borders on Bhutan, the allied Rabhas (84,000) and the Lalungs (50,000). The plains Miris (107,000) are mainly in the upper two districts, and represent Abors who have been driven from the hills by pressure on the land or other causes. They speak an Abor dialect and the process of pressure from the hills is still going on.

18. The second group consists of the Ahoms who are concentrated in the upper two districts of the Assam Valley and number about 300,000. They are of Shan origin and represent the conquerors of the Assam Valley in the XIIIth century and its rulers until the advent of the British in the XIXth. They are tending increasingly to emphasize their tribal distinctness. The Chutias, a Bodo race scattered over the same area, were predecessors of the Ahoms in the Upper Valley.

19. The third group consists of the tea garden tribes. Labourers have been imported steadily for nearly a century, largely from Chota Nagpur, and now form a large settled community, mainly in the upper two districts of the Assam Valley and to a less extent in the Surma Valley. Of those living on tea estates, who number 1,162,000, over 700,000 were enumerated as tribals. The tribal population of former tea labourers settled elsewhere is put at 270,000 but all the figures relate only to five main aboriginal tribes—Mundas, Oraons, Gonds, Konds and Santals, and omit smaller groups. A number of other Santals, who emigrated from Bihar on their own account, are settled in the lower part of the Assam Valley.

20. There are minor racial or cultural connections between some of the hill tribes and those of the plains. The Ahoms being originally Shans ('Ahom' and 'Assam' are both corruptions of 'Shan') have racial affinity with the Hkamptis in the Sadiya Frontier Tract, and the Shans in Burma and some of the tea garden tribes belong, like the Khasis, to the Mon-khmer linguistic group. The connections between the Kacharis, the Garos, the Rabhas and the Chutias have been noted. A more important affinity is the religious one. Although all the plains tribes have been Hinduised to a considerable extent and have lost nearly all of their tribal organization, they all sit lightly to Hinduism and,

except the Ahoms, include a good many Christians. The non-Christians do not acknowledge any Brahman supremacy and are much less strict than the Hindus in matter of caste. The Ahoms have still some Buddhist sympathy and their influence has probably helped to modify in a theistic direction the Hinduism of the Assamese with whom they live.

21. Between hills and plains, there is a slight overlapping of tribes. The Kacharis, who are mainly in the plains, still live in the North Cachar Hills also. The Mikirs and Garos, who are hill people, have spread into the plains and there is a substantial Manipuri colony in Cachar and east Sylhet. Reference has been made to the Miris, who are Abors settled in the plains. The Hkamptis are a Burma hill-tribe who have taken to the plains in Assam. The other hill tribe have no footing in the plains, though they visit them in fair numbers in the winter months. Except for the intermingling of the Nagas and Kukis, mainly in Manipur, and some mixture of tribes in the North Cachar Hills, practically every hill tribe has a well defined country of its own. This is largely true of the older tribal peoples of the plains but much less true of the Ahoms and the tea-garden tribes.

22. The table on page 2 [page 140 of this book] shows that if the Northern hills are treated as a tribal area (*i.e.* excluded from the province), the plains tribes in Assam outnumber the hill tribes by two to one. The former are about 1,670,000 and the latter about 810,000. Even if the States are included, the plains tribes have still a substantial majority. The Manipuris, who can be regarded either as a hill tribe or a plains tribe, are excluded from this calculation.

D. Relations with the Hill Tribes

23. It is impossible here to enter into the history of relations with the hill tribes; a brief outline is given in Sir Edward Gait's "History of Assam" and the record can be studied in detail in two

books. Sir Alexander Mackenzie's "History of the Relations of the Government with the Hill tribes of the North-East Frontier of Bengal" covers the period before 1883 and Sir Robert Reid's "History of the Frontier Areas bordering on Assam" carries the record on to 1941. But a few historical facts have a close bearing on the subject under discussion here and should be noticed.

24. British rule over the plains of Assam was virtually complete with the cession of the Ahom territories by the Burmans in 1826 and the absorption of outlying areas, including Silchar, in the next decade. From then onwards, as Mr. Mills has pointed out, the central and southern hills were secured in three periods; a fourth period may be said to have begun in 1943 with the extension of administration to the northern hills. In all the three periods, the main object was the security of the plains; it was their welfare and not that of the hills which was in view.

25. But civilizing influences followed. The officers stationed in the hills were able, for the most part, to secure the confidence of the people, and the spread of Christianity proved a pacifying factor. Savage practices, such as human sacrifice and head-hunting, disappeared as administration was extended and missionaries followed, and a generation of administrators arose who laboured to understand and to study the tribes and whose handling of them was generally inspired by both knowledge and sympathy. The great anthropological interest of the tribes, and particularly the Nagas, attracted special attention and was the subject of valuable research.

26. Even so the record of relations which the hill tribes in recent years is largely occupied with accounts of a long series of punitive expeditions. These, unlike the earlier expeditions, were not undertaken to protect the plains, which were un-molested. They arose out of trouble in the hills, and it is a significant fact that many, perhaps most, of the larger ones can be traced to errors of judgment or misunderstanding on the part of Government or its officers. Mr. Mills (in an unpublished note) has shown how frequently incidents calling for expeditions and even rebellions have been so caused.

27. Thus in the Naga Hills, where he has been able in some cases to add to our knowledge by local inquiries, he traces the Pangti expedition of 1875, the Chang expedition of 1889, the Yachummi expedition of 1910 and the two Chinglong expeditions of 1910 and 1913 to lack of accurate knowledge, coupled in one case with lack of control over subordinates and in another to employment of an unsuitable officer. A similar weakness was responsible for the Babyiya Mishmi expedition of 1899–1900. Tactless action by subordinates led to the Khonoma (Naga) rebellion of 1879 and rendered necessary the Aka expedition of 1883–4; this last is also an example of the results of ignorant interference with tribal rights in land. The big Abor expedition of 1911 was occasioned by the murder of two officers; but that seems to have been due to an error arising out of ignorance of local custom. The Miri expedition of 1911 was intended to be exploratory, but ignorance and lack of contact made it a belligerent affair. The big Kuki rebellion of 1917–18 can be traced directly to lack of contact on the part of administrative officers and a consequent unwise step by Government.

28. Savage practices have not died out in places which are unadministered but elsewhere life is generally as safe as in the plains. And, as a result of more experience and sympathetic study, the viewpoint of the tribesman is better realized. In the early stages he not unnaturally objected, and he still objects, to intrusion and particularly armed expeditions or promenades, as they used to be called. After administration is established, he is prepared to welcome officers who understand him, especially if they can bring the benefits of civilized life. Sir Edward Gait, when history was first published in 1906, described the Abors as "the most ruthless savages in the whole of the Northern frontiers", but no one would be disposed to describe them in these terms to-day. Here as elsewhere knowledge and understanding have brought greater appreciation and better relations. But the hillman still lives in a world that is very much his own and, even in areas where he has settled down to peaceful ways, errors in dealing with him can have very serious consequences.

CHAPTER II—THE PRESENT SYSTEM OF GOVERNMENT

A. Constitutional Arrangements

29. The whole of the two Valleys is subject to the ordinary ministerial Government, with the exception of a few small areas adjoining the Northern Hills. The only recognition of the tribal peoples of the plains is the grant to some of them of separate constituencies, of which there are four. The system should be extended to the plains tribes generally, other than those on tea gardens. Tea garden workers secure some representation in labour constituencies, although the system of rotation adopted here detracts from the effectiveness of their representation and should be abandoned.

30. The small excluded plains areas lie in four Political Tracts. Three of the Tracts, the Balipara, Sadiya and Tirap Tracts, so far as they lie in the plains, are essentially bases for the administration of the hills behind them. Of these only the Sadiya Tract contains a substantial area of inhabited plain. As administration extends, it will probably be preferable to establish headquarters in the hills. The fourth, the Lakhimpur Frontier Tract, is a vestigial area unconnected with the hills, and there now is little reason for its exclusion from the ministerial province.

31. As has been already stated, there was practically no government except that of the tribes themselves in the Northern Hills till two years ago and only the beginnings are visible now. It will be a long task requiring much patient thought, and arduous travel will be needed even to penetrate the area properly. The outlines of a sound administration can hardly be laid without much more knowledge of the tribes than we now have. Although the area has been an Indian responsibility since the MacMahon Line was drawn in 1914, it was not till 1937 that the Government of Assam was told of this line. Till then they assumed that India and their interest ended much nearer the plains. The Southern tribes have nearly all been subjected to close study by skilled and experienced

officers, but in the north practically all this work has yet to be done. Among the earliest tasks will be the suppression of slavery and the bringing in of some medical benefits. The whole area was supposed to be, constitutionally, a tribal area until very recently when it was discovered that the accepted line of demarcation had no statutory sanction. It therefore lies technically within the Province.

32. The constitutional arrangements to which the remaining hill tribes are subject exhibit an extraordinary medley of conditions; Ministerial Government is in full force nowhere in the hills, except in part of Shillong. The Naga Hills is a regular district and is totally excluded. Adjoining it and almost separating it from Burma lies the Naga Hills Tribal Area, which is the only statutory tribal area in Assam at the moment. It is a responsibility of the Central Government, which acts through the Governor as its agent, but is practically unadministered. Manipur which comes next is an Indian State with a Maharaja and is divided into (*a*) the plains, which are administered by the Darbar (*b*) the hills where the administration is, for practical purposes, under the Governor as Agent to the Crown Representative and (*c*) a British reserve in Imphal administered for the Governor by the Political Agent. The Lushai Hills constitute a district and are totally excluded.

33. The Mikir Hills are a partially excluded area and are divided between the two districts of Nowgong and Sibsagar with not even a subdivisional officer exclusively concerned with or resident in them. The North Cachar Hills are a totally excluded subdivision which forms part of the otherwise entirely ministerial district of Cachar. The Khasi and Jaintia Hills consist of (*a*) 25 States of varying size containing most of the Khasis, (*b*) the Jowai subdivision, a partially excluded area which includes most of the Syntengs, (*c*) small partially excluded areas scattered among the Khasi States and inhabited by Khasis and (*d*) Shillong, part of which is British India and subject to ministerial government and part of which, through lying in a State, is more or less administered. The Garo Hills constitute a district and are partially excluded.

B. Administration in the Hills

34. The most important feature of the administration of the hills, as contrasted with the plains, is that the hill tribes, to a very large extent, govern themselves. In most of the Northern hills they have been left to govern themselves entirely and this section will not deal with them further. But even in the Southern and Central Hills where Government has long had control, the bulk of the power rests with the people themselves. Whereas the plains, including the tribes there, are subject to the ordinary direct rule of Government, the rule exercised by Government officers in the hills is largely indirect. On the side of law and order, the hills police themselves; police forces are limited to very small groups at headquarters retained mainly for such purposes as treasury guards and the duties of a headquarters station. In the Naga and Lushai Hills and in the Frontier Tracts the district officer has behind him the Assam Rifles, the Political Agent has a similar force for the Manipur Hills and small detachments of them are normally located at subdivisional headquarters and some other places; but these afford an ultimate sanction in case of trouble and do not serve the purpose of day-to-day administration. In the other hills there is no such force.

35. The systems of self-government are very varied. The Konyaks, who live mainly outside the range of administration in the Naga Tribal Area, are organized under chiefs who wield fairly wide authority. Most of the Naga tribes are democratic, and so are most of the Northern tribes. The Kukis and Lushais have chiefs who are at the head of villages or very small groups of villages; they are in theory autocratic within the sphere left to the people by Government, but their authority is in practice shared by the village elders, especially among the Lushais, where Christian influence strengthens the democratic instinct. The Khasi Siems have to work with elected Darbars who may, however, be limited to certain clans or families.

36. In most areas, the system can fairly be described as distinctly democratic and even where it is not democratic in form,

it is largely so in practice. The position has been well put by Dr. Hutton, who wrote:—

> "......self-determination actually exists in a tangible form, through in some cases a transition is in progress from a village to a tribal consciousness. Organization varies from that of a Greek city state with complete democracy through a feudal to a purely monarchical system, but even these are essentially self-determined."

This requires some qualification in unadministered areas where slavery survives: there as in classical Greece, the democracy is limited to freemen. The Imphal plain is perhaps the area where the people have least voice in their Government.

37. Generally, the village is the governing unit: in some of the less democratically ruled tribes it is larger and some tribes have been moving towards greater cohesion. But normally the system is effective mainly for maintaining peace and justice in the village. It is less effective where inter-village disputes are concerned. These are, as far as possible settled by discussion, but they have frequently to be referred to an officer of Government, and where there is no administration available, as among the Daflas, may easily lead to strife. An account of the system with some valuable comments on its actual operation, has been given by Mr. Mills: this is written primarily with the Nagas in view, but the main features are common to most tribes.

38. Criminal jurisdiction in the hills is everywhere left largely to the tribal organizations. In the administered areas, heinous crimes, and especially murder, come before the district officers' courts, and small jails are maintained for the few offenders with which these courts deal. But the great bulk of offences never come before a higher official. They are dealt with by the tribal authorities, normally those of the village, who impose fines in kind or in money and, in grave cases, sentences of banishment. The tribal authorities may or may not be assisted by an agent of the district officer.

39. These agents although their functions are in some respects similar to those of magistrates or pettier bureaucrats in the plains,

are different in character. They are drawn from the tribes and the areas which they serve and are essentially intermediaries between the tribe and the district officer, or the subdivisional officer where there is one. Among the Garos, each village has a hereditary *nokma* and a group of *nokma* elects the *laskar* for the area, who has magisterial and tax-collecting duties. Among the Syntengs there is a *doloi* for each area, who is normally elected by certain clans; among the Khasis of British India the *sardars* occupy a similar position. Among the Lushais, the system of chiefs makes other agents unnecessary. In the Naga hills *dobashis* (*i.e.*, men of two languages) are proposed by the people and selected by the Deputy Commissioner; the younger ones stay at his headquarters and the older ones in their areas. They may hear and decide cases which the village cannot finally settle, but an appeal can always be preferred against their conclusion to the district officer. In the Manipur hills *lambus* have the same functions, and the arrangements with such of the northern tribes as have close contacts with Political Officers are very similar.

40. On the civil side, disputes rarely require official intervention, and these only because they may involve strife. The litigious Khasis who are influenced by the existence of a civil bar in Shillong are a partial exception. Tribal laws, which are all unwritten, except in so far as anthropological studies and one text book of Khasi law have attempted to give an account of them, are often elaborate. They regulate the life of the people in respect of marriage and divorce, inheritance, moveable and immoveable property. There is nothing corresponding to the land revenue system of the plains. Following British (and Moghal) tradition, Government has made a theoretical claim to ownership of the land. But as Dr. Hutton pointed out, this is totally irreconcileable with tribal history in the hills, and land is owned by the village or by members of a clan within the village or by individuals.

41. It follows that officers of Government in the hills are few; but there is difficulty in providing them. For the Indian official is neither happy nor acceptable in the hills, save in very rare cases. He regards life there as an exile, if not a punishment, which it has been in some cases, and provincial officials threatened with

posting there, unless they are themselves hillmen, usually leave no stone unturned to prevent that calamity. Lacking sympathy or real contract with the hillmen, they lack influence and authority. In consequence the superior posts have almost always been filled by Europeans of the All-India services. At the provincial level, Government has depended as far as possible on Anglo-Indians and the small band of hillmen who have as yet got into the services.

42. The need for separate cadres of officers for hills and plains in the services now classified as provincial has been obvious for a long time, and has become more acute with the steady disappearance of Anglo-Indian officers. The hillmen are aliens in the plains as the plainsmen are in the hills, and each section is nearly always unsuitable and happy outside its own *milieu*. When it is realized that hillmen and most of the plainsmen are more distinct from each other than the people of any two adjoining provinces in the plains, this will be easily appreciated. This is a change which should be made whatever form of government is devised. Officers of the type recruited for the All-Indian services will also be required, and these ought to be mainly Europeans until a stage is reached when hillmen of the requisite education and calibre are available.

43. The higher judicial arrangement for the hills are entirely different from those of the plains. Supreme criminal jurisdiction in Shillong is vested in the Calcutta High Court, which has both civil and criminal jurisdiction in the plains districts. Everywhere else in the hills of British Indian and in the Frontier Tracts, the highest civil and criminal court is that of the Governor, who is also the supreme civil court for Shillong and has a limited jurisdiction in the Khasi States. Except in Manipur, there are no whole-time judges: the powers vested in civil and criminal judges in plains districts are held partly by the Commissioner and mainly by the District or Political Officers. Manipur has recently established a Chief Court for the plains, but the Governor retains power in respect of confirmation of certain sentences and other matters, and wider authority in respect of the hills.

44. Justice is, on the whole speedy, straight-forward and readily accepted. The hillmen are normally very truthful: even murderers frequently plead guilty. The least satisfactory part of the present arrangements is that which makes the Governor, with the Commissioner as the next lower court, the chief civil court for Shillong, when there are a number of commercial and other cases unconnected with Khasi tribal law. A Bill was carried through some stages in the legislature before it was dissolved to transfer this jurisdiction in British Shillong to the Revenue Tribunal and a District Judge.

C. The Effects of Exclusion

45. The plains tribal peoples live in the ministerial province and have not been noticeably injured thereby. On the most controversial issue of Assam politics, the settlement of waste lands, all the ministries have professed care for their interests and have, to some extent, made that care effective. While this has been partly due to the fact that all the Assamese peoples are anxious to representation in the legislature and in the ministry. So far as appointments are concerned, they have fared badly, but this is due much more to their own backwardness than to any prejudicial measures on the part of the ministry, whose record in the matter compares not unfavourably with that of the earlier bureaucratic rule. It must be recognized, however, that the life of the plains tribal peoples under a popular ministry throws hardly any light on the effect which inclusion of the hill tribes would have. The former have always been intermingled with the other plains peoples and subjected like them to direct government.

46. The system of partially excluded areas has had only very partial success. The Governor cannot, and was not intended to, control day-to-day administration which rests in the hands of Ministers, and while the existence (more than the use) of his special powers has had some influence in preventing prejudicial acts, it would be difficult to claim that the standard of administration

has been higher in the partially excluded areas than in the ordinary ministerial province. In the Mikir Hills, at least, it has been lower; but here other factors than constitutional status have been at work. It is difficult to resist the impression that the partially excluded areas have fallen between two stools. The Ministry (none of whom has lived in them) have had little interest in them and the Governor has not been able to administer them.

47. Against this can be set some advantages, negative and positive. The system of partial exclusion has prevented the legislature from adopting measures which would run counter to tribal laws and customs; and in the absence of some safeguard, there would have been a real danger of legislation being attempted which would have been injurious to tribal interests. That danger will be considered in more detail when the question of the legislature of the future is examined.

48. The presence in the legislature of a few representatives has been of some help to the people. It has given some of the tribes experience in representative government and the Khasis in particular have gained thereby. With the advantages of the provincial capital in their midst, and of fairly good education, they have supplied more than one Minister and have counted for more than their numbers would justify. Their representatives and that of the Syntengs, who have been Christians, have been if anything above the average of the Assam Assembly. The representatives of the Garos and Mikirs and those of the plains tribals have been distinctly below it, and have lacked both capacity and political dexterity.

49. They and the plains tribals have not made up for this by cohesion; for they have sat loosely to party ties, some have been easy to buy, and they have shown little inclination to accept or be loyal to leaders. But there has been a slight tendency on the part of the plains and hills tribal representatives to make common cause. Among the former, who have provided two Ministers, the Ahoms show signs of taking the lead. There is also a tendency to look to the excluded tribes as possible allies of the future. The tribal representatives have also acted to some extent, as a

balancing factor between the big communal parties, and would probably have been more effective with greater voting power.

50. In the totally excluded areas, protection has been more effective. The administrative machinery has been untouched by political influence and it has been strengthened by the constant tendency to post a high proportion of the more capable officers to the hills. So far as relations with the Ministry are concerned, what Sir Robert Reid wrote regarding 1937–41* remained broadly true in 1941–4. The system has worked without friction, and Ministers, while ready to give the excluded areas what they could claim on a population basis, have shown no desire to interfere with the administration. The funds readily given were sufficient for all that could be attempted in war-time.

D. Progress and Development

51. So far as progress and development are concerned it is impossible to form a far judgment on the effect of exclusion in the last few years, because the war has had effects which obscure all other factors. Its main effect has been an immense quickening of life among the hill peoples, some of whom saw it within their own territories, and nearly all of whom participated in it in various ways. This quickening is reflected in a desire, scarcely existent before, for advancement. For example in that part of the Naga Hills which saw the main fighting, the Deputy Commissioner reports that the desire for education has increased a hundred-fold and some Nagas are even talking of applying compulsion for this end. They are also, like the Lushais, more concerned about their future and tending to take interest in political developments. Progress in other directions has naturally been retarded; conditions placed almost insuperable obstacles in the way, even if all the officers available had not been overworked with more immediate tasks.

---

* Pages 12–13 of his Memorandum.

52. Taking a longer retrospect, there are reasons for thinking that the hills have lagged behind the plains in progress and development. In the past energy and enthusiasm were displayed in maintaining the peace and in studying the life of the people, both tasks of greater intricacy than in the plains; but the general outlook in other ways seems to have been static rather than dynamic. Dr. Hutton who admitted in 1928 that "educationally the hills stand where they did in 1919", added "some form of education is required to forestall exploitation by the unscrupulous." He was perhaps not exceptional among the older officers in regarding education as the lesser of two evils.* All the earlier discussions of the problem of the hill tribes are marked by this negative idea of preservation and protection; and one finds little thought on possible ways of progress, or even recognition of the fact that in a rapidly changing world the tribes cannot afford to stand still.

53. This is reflected in the statistics of education which is the most vital subject, if the hillmen are to be enabled to hold their own. In the excluded areas the expenditure from public funds on education was in 1944 just over 1 percent of that in the province. This is much less than their population (not to stress their condition) justifies. In the Khasi Hills and the Garo Hills combined, the number of institutions has actually diminished between 1922 and 1944, although it has been more than doubled in the rest of the province. The Lushai Hills make a much better showing with the number of institutions more than trebled; but this is almost entirely due to missionary activity: the expenditure from public funds there is about Re. 1-8-0 per pupil as against about Rs.9 in the ministerial province. This last figure excludes the expenditure on colleges (nearly Rs. 200 per head) in which men from the hills which have no colleges, are unrepresented. In the Naga Hills the figure per pupil is about Rs. 6 per head but there were less than 7,000 pupils in all, and the increase in institutions in the

---

*Recently Dr. Hutton, while suggesting that the first motive behind the Nagas' demand for education which, he says, has long been insistent is (as it is in the plains) a desire for Government employment and will bring disillusionment later, has affirmed that "the demand for education is one which cannot be denied if anything is to be granted at all" [Presidential Address to the Royal Anthropological Institute, 1945].

20 years was less than 50 per cent. The increase in pupils in the hills has been substantially below that of the plains. If the principal hill districts can still show, in the lowest classes, a proportion of pupils comparable, on the basis of population, with the plains, credit must go largely to missionaries, working with too little assistance from Government. Where there are no missions, as in the Northern Hills, there has been no education.

54. Individual officers, particularly in more recent times, have been anxious to secure advance in particular spheres; for example there has been some notable progress in agriculture in the Naga Hills. But such progress has tended to depend on individual inspiration rather than on settled policy and has in consequence been somewhat spasmodic. Among handicaps under which officers wishing to secure progress have worked has been a lack of assistance from the heads of technical departments. The evolution of policy in such matters as education, health, agriculture, communications, forests depends largely on departmental heads, and the district officer is not expected or as a rule qualified to guide Government in such matters. But the heads of Departments have tended to neglect the hills. Touring there was difficult and conditions strange to them, there was plenty to do in the plains, and the pressure exerted by Ministers, the Legislature and public opinion generally also encouraged the tendency to concentrate too exclusively on them. In the northern hills the functions of the head of the district were entrusted to police officers, who were intended to serve as 'keepers of the marches' rather than agencies for development, for which they were given no resources.

55. The lack of a Commissioner, has been another factor operating in the same direction. The Commissionership which included the hills was abolished as a measure of economy in 1938. In 1943 the Governor was given an Adviser for the Tribal Areas and States, but although Mr. Mills, who has filled the post, has generously given assistance with the excluded areas when required, this is no part of his functions. Whatever form the Government takes, its head should have an experienced administrator, holding a position analogous to that of Commissioner, to assist him in respect of the hills.

56. On the whole, it would be difficult to rebut entirely the charge that the effect of policy in the past has been to keep, the tribes as a 'human museum'. They have benefited by the lack of unwise interference, and the history of the hills shows how frequently unwise acts have led to serious trouble. Sympathetic officers and missionaries have won their confidence by patient understanding and helped them to more peaceful and kindly, and in some cases more prosperous, ways of life. But there has been too little regard for the future. Mr. Mills' view that the hillman of to-day is more separated from the plainsman than was his great-grandfather has much to support it. It should be added that no officer now serving in the hills would endorse a static policy, nor would those tribesmen who have come in contract with the outer world.

CHAPTER III—PRELIMINARY FACTORS

57. Before going on to consider possible arrangements for the future government of the hills, it is convenient to consider five preliminary factors. Each of these raises an issue of importance with an intimate bearing on the soundness of any scheme that may be devised. They are:—

(1) the actual and potential scope of tribal institutions;
(2) the capacity of the tribes for self-government;
(3) the desires of the people concerned;
(4) the extent of cohesion among the tribes;
(5) the relationship of the tribes with the outer world.

A. The Scope of Tribal Institutions

58. In dealing with the present system of government in the hills, reference was made to the fact that to a large extent the tribesmen govern themselves and this has rightly been stressed by all who have written on the subject. Sir Robert Reid, indeed, has described the hills as a 'block of self-governing communities'

and the survival of tribal institutions as organs of government is one of the big differences between hills and plains. Among the tribal peoples of the plains, while in most cases the tribal feeling remains and affects the social structure, government has passed to official hands or to a local bodies in which, at the best, they have only a minority of the members.

59. In the areas to which administration has not penetrated, Sir Robert Reid's description is substantially correct. Throughout nearly the whole of the northern hills and in most of the Naga tribal area the tribes have maintained their own government for periods going back further than any historical record. In the Momba country on the Bhutan border a certain amount of suzerainty has been exercised by Tibetan monastic or civil officials, but generally speaking, the tribes have had no overlords and our intervention has been confined, until very recently, to expeditions of an exploratory, pacificatory or punitive character. Elsewhere the ultimate responsibility for law and order has been exercised everywhere (not excepting the Imphal plain) by officers of Assam Government (or Governor). Serious crime comes within their cognizance; in their excluded areas the Assam Rifles, of whom at least three quarters have always been 'foreigners' (Gurkhas), have been maintained to keep the peace, and in the partially excluded areas there are other agencies.

60. In all areas self-government is subject to two further limitations. One relates to its functional and the other to its territorial range. So far as functions are concerned, these are limited to the provision of civil and of criminal justice, between which the tribesman draws no real distinction, and to the regulation of land. So far as education is concerned, the institution of the 'Morung' or Bachelors' Hall, which is found in nearly all Naga tribes and has some survivals in others, can be regarded as a kind of 'boarding-school' giving education in tribal life and warfare and serving economic as well as social purposes. But the tribal organization has had no share in education in the sense of literacy or anything higher: indeed the tribal languages, except that of the Hkamptis, were unwritten till the missionaries came. Communications are a matter; at most of the maintenance of

bridle tracks and even these are not usually the care of the tribal organization as such. The economic life of the tribe centres in the land and apart from that it is not regulated, much less stimulated, by any tribal body. There is thus a limitation to functions which are very vital but essentially primary, and which include none of the new functions that have been assumed by civilized Government in the last century or two.

61. The second limitation is that tribal Government is local self-government, with the accent very much on 'local'. In nearly all cases the unit is the village, and in most cases the organization envisages no larger unity.* In 1928 Dr. Hutton, wrote:—

"If it be found necessary to devise mechanism for the expression of tribal as district from village life, the proper method would be by tribal councils, with a view to the creation, ultimately, of autonomous tribal areas."

The "If" is significant, and unfortunately the static outlook which has been a feature of policy in the hills seems to have led to the conclusion that the devising of a larger mechanism was not necessary; for no official steps were taken in this direction.

62. In some areas, there have been larger units than that of the village. As a rule this larger unity has been associated with a less democratic form of rule. Among the Konyaks there are chiefs of fairly wide and rather autocratic jurisdiction. The Lushai chiefs have a considerable amount of power and a number rule over small groups of villages, though many have only one village. The recognition of most of the Khasi country as Indian States has crystallised it into units, most of which are much bigger than villages, and there are other instances. In the northern hills, the Apa Tanis, a compact tribe with few villages, have a tribal council. The plain of Manipur, where conditions are to some extent artificial, is the largest unity in the hills.

63. Where the village remains the unit the tribes themselves have made some progress towards greater cohesion. Particulars

---

*Among some of the most primitive tribes, such as many of the Mishmis, even the stage of village government has not been reached.

of some developments were given by Sir Robert Reid and these, among the Naga tribes at least, have gone further since he wrote. The Aos have formed a central committee and their range committees have extended their functions. They now maintain schools and teachers, and have dealt with such subjects as sanitation, the upkeep of roads, the development of village industries and the improvement of agriculture. The Semas have a central committee and one has recently been formed among the Tangkhuls of Manipur. An Angami committee is in process of formation and four tribes in the Mokokchung subdivision have combined to form a subdivisional committee which has started a High School. Most of these committees tax their people, especially for education, as do the Lushais.

64. This movement is of especial interest as illustrating how the innate democratic instincts of the tribes can be widened and made effective by the spread of education. Tribesmen who get some sense of the richer life of the bigger world seek larger horizons, and Christianity with its conception of fellowship is probably another influence here. A number of the tribes are thus coming to recognize that the village can no longer be the unit, and are feeling their way towards self-government on a bigger scale. An officer has been appointed to report on the existing situation and to make recommendations for the establishment of councils of wider jurisdiction.

65. Such councils, which would normally be formed on a tribal basis, could and should be given wider responsibilities, and should have powers of taxation to enable them to undertake constructive duties. They would naturally settle inter-village disputes which among some tribes are a constant source of friction and even bloodshed. They could probably be given a larger scope in respect of law and order and might deal, with the assistance of officials of Government, with heinous crime as well as petty crime. They could be made responsible for all but the leading routes of communication. They might be given duties in the realm of primary education, and perhaps even secondary education in some areas. They could probably maintain the elements of medical

attention and be given responsibility for public health, including water supplies.

66. But they cannot hope to maintain the services on which the progress of the tribes must depend. They could not provide higher education, to which the tribes must look for their leaders of the future. They could not be granted the authority to exploit the forest wealth on an economic scale, for this requires trained experts, nor can they do much in the direction of industrial development. Still less could they undertake the harnessing of the water power. The higher medical facilities will require to be provided by a larger authority, as will the maintenance and extension of modern communications. They can be taught to apply the benefits of agricultural research, and to assist in the conservation of the soil, but the direction and development of agriculture will require experts whom they cannot employ.

67. These limitations will not disappear with the growth of education in the hills, for they are fixed by territorial considerations. No tribe occupies a large enough area or has large enough population to be able to maintain the services which are necessary for the well-being of the community. Nor is there any likely combination of tribes, assuming that the language-bars and antipathies could be overcome, which would be large enough to do so. In short, it is only so long as life is primitive and unprogressive that peoples governed by tribal organization can be self-governing communities. For anything of a more advanced type, there must be guidance by a governmental authority transcending the tribe, and the wider collective functions of Government must be largely vested in such an authority.

B. The Capacity for Self-government

68. The plains tribal peoples already participate in the Government of Assam and, as there can be no question of separating them, their capacity in this respect need not be examined. The peoples of the northern hills are incapable of sharing in any

Government at a level above the tribal level for a considerable time to come. They are all in an almost primæval state, and most of them have no educated men who could represent them in any sense. There is, therefore, no alternative to a system of tutelage in their case.

69. The tribes of the southern and central hills are at varying stages. Some have had a little experience of self-government by being in partially excluded areas; but the allocation of areas as excluded or partially excluded bears little relation to the stage of progress reached by the tribes. The Mikirs, who are partially excluded, are about as backward as any tribe within the administered boundaries, and the Garos are also backward: the Lushais and some of the Naga tribes are considerably more advanced. There are Lushai and Naga doctors, schoolmasters and pastors; they have provided officers who have distinguished themselves in the army and administrative officials in the provincial cadres.

70. There is thus no area that is incapable of furnishing the limited number of men which the area would be entitled to send to a provincial legislature; and the representatives from the areas now excluded might well be better than some of those sent by the partially excluded areas or even some of the plains representatives. As a whole, they would lack experience at the start and, educationally they might for some time be weaker than the average Assam politician. But, if proper selections were made, they might bring gifts of character which would be an asset to a legislature. A minor difficulty arises from the multiplicity of tribes, especially among the Nagas, who could, on the basis of the present Assam Assembly, have at the most two representatives. With an Assembly of the tribes alone the numbers could be increased, but the difficulty of finding suitable men and of their taking common counsel would also be increased.

71. Mr. Mills has some interesting and uncomplimentary remarks on the Khasis, who, in any Government centred in Shillong, might expect to have a considerable influence, and is anxious to exclude the more educated and detribalised Khasis. The Khasis are not typical and good many of them are more

sophisticated than other tribesmen. But it would be difficult to select any tribe that is typical; for there is a great diversity among them. Indeed one of the difficulties in dealing with this subject has been that much that has been written about the Assam tribes was written with the Nagas filling the view and they, like the others, are not typical. The money-seeking tendency of the Khasis represents largely the natural effects of changing from a self-contained economy in 'kind' to a money economy resulting from better communications. There have been signs of the same tendency in other tribes to whom the war brought large sums of money.

72. The individualism of the Khasis, of which the money-seeking tendency is a symptom, represents a stage which is inescapable if modern civilization is to reach the tribes, as it must. There is, with sophistication, a change which weakens the herd instinct and increases the acquisitive instinct; and the Khasis have been exposed to the impact of civilization much more severely than the other tribes, who are fenced off by lines which not even a man of another tribe can cross without official permission. The Khasis are learning, partly under Christian influence which has permeated them more fully than any other tribe except the Lushais, the idea of a wider unity and, despite the fact that the woman is generally 'the better half', are producing men of some character and capacity. Their experience would be valuable at the start, but they would certainly not monopolize even a tribal government. Other tribes like the Lushais tend to look down on them somewhat and would not be slow to assert themselves.

73. One difficulty would be that of securing representatives who are representatives, *i.e.* who are in sufficiently close touch and sympathy with their constituents to be able to speak for them and pursue their welfare intelligently. Any individual now coming, say, from a Naga tribe, if he has sufficient education to discharge his duties well, must be to some extent divorced from them. He may have been educated at a school outside his area and, even if he has not, his contact with a world which most tribesmen can scarcely imagine will inevitably create a gulf. But that gulf exists to some extent in all legislatures. No parliament

has many 'men in the street'; if they were merely typical citizens they would not normally be in Parliament. The M. P. who started work in a coal mine is greatly changed by years of public life. But he seldom on that account loses his sympathy for and understanding of those from whom he came. A legislator from the tribes may be separated to a greater degree from his constituents; but the gulf will diminish with the spread of education; and if care is taken with the method of election, it need not be deep. Tribal councils, if they can be established, would probably be much better constituents than individuals; failing them the village councils could select the constituents to exercise the franchise.

74. There would be greater difficulty in securing persons to serve as ministers than in securing legislators. Among the hill tribes, if the Manipuris are excluded, only the Khasis as yet have participated in their own Government. The two ministers they have supplied to the Assam ministry belong to the urbanised Khasis whom Mr. Mills wishes to exclude as having "nothing to contribute to the welfare of the tribal peoples as such", a judgment which is open to serious question.

75. On the capacity of the tribes to furnish ministers, there is thus insufficient experience to justify dogmatic assertions; the position would depend to some extent on whether the tribes, or any section of them, had to form their own ministry or merely to contribute a minority to an all-Assam ministry. In the latter event, they should be able to furnish their share in the ordinary way. At the start, their lack of political experience might be a handicap, as it is now to ministers from the Scheduled Castes, but they would probably overcome this more quickly than Scheduled Caste ministers, as they have not the burden of a depressed history behind them and would be more independent.

76. If the tribes, or the hill tribes, had to form their own ministry, the initial difficulties would be much greater. There are probably to-day men in the more advanced tribal groups—Khasis and Syntengs, Nagas and Lushais—who are capable, with guidance, of forming a small ministry; but an electorate which would be, in the main, new to political life might not throw them up.

The Garos and Mikirs would have greater difficulty in finding men. The question would appear to be one of time; given a period of guidance, there seems to be no reason why a tribal ministry should not be formed which might possess less political astuteness than the average Indian ministry, but might well be stronger in other qualities. The democratic spirit inherent in the tribes should prove a buttress of representative government.

C. The Popular Desire

77. There are few tribesmen who are in a position to give a reasoned judgment of their future in the light of all the factors involved. The interest of the plains tribes clearly lies in the inclusion of as many of the hill tribes as possible, and their leaders would advocate this and welcome closer ties. Those plainsmen who do not belong to the tribes have no strong interest, but would probably oppose a partition of the province and support the idea of closer unions with the hills. Some of the hill tribesmen, and particularly of the Khasis, would incline to this also, but practically none would support complete assimilation.

78. As regards the bulk of the hillmen it is difficult to dogmatize because they have no real appreciation of the possible alternatives. Mr. Mills claims that the hillman "does not join in the cry for political freedom" and cites in support two 'genuinely representative meetings'. Both were limited to Nagas and in one there was demand for a Legislative Council with power to take full autonomous control whenever it chooses. Sir Robert Reid's advocacy of his scheme for a British colony has evoked some support and some opposition. Occasional meetings in Shillong demand union with Assam, but as Mr. Mills observes these are generally led by urbanised Khasis, other tribes being represented, if at all, by immature students. A federation of tribesmen which includes some more responsible men has been feeling its way towards closer union of tribesmen in the hills and the plains.

79. Mr. Mills is on safe ground in asserting that the average hillman wants "a government which will let him alone except when he requires help" but this is not of great assistance, for practically every one would like such a government if it were possible to create it. Most of the hillmen would probably rather be let alone than have the help; and their wishes in this respect have, with results that are not altogether happy, been largely respected in the past. But this attitude is changing. The leaders at least have come to feel that their people are in danger of being left behind, and consequently of proving unable to cope with the incursion of a more modern world; and they would be prepared for some sacrifice to secure the help they need.

80. Hitherto the hillman has not been given much, but he has got more than he has paid for. Of the hill districts, the Garo Hills alone is more or less self-supporting; all the others are a drain on the province. Manipur supports itself at a moderate level of administration; the Khasi States have practically no taxation and provide hardly any service. There are resources in the hills capable of being developed. Mineral resources appear to be mainly in the central hills and there are everywhere possibilities from forests. But it is certain that the hills would not want to pay for their own government, and they could not be made to pay for a government able to give them real help without serious hardship in present circumstances. The desire for a government which will help but not interfere is, to a considerable extent, a desire for free benefits.

81. Probably the nearest approach to the preference of educated tribesmen of the hills who are able to appreciate the issues is somewhat as follows. They do not desire to be subjected to either Hindu or Muslim rule, or to be administered by officers of these communities or by plainsmen at all. But they do not want to remain in a backward state and realize the need for better education, for communications and for other modern facilities. They would like to retain their tribal outlook and culture and general way of life, so far as that is consistent with political and economic progress. And they would welcome the assistance and indeed guidance of European officers if that is not to involve an oppressive or a permanent tutelage or a heavy burden in taxation.

D. The Cohesion of the Tribes

82. Between the tribes of the plains and those of the hills there are, as has been noted, minor connections, but there has been no extensive contact. The presence in the Assam legislature of representatives of the plains tribes and of some of the hill tribes has helped to establish a limited contact, and both are beginning to realize that cohesion has advantages. A tribal federation has recently been formed to secure closer union, but it cannot claim a representative character and its ideas would appeal to very few tribesmen.

83. Between the tribes of the northern hills and those of the southern and central hills there is no contact whatever. It is doubtful if a Naga has ever seen a Momba or if any Lushai has met a Dafla. Where the two series of ranges meet, there is of course some intermingling, and the war and its needs bought Abors and Mishmis into contact with some Nagas. The most that can be claimed for treating these two divisions collectively is that there are affinities of race and of social structure and that they present, to some extent, the same problems.

84. The tribes occupying the southern and central hills have, among themselves, a good many points of contact, and these have been greatly increased by the war. Prior to the war, higher education for Nagas, Lushais, Khasis and some others tended to be concentrated in Shillong, which is still important for this purpose. Hillmen who were officers in various Government services were not confined to their own hills, but frequently served with other tribes. The war brought Khasis, Syntengs and Garos to the Naga and the Lushai Hills and it united men from most of the southern and central hills in service. The constitution of the Assam Regiment, which has consisted very largely of hillmen, has probably had some effect in stimulating the sense of common interest among the tribesmen. Christianity which has affected all these tribes considerably is also a unifying force, and seems likely to have greater effects as communications improve.

85. With all this, it must be admitted that cohesion does not go far as yet. It will be a long time before the tribes can claim to be a people: even the Nagas, by themselves, could not make that claim to day. The tribesman tends to think primarily in terms of his village or clan; even the tribe itself sometimes means little and it is only the few who have conceptions of any larger unity. Between the tribes too, as indeed between villages in some areas (notably the Naga Hills) there are some traditional hostilities. Mr. Mills has referred to a case where some Khasi areas have federated to form a small State. Adjoining the State is another where the difficulty is to hold several groups of villages together. Here there are no linguistic or geographical barriers, but both are serious obstacles to cohesion among the hill tribes generally.

86. No group of peoples of the same size, and perhaps none in the world has so many distinct languages: the number of known ones is in the neighbourhood of 90. The hillman is a good linguist and the men of one tribe have normally some acquaintance with the language of a border tribe; but none of these languages can hope to become a *lingua franca* and any large gathering of tribal representatives would have serious difficulties in reaching a common basis in present circumstances. The tribes must therefore depend on an external language and Assamese, and to a lesser extent English, already serve the purpose of communication among the educated and those holding position of authority. As education spreads and travel becomes more general, the knowledge of both will increase.

87. In considering possible schemes for the Government of the hills, it will be necessary to face the great difficulty in the way of keeping them together and this section can be concluded with observations on possible lines of partition. All those who have dealt with the subject have started by separating the hills from the plains tribes; and for reasons that should be clear from the descriptive chapters; this is the most prominent dividing line. There is another between the northern hills and those of the south and centre: the many points of difference need not be summarised here. The least defensible line of partition is that chosen

by the framers of the Government of India Act which treated the British Indian portions of the Southern hills as excluded areas and nearly all the central hills as partially excluded. The division into States and British India is of much longer standing, but, so far as the Khasi States are concerned, it is entirely artificial. The Manipur plain can be regarded as *sui generis* in the hills; but, the line which separates the other parts of the State from the adjoining hills is artificial.

E. The Hills and the Plains

88. There has been a tendency, in discussing the hill tribes to treat them, as it were, *in vacuo*. Their connections with the outer world have been ignored or regarded as unimportant. In the distant past, this might have been justified, for they led a life which was both primitive and isolated. The policy pursued towards them tended to encourage isolation; to this day most of them are protected by an 'inner line' which no outsider can cross without a permit. It could be maintained that the tribes did not desire outside contact to any appreciable extent, but in the modern world no people can live in isolation. The links of the hills with the plains constitute a factor of importance to them, and are not without relevance from the point of view of the plains.

89. The most obvious link is furnished by geography. Of three belts of hills the northern one drains into the Assam Valley from the north, and the southern, with the exception of much of Manipur which drains into the Chindwin, drains into both the Valleys of the province. The third belt consists of a long peninsula completely separating the two Valleys and containing in its centre the provincial capital. The Mikir hills form an outlying mass stretching from the bank of the Brahmaputra to the Southern hills, and practically bisecting the Assam Valley, so that the province, without the hills, consists virtually of three separated areas. A glance at the map shows how interconnected the hills are with the plains.

90. But the ordinary map is far from exhibiting the complete lack of cohesion in the hills. It shows an area which, though of very irregular shape, is connected. In actual fact the connections are illusory. For practical purposes the Garo Hills cannot be reached except through the plains, the Khasi Hills are connected with the Jaintia Hills only by bridle paths, and the Lushai Hills cannot be reached except through the plains of Cachar. The North Cachar Hills are almost unconnected with any other area except by the railway from the plains. The Mikir Hills are a peninsula almost surrounded by the plains and the Naga Hills cannot in practice be reached from any other hills except those of Manipur. Even between some points of the Naga Hills themselves the easiest way of contact is by the plains. The northern hills have even less connections, for the people live in a series of deep Himalayan valleys separated by forbidding ranges and accessible to each other and to any other hills only through the plains. All the hills can be compared to blocks of small rooms which open on both sides of a broad central corridor or hall but which have no connecting doors between them. More strictly there are two such corridors represented by the two Valleys.

91. From the economic point of view the hills are naturally linked with the plains and prosperity will depend largely on interchange. From the point of view of the plains the hills are the source of water-power which should play a vital part in the economic development of Assam; and they provide products, such as cotton and potatoes, which the plains need badly. The important forests lie either in the hills or in the submontane tracts which are largely inhabited by plains tribes. Erosion in the hills, which is a much neglected and very urgent problem, is also of vital concern to the plains, which are threatened with the prospect of increasing damage by floods. Manipur and part of the Naga Hills can now hope for one good road to Burma, but it seems likely that the main trend of trade will continue to be with Assam. The northern hills will always have some interchange with Tibet, but there are only two routes to that country which can be regarded as even tolerable and the main one will serve trade

between China and the plains rather than the trade of the hills through which it passes.

92. There is thus danger on the economic side in any separation of the hills from the plains. Experience has already shown that provincial boundaries are an economic handicap, and with the tendency to increasing State control of economic life, their economic effect is likely to grow. Nor is any new constitution likely to curtail the power of provincial governments to do each other mutual injury in this respect. The Assam hills are a series of economic islands, joined only by the plains. As a separate province they would be much more vulnerable on the economic side than a better connected and larger province, and they would be in a much weaker position than the plains in the event of economic differences with them.

93. Administratively, the hills have been closely linked with Assam. Their penetration, so far as it has gone, has been effected from Assam and almost entirely by the Assam administration; and they have depended throughout on the Assam cadres to man their services. It cannot be claimed that the arrangement has been altogether satisfactory and possible changes will be considered later. But the hills are not capable of maintaining an entirely separate administration and it is to Assam that they would most naturally turn for assistance.

94. Politically, the southern and central hills have for long had connections with Assam; the northern hills have had practically no political history. All the areas were a responsibility of the Assam Government until 1937. Since then the Government and the Governor of Assam have shared responsibility for them, the latter acting as an agent of the Crown Representative or the Governor General in Council in some areas. The peoples of the central hills have taken part in the political life of the province. Assamese is the *lingua franca* in a large part of the hills, including the Naga Hills, and the location of the capital in the hills has acted as link between them and the plains, and provided a meeting place for their peoples.

CHAPTER IV—RETENTION IN ASSAM

A. The Possibility of Fusion

95. In the three preceding chapters an endeavour has been made to set out the main facts and conditions of the problem of the future place of the tribal peoples. The remaining chapters deal with possible solutions, and it is natural to begin with the possibility of the fusion of the hills and plains of Assam. It is convenient to leave for a later stage consideration of those areas which are not parts of the province or are not treated as such, *i.e.*, the States, the Naga Tribal Area and the whole of the northern hills. The discussion is therefore confined at present to areas which are, both *de jure* and *de facto*, parts of the province.

96. The links with Assam have just been discussed; they are very relevant and they are likely, in the absence of artificial barriers, to grow steadily stronger. In recognition of this, and despite the pleas of separatists, there has been a tendency to regard fusion with Assam as the ultimate goal. That fusion has gone some distance already and the Government of India Act, 1935, can be regarded as endorsing the idea to a large extent. For, accepting the areas as part of Assam already, it contemplates the conversion of the excluded areas into partially excluded areas and the conversion of the latter into ministerial areas, but does not countenance the reverse process. A merger would in some ways represent the least radical change from the *status quo* and it would meet some of the difficulties inherent in any other proposal. But as Sir Robert Reid and others have emphasized, it creates other difficulties and has potential dangers.

97. Before dealing with these, one preliminary point deserves attention, particularly because it appears to have been overlooked in the earlier discussions of the question. This is that the question of the inclusion of the hills in Assam or their separation is not one that concerns the hills alone. The exclusion of the hills would affect the position of the plains in various ways. Financially, it would probably be of advantage to them, at the start at least. But in other ways it would be a disadvantage. It would leave a province

of somewhat inconvenient shape with, unless it was deprived of Shillong, an isolated capital. It would tend to produce undesirable economic effects and it would bring political disadvantages. At present the representatives of the hills, who are neither Hindus nor Muslims, exercise a moderating and balancing influence; if all the hills were included this influence would be more marked. Further the position of the plains tribes would be substantially weaker if the hills were taken away and appreciably stronger if the excluded areas were included. This is probably true of the under privileged generally, and will be clearer when the comparative strengths of the communities are analysed. While the issue of fusion or separation is one that affects the hills much more than the plains, it is a mistake to think only of what benefits the hills and to ignore the real interest of the plains in any conclusion that may be reached.

B. Dangers and Difficulties

98. Passing to the dangers and difficulties of a merging of the hills in the ministerial province, officers interested in the hills have been apprehensive lest the tribes living there should have their cultural traditions distorted or destroyed by contact with the plains; and this fear has contributed to the tendency in the past to keep the tribes as an anthropological museum. The lot of the déracinés is usually unhappy, and tribes which lose their culture are in grave danger of falling into this condition. For the same reason, the older hill officers generally tended to look on Christianity, especially in the form in which it was presented by American missionaries, with grave misgivings if not hostility. There is undoubtedly much in tribal culture which it is desirable and indeed important to preserve, and in some areas missionaries themselves would admit that they and their converts were too iconoclastic in the past. There are signs in some areas of a more accommodating spirit among Christian tribesmen themselves. One American missionary* has written "In opposing or

---

* Rev. F.W. Harding, D. D.: Indigenous Christianity in Assam.

abandoning some tribal laws and customs indigenous Christianity has sometimes ignorantly 'thrown the baby out with the bath water'. On the other hand administrators have occasionally hung on to both the baby *and* the bath water."

99. He might have written 'kept the baby *in* the bath water', for not all the features of tribal culture are worth preserving: some are definitely harmful and degrading. Moreover cultural change—it would hardly be going too far to say cultural trans-formation—is inevitable. Except is the northern hills the growth of Christianity has been striking and is going on. The war has brought almost a revolution in the thought of all but the north-ern tribes by bringing them into close contact with men of other races and by showing them the power of modern invention. A number, and especially the southern Nagas and the Kukis have seen war in their own lands; others have come into contact with it in various ways. With the gradual growth of education which in its higher forms must be sought in Shillong or outside the hills altogether, there is an increasing change in cultural outlook. The better features of tribal life, however, have a high degree of vital-ity; and from the cultural point of view, there would seem to be no grave danger of harm and some possibility of good in fusion with a larger unit.

100. The greater dangers lie in the political field. If the hill tribes are included in Assam they will form a minority and the Government will be largely dominated by persons who will have little sympathy with them and no great understanding of their life and their needs. Sir Robert Reid has forecasted "rebellion, bloodshed and ultimate ruin" and the hills have seen a good deal of bloodshed. The original advances and annexations, which were seldom peaceful, were made mainly with a view to security in the plains. To the larger expeditions of later years errors on the part of the paramount power or its officers made important contributions, and there is no doubt that a Government with no hostile intentions might easily blunder into acts which would precipitate serious trouble.

101. The risk of such trouble would be greatly reduced if the tribes could feel that they were represented in the Government

and that, in matters peculiarly concerning them, their will would prevail. As has been pointed out already, there could at present be no representation of the northern hills. The peoples of the central hills are already represented in the Assam Legislature, and it would not be difficult to secure, on a limited franchise, representation of most of the peoples of the southern hills.

102. Although they might not all be effective at the start, the tribal representatives could secure a position of some strength in the Assam Legislature if they held together. In 1941 caste Hindus numbered 3,864,000 and Muslims were 3,474,000 and have probably added a fair number since. The tribal peoples (*vide* table on page 2 [page 140 of this book]) of the hills and plains, excluding the northern hills and without taking any part of the Naga tribal area, are 2,824,000. In these figures the Manipuri non Muslims who are about 340,000 are reckoned as caste Hindus. The remaining million are mainly Scheduled Castes who, if they were freed from the shackles of the Poona Pact, would be more friendly to the tribal than to other sections. On any fair system of representation the tribals would be one of the three large and almost equal sections, and might well aspire to hold the balance between the other two. Despite the exclusion of important sections of the hill tribes and the fact that separate constituencies are given to only part of the plains tribes, this effect has begun to appear already and the plains tribals are tending to look the hills for potential allies.

103. But this offers a precarious and inadequate security. The bulk of the legislators would always be plainsmen and on questions of conflict between hills and plains, the hills would be in a minority. Nor could they expect to wield great influence in a ministry; for they would be handicapped not merely in numbers but, for a time at least, in quality. And there are many directions in which a ministry and a legislature composed predominantly of plainsmen could take action which would be injurious to the hills and which could lead, sooner or later, to serious discontent and revolt.

104. In the sphere of legislation, three examples may be taken. So far as criminal and civil law is concerned, there would probably be a move to extend to the hills the 'blessings' of the Indian

judicial system. Nine out of ten Ministers in both the recent ministries have been lawyers, and as a large proportion in every legislature is drawn from the bar this idea would make a strong appeal. But the effect would be calamitous, not merely because it would introduce to the hills the grave abuses which dog the Indian judicial system, but because it would tend to sweep away the whole tribal system of Government. As a second example, grave errors are possible in respect of revenue legislation. Bengal, Ireland, Scotland and South Africa can all testify to the lamentable effects of misunderstanding by foreign rulers or 'the predominant partner' of the indigenous system of land-tenure, and the Assam legislature might well be tempted to make Government's spurious claim to tribal lands a real one, or to introduce an alien system of land revenue. Thirdly in the realm of taxation, plains legislators may well be tempted to secure what they would regard as a greater equality of burden between the hills and the plains and to make the former less of a 'drain' on provincial revenues.

105. In the realm of administration, serious errors can easily be made. As it is, ministries are liable to try and 'punish' officials by relegating them to the hills, and they are not likely to accommodate themselves easily to the idea of letting the tribesmen rule themselves to a large extent. This danger would admittedly be minimized by the establishment of separate provincial cadres for the hills and the plains; but even the hill cadres would be subordinate to a ministry composed largely of plainsmen, and those who proved most accommodating to their ideas would have a happier career than those who stood up for the rights of the tribal peoples.

C. Arrangements for Joint Working

106. This leads to the broad conclusion that the fusion of the southern and central hills with the plains, without some special arrangements by which the special needs and separate conditions

of these hills are recognized, would be most unwise and unsafe. The possibility of devising such arrangements has now to be considered.

107. In respect of legislation protections is at present afforded by section 92 of the Government of India Act, which has virtually the effect of making the Governor the legislating authority for both excluded and partially excluded areas. No central or provincial legislation can be extended to them without his direction, and he can amend the laws in issuing such a direction. He has further the power, with the approval of the Governor General, to make laws of his own, which are styled regulations. In practice central and provincial laws have been extended as a rule except where they appeared likely to be nugatory, and amendments have generally been merely formal. A small number of regulations have been made, mostly for the excluded areas. The more important ones have related to judicial matters. The value of the section as a protection to the tribes has lain more in the existence of the bar to unsuitable legislation than in the positive use made of it.

108. Although the working of section 92 has been simple and satisfactory on the whole, it can hardly be regarded as more than a temporary provision. Indeed the whole system of exclusion was in intention temporary and a situation has to be contemplated in which the autocratic powers of the Governor will disappear. They are inconsistent with a full measure of self-government and with any real merger of the hills and plains. Such a merger, moreover, must involve a common legislative chamber in which all the peoples could be represented. There could not be completely separate legislatures in a united province.

109. It is, however, possible, to have two separate upper chambers and this is perhaps the least unsatisfactory way of meeting the legislative difficulty. The present Legislative Council contains only one representative of the hills and he is a Bengali. It would be possible to create a separate Legislative Council for the hills, and there should be no difficulty in securing adequate representatives. Bills passing the Legislative Assembly would apply to the plains and the hills respectively only when they had been passed by the upper chambers concerned. Some provision for joint sessions

to resolve deadlocks might have to be retained. If the Councils were made reasonably large, joint sessions could consist of the Council concerned with the whole of the Assembly; otherwise it might be necessary to let the appropriate Council to sit with the corresponding members of the Assembly as the final tribunal.

110. In the executive sphere there would have to be a joint ministry, but some special provisions would be necessary. In the matter of selecting ministers, the Governor would have to be free to choose the sections separately and probably to dismiss them separately. If he had to be guided throughout by the Prime Minister, who would normally be a plainsman, hill ministers might be chosen for their readiness to subordinate the interests of the hills. On the basis of their population, the hills could claim only one minister in a cabinet of seven and, left to themselves, might secure no more in a larger cabinet. At present they have none in a cabinet of ten; but only part of them is represented in the legislature. They should have a larger share guaranteed, not merely to give them a reasonable voice in the Council of Ministers, but because it would be impossible for a single minister to represent them effectively. The hill peoples differ more and have less cohesion than the people of the plains; a Khasi, for example, is very different from a Naga and neither is like a Lushai. Two ministers, one from the central and one from the southern hills, would be essential and three would be a better minimum.

111. There should also be some system by which the inevitable majority of plains ministers could not overrule the hills ministers on matters concerning the hills. In such cases it might be possible to provide that the Governor shall be guided by the appropriate section of his ministers. Such a provision is likely to give some difficulty in working, for there may be cases where confusion would be caused by following two different courses in the hills and the plains. But the separation of the areas makes the difficulty a great deal smaller than that a rising from Hindu-Muslim differences in the Central Cabinet, where some such system has been proposed and may have to be evolved. It would seem that a certain amount of discretion will have to remain in the Governor's hands.

112. The difficulty is likely to be most serious in respect of finance. There could not be separate budgets, for large items of expenditure will be of an all-provincial character. Nor could there be separate financial departments or Finance Ministers. It would be possible to separate certain items in the budget; the expenditure on the excluded areas is shown separately now. But two separate authorities are responsible for these two separate sets of entries and one of these authorities, the Governor, exercises arbitrary powers. Assuming a continuance of the system of a central subvention, its allocation between the plains and the hills should reduce the possibility of friction. But there would have to be some procedure for resolving deadlocks, and it would seem necessary that the Governor should have power to act on the advice of either section of his ministry in differences over finance.

113. Heads of departments would have responsibility throughout the province and there would be a single secretariat. But for reasons already given, the cadres of what now correspond to provincial services should be, as far as possible, separate. In the sphere of administration matters concerning the plains and the hills should as far as practicable be the concern of ministers of the plains and hills respectively. This applies especially to questions of personnel relating to the selection, postings, etc. of officials of the separate cadres. The system would probably start with a fairly sharp bifurcation in ministerial duties, and it might be desirable to give one of the hill ministers no regular portfolio but a general responsibility for hill affairs. But the practice of bringing all important matters before Cabinet and of constant consultation should produce mutual trust and thus make it possible gradually to reduce the dichotomy.

114. Arrangements such as these cannot be regarded as ideal, but it is difficult, with a joint province, to see alternatives to which more objection could not be taken, short of giving some authority like the Governor increased powers. To that the objections are that it reduces the scope of self-government, and it makes too much depend on one personality, who may not have the administrative experience usual in the past and is not likely to

be subject to the controls now in force. One merit can be claimed for a scheme of this kind, namely that it treats the plains and hills alike and that the protection given to each lies, as far as possible, within the actual constitutional arrangements. While the effect of protection would be more felt in the hills than the plains, because it is most needed by the smaller partner, the scheme is as free as seems possible from artificial and arbitrary "safeguards". But before reaching a conclusion, it is necessary to analyse the possibilities offered by schemes involving the separation of the hills from the plains.

D. Provincial Boundaries

115. It has been assumed, in the foregoing discussion, that the province of Assam will retain its existing boundary with Bengal. But it is possible that, to secure a settlement of the communal problem or for other reasons, provincial boundaries may be redrawn. So far as Assam is concerned, the most obvious adjustment would be the exclusion of the Surma Valley or at least of Sylhet which contains five-sixths of its population. Sylhet is ethnologically, geographically, linguistically and economically part of Bengal. Most of it is part of the original *dewani* and it was cut off from Bengal in 1874, presumably to make Assam a large enough province; these were days when provinces of 3 or 4 million people were not regarded as possible. Its return has been mooted from time to time and was at one time approved by the Assam Legislative Council. It would mean the exclusion from Assam of 1,892,000 Muslims, *i.e.*, more than half the Muslims of the province. Only 70,000 tribals would go: no Assam district has so small a number. The others excluded would number about 1,150,000.

116. This would probably strengthen the position of the tribes. Although there would not be so close a balance between Hindus and Muslims, they would form a much larger proportion of the population—about 3 million out of less than 8 on the 1941 figures. The removal of parts of the lower Assam Valley, which

have now a large Muslim population, would exclude also some tribal people, but it would strengthen further the position of most of them. Most of Goalpara is also part of the original *diwani* of Bengal, it is largely Bengali-speaking and its Bengali population, always substantial, is large and increasing. It is worth noting that the Assamese are a more tolerant and easy-going race than the Bengalis, and would be likely to work better with the tribes.

117. A more radical partition, which would be distasteful to many Assamese Hindus but for which a fairly good case could be made, would be to transfer most of the land north of the Brahmaputra as well as Sylhet to Bengal. This would unite the great bulk of the Muslim population to Bengal, and although it would remove a good many plains tribals, it would leave a province in which the tribes should be well able to hold their own. Such a province would also be better off financially, as Sylhet and the bulk of Goalpara, the two districts belonging to the permanent settlement of Bengal, would be cut out, while the heart of the province would be the two upper districts of the Assam Valley, which contain the bulk of the tea area, the oil and the coal.

118. The only other partition line that need be considered, short of the entire separation of the hills, is a line cutting off all the plains West of the Mikir Hills. This would mean a province confined to the hills and the upper two districts of the Assam Valley. Owing mainly to the large number of tea gardens in these districts and the fact that they contain nearly all the Ahoms, no districts in the plains or the hills have such large tribal populations, and in a province so constituted the tribal peoples would have a majority. From such a division, therefore, the hill tribes would have much to gain and little to fear, and it is possible that the Assamese, the majority of whom would dislike it at present, would gain in the long run. For it seems likely that they will be swamped in the lower districts by the increasing immigration of Muslim from Mymensingh, a people whom they fear and dislike and who bring much lower standard of living with them.

119. In connection with the adjustment of provincial boundaries, the possibility of adding the Chittagong hill tracts to the Assam hills deserves notice. The inclusion of this area was part

of Sir Robert Reid's and Dr. Hutton's scheme, and they have been followed by Mr. Mills. The people are doubtless allied and this area has some similar problems. But there is no geographical connection; that which appears on a small scale map is illusory. Further they belong economically to Bengal and union with Assam would be artificial in many ways. Those who are politically minded among them already look towards fusion with Bengal, and the people as a whole have closer relations with Bengal than the Assam hill tribes have with Assam. Except that the addition of this area would increase the tribal population and consequently the tribal strength, the proposal has very little to commend it.

120. Mr. Mills has also suggested the inclusion of Tripura State. The bulk of the people are Mongolian in origin and the Tipperas, the largest of the many peoples, are allied to both the Kacharis and the Garos, while the State has also some Manipuris and Kukis. But the State is geographically and economically connected with Bengal, Bengali is the dominant language and there is a considerable population of Bengali immigrants, mostly Muslim. The case for its attachment to Assam or to the Assam hills, if separated, cannot be regarded as strong.

121. On the other hand, the transfer of that part of Bengal which borders on the Garo Hills should be considered. Here there are some partially excluded areas peopled mainly by Garos. Some adjustment of boundaries seems desirable, and would be welcomed by the Garos, to whose district any transferred area would be added. Within Assam also, some minor adjustments of boundaries between hills and plains are desirable if special arrangements are made for the two areas. The Mikir hills should in any case be separated from the two subdivisions in which they now lie and constituted as a separate subdivision.

CHAPTER V—SYSTEMS OF TUTELAGE

122. The possibilities of separation fall into two classes. In the first place, the hills could constitute an agency of a higher

authority in Whitehall, New Delhi or elsewhere. This would, in effect, involve a fairly complete state of tutelage. In the second place, the hills could, in separation from the plains, form a unit enjoying the largest possible measure of self-government. The suggestions made in the first category are discussed in this chapter and the possibilities of the second type are considered in Chapter VI.

A. A Separate Colony

123. The formation of a new colony is the solution advocated by Sir Robert Reid who was inspired by Dr. Hutton and has been followed by Mr. Mills. His conclusion was in favour of what would be, in essence, a separate country "divorced (as is Burma) from the control of the Government of India." This would include not merely all the hills, north, south and central, of Assam, but the adjacent hills of Burma and Bengal and perhaps the Shan States. The United Kingdom, perhaps assisted by contributions from Indian governments, would meet the inevitable deficit. Sir Robert Reid emphasized the extent of self-government among the tribes, and added "The amount of control would undoubtedly have to be very considerable for a time, but it is essential that it should come from Whitehall and not from India, to which the hill tracts are entirely alien." He added that he saw "no other line along which we can fulfil our duty to these primitive peoples. They will not get a square deal from an autonomous Indian Government and the sequel would be rebellion, bloodshed and ultimate ruin."

124. These are strong words and, coming from one who had devoted special study to the Assam hills, may well give pause to those who favour less radical solutions. But the solution seems open to serious objections. To put it at its lowest, it seems most unlikely that a British Government which is prepared to set India and Burma on a self-governing footing should now undertake the administrative and financial responsibility for a patchwork of sparsely populated hills lying where these hills do. Indian

opinion would be equally strongly opposed to the constitution of a foreign territory with its natural boundaries. To ask an Indian Government to contribute towards the maintenance of the amputated member would be regarded as adding insult to injury.

125. Apart from possible political difficulties, there are cogent objections to such a scheme. Geographically the proposed colony would have a fantastic shape and be completely lacking in cohesion. Economically it would be isolated and its interests would almost certainly be ignored by both Burma and India, so that it would have to relapse even further into an economic self-sufficiency of a primitive type. Administratively, there would be grave difficulties in securing and retaining suitable cadres of officers. Further the hills, to the north and east at least, are an integral part of India's defence and although Great Britain may co-operate in that defence, the complete removal of the area from Indian control would complicate the question of defence on the East. Finally the proposal would involve a postponement of responsibility in Government and an actual step back for the partially excluded areas.

126. It seems unnecessary, on this view, to discuss in detail the situation of the High Commission territories in South Africa: but it is perhaps desirable to refer to them briefly as their constitution might appear to offer some analogy to Sir Robert Reid's scheme. They can be regarded as backward tracts, and the British Government still accepts responsibility for their administration and for meeting their regular deficits. But they would not have survived if their peoples could have secured full rights of citizenship in the Union, and although one of them was under the Cape administration and another was, for a few years, a protectorate of the South African Republic, they have never been within the Union. There is no real parallel between the position of the Assam tribesmen and that of the negro peoples of the High Commission territories; still less can the Indian or Assam electorates be compared with the minority which monopolizes political power in South Africa. One point, however, which the South African situation appears to underline, is that of the economic difficulties which confront small segregated areas. If parallels

are to be sought abroad, the Indian reservations in the United States afford a somewhat closer analogy. But these reservations lie within the Federal Government's fabric and do not belong to an outside power.

B. Union with Burma

127. The suggestion of union with Burma was put forward at one time by Dr. Hutton, and Mr. Mills has referred to the affinities with that country. It deserves notice for several reasons. First, if the separation of the Assam hills were accepted, it would reduce somewhat the series of difficulties inherent in the creation of so small a unit. Secondly, the peoples of the Southern and Central Hills are ethnologically more akin to the Burmese peoples than to the Indian peoples, and they came to Assam *via* Burma. Thirdly, except between the Lushai Hills and the Chin Hills (and even there the peoples are allied), the tribal areas run across the political boundary. At the extreme south the Lakhers are arbitrarily divided. Kukis live in considerable numbers in the Burma areas bordering on Manipur and in the Somra Tract, and the Nagas are on both sides of the watershed. This is particularly true of the Konyaks who occupy a considerable area lying north of the Hukawng. Most of the country between the Assam plain and the Chindwin can be regarded as connected from the ethnological point of view.

128. On the other hand, the economic and geographical connection between the Assam Hills and Burma has been slight, and such connection as there has been has naturally been limited to the Southern hills. Prior to the war, there was no connection by road. During the war the road connecting Assam with the Manipur plain, which lies on the Burma side of the watershed, was carried through to Burma and is likely to be maintained as a national highway. It should stimulate trade between Manipur and Burma but seems unlikely to have a large effect on any other part of the Assam Hills. A second road, the 'Stillwell Road',

leads from the extreme east of the Assam Valley to the Hukawng Valley, Myitkina and China; but it is most unlikely that it will remain open and, if it does, that it will carry any appreciable traffic. Schemes of connection by rail have never got beyond projects and seem now unlikely to materialize. A military road was constructed from Manipur to Tiddim in the Chin Hills, but this will not remain able to carry mechanical transport across the border and cannot have much importance for trade purposes. Even the Southern hills will look towards Assam for trade and the other hills have no choice.

129. Further the constitution of the whole area as a political unity is not acceptable to Burma and would run counter to the policy announced in the Burma White Paper. Apart from these objections, there are grave objections to any scheme under which Burma would come down and into the middle of the plains of Assam or stretch along India's northern frontier to Bhutan and the separation of the southern from the central hills, for reasons given in Chapter III, would be most undesirable. It seems unnecessary to enter, therefore, on a discussion of the other difficulties which union would create.

130. But some adjustment of boundaries between India and Burma is very desirable. In particular the Konyak Nagas should be united and also the Chang Nagas, and in view of the fact that the other Naga tribes are on the Indian side, they should all be included in India. At the other end the Lakhers, a minority of whom are in Assam, might be transferred to Burma, thus shortening somewhat the long peninsula formed by the Lushai Hills district. These changes have been discussed with Burma representatives and detailed proposals have been prepared.

131. It is conceivable, particularly if the Assam hills became a separate province, that at some future date the northern Burma hills might wish to amalgamate with Assam, instead of with the rest of Burma, as contemplated in the Burma White Paper. But there is only one contingency which might make the possibility of union of at least part of the Assam hills with Burma a question for the nearer future. That is the establishment of Pakistan and the inclusion of Assam in it. The lot of the hills if joined to

Burma would be better on the whole than their incorporation in an avowedly Muslim dominion, and the same might be true of the upper part of the Assam plain. But it would be a very uncomfortable arrangement and the fact that it might be somewhat less disastrous than inclusion in Pakistan is not an argument for such a course so much as one of the many arguments against that political theory in its crude form.

132. Even in this contingency, there could not be a real amalgamation with the hills on the Burma side. These, generally speaking, are far more backward than the Assam hills or any part of the Assam plain. The Assam areas could not be relegated to the tutelage of the Governor of Burma. Even in this event, therefore, some separate arrangements, on lines discussed in Chapter VI, would have to be evolved.

C. A Federal Agency

133. The next solution to be considered is that of constituting the hill areas as an agency directly under the Federal Government. This would be the effect of Mr. Mills alternative scheme, for although tribal representatives are to be associated with the authority in charge of the area, their association would be only for a brief period of each year and their function is to be merely advisory. The authority would thus be responsible to the Federal Government and through it to the Federal Legislature. The valid arguments in favour are the distinctness and backwardness of the area, which make both absorption in Assam and the constitution of a separate province difficult. The Centre is already responsible for parts of the hills and its assistance is necessary to secure the development of the northern hills. Finally the fact that all the hills are a deficit area which must depend on financial support from elsewhere can be regarded as pointing to central control.

134. But there are the gravest objections to such a scheme, for it would not remove the tribal peoples from political influence; it would merely remove from them any share in that influence.

They would be governed by ministers and politicians at Delhi who would have far less knowledge of their conditions and needs than those in Assam. And they would have no prospect of being themselves among the ministers or among the politicians who counted. They might have one representative in the Central Assembly, but what is one among so many diverse tribes? And they would have no hope of getting the ear of the Ministers. These Ministers would be drawn from men of other races and communities and provinces and, in so far as they were prepared to listen to men from Assam, they would be guided by men from the plains of their own castes and creeds, who would then have power without responsibility.

135. Mr. Mills contemplates an arrangement under which an officer, whose experience would virtually be confined to these hills and who would be removed to Imphal, would be subject to "as light control as possible" by the Central Government, and would not be required to maintain close touch with it. As 'the man on the spot' he would be left alone 'as far as possible', 'subject to the inherent power of the Central Government to issue direction on major points of policy'. Even if there were no objections on the merits to such a scheme, the idea of its being realized in practice would seem to be an illusion. The Indian politician does not believe in the principle of extensive delegation, and would not be willing to give all this liberty to 'the man on the spot'. Even a federal minister who was anxious to limit interference would be likely to face steadily increasing pressure from members of the legislature and from those within the Governor's charge who had occasion to differ from that official's ideas or to dislike his decisions.

136. The real effect would be to subject the hillmen to a rule which, so far as they are concerned, would be both irresponsible and ill-informed. It would have practically all the dangers of fusion with Assam with none of the benefits which that offers and would render the tribes politically impotent. Fusion with Assam has difficulties and dangers, but in Assam the hillmen could play a big part. They would have a substantial voice in the legislature and they could expect, or be guaranteed, a share in

the Ministry. And all ministers would be accessible to them and would have some personal knowledge of their conditions, while Delhi ministers would not.

137. Nor should the fact that about half the tribal peoples are already represented in the Assam Legislature be overlooked. They would object to what would be, in effect, disfranchisement. To meet this difficulty, it was suggested in the discussion at Delhi in March 1945, that the partially excluded areas, which would remain in Assam, should be separated from the excluded areas, which would be reduced to the status of tribal areas. This would be a deplorable arrangement as, apart from the objections to a backward move for the excluded areas, the continued separation of the southern tribes from the central ones cannot be justified. The Mikirs are not less backward than the Nagas: the Lushais should be as capable of political activity as the Garos. Further, the more tribes that are included, the greater will be the strength of all.

138. All the solutions so far considered in this chapter are, in effect, schemes which exclude the tribes from any real voice in their Government and their future. Local self-government might remain, and in this respect Mr. Mills' scheme is in one respect more retrogressive than Sir Robert Reid's, for the latter put forward the suggestive idea of treaty rights for the hill peoples, which will be considered in Chapter VI. But none of the schemes gives the tribal representatives an effective share in their own Government at higher levels. Mr. Mills' Governor's Council, meeting only once a year and exercising advisory functions would, even with the most accommodating Governor, have no real control over the administration. The tribesmen will demand a share in their own Government: indeed they are already demanding it. And, except in the northern hills and much of the Naga tribal area, they are capable of using it.

139. Their only lasting protection against misgovernment must be sought in giving them the largest measure of responsibility which they are capable of discharging. In the India of the future, a responsible Provincial Government, resting on the approval of its people; should be able to resist policies that are likely to injure

the people; any other form of Government is likely to have great difficulty in doing so. If risks have to be run, it would be better to give too much than too little. In respect of those primitive areas such as the northern hills which cannot participate in any scheme of self-government, the idea of a federal agency cannot be ruled out; elsewhere it is open to much greater objection than the idea of fusion with Assam.

140. This conclusion should not be regarded as ruling out the possibility of some guidance from the Centre. A suggestion has been made that it might have a Central Board of experts in tribal matters. Such a Board could be of considerable assistance to any province and especially to Assam if, as seems likely, the Centre continues to have some financial responsibility there. If the subvention remains and if a part of it is earmarked for tribal needs, the Board could supervise the use of the money. It could provide valuable assistance in connection with educational, agricultural and economic policy, which has still to be developed. It could also watch the working of the special arrangements for the tribes which, on any scheme of Government, appear to be necessary and advise on their modification as experience was gained or conditions altered. But the Board should be careful not to interfere with the degree of self-government enjoyed by the tribes, and should rather foster the development of power in the people and work for its ultimate self-effacement.

D. A Condominium

141. Sir Reginald Coupland, in Chapter XIII (3) of Part III of his "Report on the Constitutional Problem in India" makes suggestions which reflect Sir Robert Reid's main conception but are of somewhat different character. He starts from the proposition that the hill tribes, both on the India and the Burma side "are not Indians or Burmans, but of Mongol stock. In no sense do they belong to the Indian or Burman nation." This last dictum is somewhat sweeping, for 'the Indian nation' includes an immense

variety of peoples, and it would be difficult to adopt any definition of it which would not exclude peoples who belong unques-
tionably to India, such as the Parsees of Bombay, the Pathans
of the North-West Frontier, the Jews of Cochin, the Gurkhas
settled in Northern India and various others. Further, a considerable section of those who are by all tests Indians, such as the
Bengalis, have some Mongoloid strains and this is even more
true of the Burmans. But sufficient has already been said on
the distinctness of the hill tribes to indicate the truth underlying
Professor Coupland's assertion.

142. Referring to the Assam and the Burma hills respectively
he goes on to point out that the relations of one area with the
future free India will be similar to those of the other with the
future free Burma. This is undeniable, though it should be borne in
mind that the people of the Assam hills are, on the whole, much
more advanced than those of the adjoining hills. This would seem
to be an argument against their combination rather than for it.
But Professor Coupland, pointing out that "the neighborhood of
both to China demands a common frontier policy" says that the
considerations he has mentioned "have inspired a suggestion"
(by Sir Robert Reid?) "that the areas might be united in a single
territory, the administration of which would be separated in some
way from the Government of India and Burma."

143. He does not expressly endorse this idea but says that
"since the security and stability of this frontier zone are of the
highest importance to both countries, it seems possible that India
and Burma might welcome some special arrangement." Referring
to the idea that the new Government of India might conclude a
treaty with the British Government for assistance in the defence
of India, he concludes "The new Government of Burma might
wish to do the same. In that event, might not the administration
of the area on both sides of the frontier be associated with a joint
system of defence?" This would evidently give India, Burma and
the United Kingdom all a share of responsibility for the area,
which would thus perhaps be a form of condominium.

144. Such an arrangement, if workable, would have some
advantages. On the political side, it is open to less objection

than Sir Robert Reid's proposal to divorce the area completely (except perhaps as regards payment for it) from both India and Burma. It would probably secure a better administration than can be expected from a new Government at Delhi, immersed in numerous other problems and dominated by political influences in which the tribes would not share. And it should surmount any financial difficulties.

145. On the other hand, it is open to the serious objections already stated to union with Burma, and to some others. It is based on conceptions of foreign policy and defence which seem inadequate to support it. It is only the northern hills of Assam which abut on China (or, more strictly, on Tibet). The southern hills have no such connection and the central hills, from which they should not be divorced, lie well inside Assam and India. As regards considerations of defence, the Reorganization Committee now sitting may be expected to clarify the issues. But assuming, as Sir Reginald Coupland does, that India and Burma are treated jointly for purposes of defence, it seems very unlikely that the hills lying between them will have any large strategic importance, when the conditions of modern warfare are borne in mind. The central hills have even less importance. Indeed recent considerations by the Indian General Staff has suggested that even in the Northern hills, the main consideration is to have a friendly countryside rather than any direct strategical arrangements.

146. Professor Coupland has not indicated to whom the administration would be responsible; that would presumably depend on the nature of the arrangements made for co-operation in defence. But anything in the nature of a condominium is always difficult to work, and subordination to a single authority whose primary function was defence would be undesirable. It seems doubtful, particularly with the decision now taken in the Burma White Paper, whether any such arrangement can materialize and its practical difficulties would be very great. Finally if it does not offer the tribes any prospect of a share in their own Government, except at the tribal level, it is open to grave objection on that score. If, on the other hand, the intention is that the responsibility of the paramount authority, whatever form it takes, for

foreign affairs and defence should not preclude the people from regulating, as far as possible, their own affairs in other respects, the problem of devising some form of provincial government, to which the next Chapter is devoted, remains. It would, however, be further complicated by the union of areas which have an ethnological and cultural connection, but little else in common. It is difficult to believe that any such country could have a permanent and healthy existence, and while Professor Coupland's suggestion does not go beyond an arrangement 'for the time being', it might well act as an obstacle to the natural development of both areas.

CHAPTER VI—AUTONOMY OF THE HILLS

A. The Status of the Hills

147. The separation of the hills and the grant to them of as much autonomy as possible is, on the whole, the most logical solution. For there is no provincial boundary in India so sharp as the line that separates these hills from the plains. The peoples who live on either side of every provincial boundary have closer ethnological, historical and cultural affinities than the peoples who live on either side of this line. Almost everywhere as one crosses this line, there is a change of race, a change of culture, a change of religion, a change in the social, and economic structure and a change in the method of government. And, while it is a mistake to think of the Assam hill peoples as forming a unity, there are some close affinities between all of them which they do not share with the plains.

148. Mr. Mill's scheme is based on the conception of a series of areas, holding a position analogous to that of Indian States. The idea was first put forward by Sir Robert Reid who suggested the possibility of self-governing communities of the nature of States with their rights guaranteed by *treaty* and not subject to constitutional changes introduced in the Provinces of India any

more than our ordinary States. He contemplated alternatively something at a lower level of development at the outset, with future progress towards a higher status in the background. He made it clear that treaty guarantees would not preclude control and added "I would make it quite certain that all possibility of misrule such as has disfigured so many Indian States to this day or the petty inefficiency and dishonesty which characterises the Siemships of the Khasi Hills was eliminated."

149. Although he speaks of self-governing communities, this is essentially a scheme of tutelage, and has the additional objection that the tutelage would be exercised by a Government outside India. But the question arises whether the conception of the hill areas as States does not offer possibilities of autonomy more suited to their conditions than the conception of a province, and whether it cannot be made effective now. Mr. Mills who envisages units "enjoying the greatest measure of self-government" at a later date, makes it clear that he is not using "States" in the ordinary Indian sense of the word and has in view not autocracy but self-governing units.

150. At first glance the conception has much to commend it: indeed there are grounds for the view that the assimilation of provinces to States of a democratic type might offer a sound line of development for India generally. The areas in question are not really a unity, they already include Indian States, whose union with the other areas would be facilitated, and they have enjoyed self-government of various kinds. Some of the tribes have never known any government but their own and all of them enjoy a measure of self-government. It is in some cases nothing more than an accident that areas have been treated as States. If the administration in 1890 had had the same outlook as in 1830, the Lushai chiefs would probably have been given the same status as those who were found to be heads of small areas in the Khasi Hills, and the Lushai Hills would today be a series of petty States.

151. It can, further, be urged that the hill tribes, whose self-government has nowhere been entirely lost, have a more equitable claim than most Indian princes ever had to recognition by treaties of their share in sovereignty. The Indian rulers with whom

treaties were made were autocrats and often autocrats foreign to their people, who generally owed their rule to force. The rule in the tribes is one not merely of consent but of co-operation; it is real measure of self-government. Although their rights, so far as the greater part of the area is concerned, find no place in the Government of India Act, they have existed for longer than there is any historical record, they have been recognized in practice by Government, and they are exercised to-day.

152. The recognition of tribal authority is thus a matter of justice, but it is also one of sound government. For the system is basically democratic and within its limitation it offers every prospect of smooth working. It already goes far towards giving justice between man and man, it maintains with rare exceptions peace over areas which an external authority could only rule fully with great difficulty and expense, it has behind it the authority of tradition, the experience of centuries and the cultural background which would be lacking in any new and alien system. Whatever scheme of government be adopted, it should remain the foundation of rule and the tribes can reasonably claim that developments should be framed on this basis rather than that its survival should depend on its capacity to conform to some different system of government.

153. Sir Robert Reid's suggestion to secure the autonomous rights of the tribes by treaty was a corollary of his proposal to form a British colony. If that is rejected, it is still possible to accept the main idea, but the form in which it would be embodied would be the Indian constitution and not a series of treaties with His Majesty's Government. The constitution should recognize village authorities, as the existing regulations do to some extent. Above these it would give a series of tribal or similar councils wider powers on the lines indicated in Part A of Chapter III. They would, in the initial stages at least, form the electoral colleges for any legislative body. There should be some constitutional provision by which their powers and those of the village authorities could not be encroached upon except with very general consent of the tribes. These should be an integral part of the arrangements whether the hills are joined to Assam or separated.

154. To this extent the conception of "States" is sound and helpful, but it is unsound to stretch if further. As was shown in Part A of Chapter III tribal institutions cannot maintain a modern government. They are adequate, up to a point, for the maintenance of law and order in small pockets; but they cannot sustain the services on which progress belongs. If they are to be the real instruments of government, the tribes must always remain in a primitive state. The least satisfactory Indian States are the small ones, and these hill States would always be small. Mr. Mills appears to recognize this, for he superimposes a Governor with very wide powers controlling an official structure to deal among other things with the 'nation-building' departments.

155. The fact has thus to be faced that there must be, if progress and good government are to be secured, a provincial authority which, whatever form it takes, is in essence a provincial government. And over that government the tribes ought to be given the largest practicable measure of control. It would be dealing with functions vital to their well-being, and unless it was based, as far as possible, on their will and co-operation, its authority would remain precarious. The arguments against a federal agency given in Part C of Chapter V apply against any system which would deny to the tribes authority at the provincial level, and would give them merely an advisory voice.

156. It is, moreover, inevitable, unless the tribes are always to be backward, that the provincial authority should gradually extend its functions. It will embody and it should enhance steadily the sense of unity. While tribal institutions can play a vital part, the growth of too large a measure of autonomy there has obvious perils; and if the tribes had real authority at the tribal level and not at the provincial level, there would be a tendency to enhance the degree of autonomy enjoyed by tribal institutions and thus to encourage separatism. Few things are so difficult as the union of a series of areas each of which has extensive sovereign rights. Not to go further afield, the Khasi States are divided by no geographical barriers, they are peopled by a single race with a single language and common traditions, and have no real justification for a separate existence. But ideas of federation are limited to a few of the

urbanised Khasis whom Mr. Mills would exclude; and a proposal for federation, although obviously sound, would encounter strong opposition. If union is to be secured, and all would agree that the only hope of the tribal peoples lies in wider unity, it is unwise to start by confining autonomy to the tribal level.

B. A Provincial Government

157. If therefore, the hills are to be treated as a separate unit, they must have some form of provincial government. But it is here that the main difficulties arise. The first is the backwardness of the tribes. The discussion of their capacity for self-government in Chapter III led to two main conclusions. The first is that in the northern hills and the Naga Tribal Area the conditions for self-government, except in a most primitive form, do not exist; these areas will be considered further in Chapter VII. The second is that the rest of the hills could provide legislators in limited numbers and even some ministers if a suitable method of selection were adopted. It would be an arrangement suited to tribal conceptions to make no distinction between the executive and the legislature and to have a small body exercising both powers. But numbers create a difficulty. No tribe of any substantial size could well be represented by a man of another tribe and, for this reason as well as that of providing political education, it is desirable to secure the representation of as many tribes as possible. The ministry should be a small body. A small province could not support a large ministry and the choice of ministers is likely to be very limited.

158. It would seem preferable therefore to have two bodies. There could be a legislative council to consider matters of common interest to the tribes. If, as seems wise, considerable powers are delegated to tribal councils, the function of the legislature would be limited and common laws would not be greatly needed. The main function of the centre would be the provision of the 'nation-building' activities and the council, in addition to dealing with financial provision, would be able to guide the ministers in

these spheres and to ensure that they were kept in touch with all the different areas. They would also provide a unifying body and should establish useful contact with ministers and legislators from the plains. The smaller Naga tribes would probably have to be grouped, and the aim should be a council of not more than 20.

159. From this body the ministers could be chosen, but it would be desirable in the early stages to give the Governor an entirely free choice to select the most capable men, and to make them irremoveable for a specified term. This would necessitate some provision by which supply could not, in the last resort, be withheld. Three tribal ministers would suffice and it would probably be found best to start with a Khasi, a Lushai and a Naga minister. In addition it would be wise to have an official minister for some time at least, who would act also as Chief Secretary and head of the services. This official might be able to discharge the functions of the administrator referred to in paragraph 55.

160. As both legislature and ministry would start almost without previous experience there should be some residuary powers in the Governor's hands. These might correspond to the present power of individual judgment and would include the control of the Assam Rifles. The powers could be fairly wide, but they would be, for the most part, limited to a specified term of years after which they would expire. As with the present power of individual judgment, they would not be used to control day-to-day administration, but would be held in reserve to secure a smooth inauguration of the system and fair treatment for all the tribes.

161. Some such arrangements should provide a large [measure] of ministerial responsibility, and should not occasion any great measure of control. It should be borne in mind that law and order, which is the subject giving most anxiety in Indian administration and which is the most difficult task of a popular ministry, would be largely vested in tribal institutions and should, in consequence, give much less trouble and involve a much smaller measure of ministerial responsibility than in the plains. The danger of serious outbreaks, such as have frequently occurred in the hills, would not disappear; but it should be greatly reduced by the entrustment of powers to tribal councils and by the existence of

a central Government run by tribesmen. The unwise interference
and tactless handling which have occasioned so much trouble in
the past would be much less likely with a government which was
so constituted, and whose main functions would lie in 'nation-
building' activities. The most likely source of trouble would be
unwise taxation but popular Governments in India have not
erred in the direction of seeking too much revenue, and a tribal
government would be unlikely to make that mistake.

C. Administration

162. The difficulties of a separate hill province would not be
merely political: there would also be administrative difficulties.
The southern and central hills are approaching a stage at which
they can provide men for their own 'provincial' services. But they
cannot provide men for the higher posts such as heads of departments or even of districts, and while district officers can for
some time be furnished by the I.C.S. or other agencies, there are
still two difficulties to be surmounted. One is that the hills are
not large enough to make a separate cadre workable. The other
is that such a small province could not afford the apparatus of
separate heads of departments and other expenses incidental to
its own government.

163. Mr. Mills suggests that the only difficulty created by
small cadres is that promotion is limited. This is not so: a small
cadre can sometimes offer as good prospects as a big one. The
real difficulties lie in arranging for postings, reliefs, casualties,
and providing sufficient variety of work. Assam, with its eleven
million people, is the smallest Indian province with I.C.S. and
I.P. cadres of its own, and even Assam has had difficulties owing
to the size of the cadres. Indeed, the question of joint cadres with
Bengal has been seriously considered. The hills would be a mere
fraction of Assam. This difficulty could be met as it has been met
in Orissa, Sind and the North-West Frontier Province by having
joint cadres with a larger province, the obvious province here

being the Assam plains, which would otherwise have the existing inconvenience enhanced.

164. In discussing these difficulties it is desirable to bear closely in mind the scale of affairs. The population of the hills lying within British India is less than 900,000. Thus the population is comparable with that of one average district. If it proved possible to include all the States, a total of 1,600,000 millions would be reached. To provide such a section of the population in the plains with the machinery of a provincial government would be difficult enough. But here they are scattered over the equivalent of 6 or 7 districts, and the area is cut up into a multitude of separate tracts. Moreover, this small population speaks a larger variety of languages than even the people of the largest Indian provinces, which adds seriously to the difficulties of interchanging officers.

165. Even if a separate cadre of superior posts were workable, it would be open to another grave objection in that continuous service in the Assam hills would have a most cramping effect. Under the existing system, officers serving in the hills normally have periods of service in the plains also. Even so service in pre-war Assam, which was more backward and isolated than most Indian provinces, was a handicap which only the most vigorous officers entirely overcame. And officers who spent long periods in the hills (prior to the vivifying influence of war) tended to deteriorate. The man who is dealing year in and year out with primitive peoples, and seldom has to pit his brains against other educated minds or face the currents of a wider world, and who does not lose "edge" is exceptional. The result, even when physical vigour is maintained, appears in a settling into mental grooves and, in some cases, the loss of a sense of proportion. It would seem that cadres of superior officers must be shared.

166. There would also be difficulties in providing a number of expert heads of departments, as is proposed by Mr. Mills. As there would be no cadres from which such men could be drawn, they would have to be borrowed; for a tiny province could not offer scope for a life career in a single department. As experience shows, borrowing competent officers from other provinces is a very difficult and 'chancy' affair. Incompetents are more readily

lent. Nor is the system satisfactory by which the heads of department in small provinces are borne on cadres shared with larger ones. The best officer gravitates to the larger province, where pay and scope are greater; and if a good officer goes to the smaller one he is generally marking time until he gets back. What would be possible would be for comparatively junior experts, serving under heads of departments who would have responsibility for both hills and plains, to be assigned special charge of the hill province. Junior officers could face better than senior ones the unusual physical strain of service in most of the hills. Thus a Director of Public Instruction serving both the Assam plains and the hill province could have a Deputy for the hills; and so for other Departments. A separate secretariat would be desirable but the separation need not be in all cases complete.

167. All reasonable economy in administration would be important for, at the start at least, the hills would be seriously in deficit on the ordinary expenses of administration. Further, if they are to make up the leeway which separates them from most of India, considerable expenditure on development will be required. Much of this might prove ultimately profitable, but the province could not be self-supporting at the start and it is doubtful if it ever would. Assam at present gets a central subvension of 30 lakhs which more than covers the deficit on the excluded and partially excluded areas, although none is earmarked for that purpose. In any new settlement, separate provision would be required for the hills.

168. The necessity of sharing cadres and other considerations point to the desirability of the two provinces having one Governor. The task should not be beyond the capacity of one man, for in normal times Assam is a smaller charge than most provinces. This would minimize the inevitable administrative difficulties and it would tend to secure some co-ordination of policy. Both the hills and plains would probably suffer on the economic side by separation; but a common Governor should have some influence in preventing undue injury.

169. Another valuable influence in preventing friction in all fields would be the presence of the two Governments in one

capital, where mutual discussions would be easy on the numerous issues of common interest, and where those responsible for legislation could also share ideas and experience. Shillong, which is in the hills but easily accessible to the plains, which lies partly in the ministerial province and partly in the Khasi States, and which is already a meeting place of plainsmen and hillmen, is the obvious site.

170. The removal, proposed by Mr. Mills, of the hill government to what is (except in war-time) the lotus-land of the Imphal plain would be a most unfortunate step. The Manipuris who would surround it there are much less typical hillmen than the Khasis. Indeed, there is probably a bigger gulf in feeling between them and the Nagas of the surrounding hills than between Nagas and the plainsmen of Assam. Moreover the isolation would be deadening. The presence of aerodromes (even if they are kept up would be a very minor advantage, for there is no aerodrome in any other part of the hills, and as the use of helicopters or very small planes seems likely to develop, it should prove a fleeting one. Further if the view is held and there is much to support it—that the best interests of the hills and plains lie ultimately in union, it is important to maintain close contact. A common Governor and a common capital will both serve this end.

D. A Sub-province

171. A suggestion for what would be in effect a sub-province of the hills has been made tentatively by Mr. H. G. Dennehy, who has experience of the hills and an intimate knowledge of the political and administrative aspects of government in Assam. He starts from the position that with Indian self-government there are only two possible alternatives, a separate administration in which the hill peoples may hope to become in some way their own masters, and amalgamation with Assam. He considers that the main principle of self-determination dictates that the possibility of forming a separate administration should be kept in

view, but the ultimate needs may equally dictate a union with an economically stronger neighbour when the hill peoples are able, educationally and politically, to utilize the strength which their numbers, character and vitality promise them.

172. He accordingly proposes to have two legislative bodies, one in which the peoples of the hills can deal with their own domestic problems and learn the rudiments of self-government, and another the Assam legislature, where selected representatives from the hills can learn how to cope intellectually with neighbours with whom it may ultimately be necessary for them to amalgamate. This latter would be for primarily for the removal of grievances. There might be a separate Ministry for hill affairs but legislation would, as at present, not extend to the hill areas except by separate act of the Governor. The hill representatives would not be able to vote on bills or to control the Ministry except by way of taking part in a vote of no confidence in the Ministry of hill affairs.

173. The main idea has some attractions. It would secure for the hills a large measure of self-determination, for their internal security and other matters of importance to them in their present way of life would be in their own hands. It would offer them an opportunity for political education in both the local and the wider field. It would avoid most of the difficulties inherent in a separate administration and the dangers inherent in a complete union, and it might help to secure closer fusion between areas that must lose something by separation. Nor is it entirely without precedent, as the present position of Northern Ireland can be regarded as presenting some similarities.

174. But it is open to serious objections. If the powers of other legislators were withheld from the hill members, some of whom already have these powers, they would have no real control over the 'nation-building' department, on which their progress must largely depend. Ministers, not being subject to their votes, could safely brush aside their demands, and they would have a constant feeling of inferiority. On the other hand the grant of equal powers would be resented by the plainsmen who could justly complain that, while the hillmen had a voice in all their affairs, they had

no voice in important functions of Government in the hills. The present position of Ulster vis-a-vis the Imperial Parliament is not logically defensible, and would not be accepted even by the illogical Englishman if Ulster were not so small. Here the hillmen would constitute a much larger proportion and the tribesman generally would be in a position to sway decisions.

175. There is a further important difference between the suggested arrangement and that now subsisting in respect of Ulster. For below the joint tribal legislature there would be the separate tribal authorities and above the Assam legislature is the Indian legislature, giving four stages instead of two. This would mean a very complicated structure and it would be difficult to provide adequate functions for the three 'storeys' in Assam out of any provincial list. It would seem that either the plains and the hills should be co-ordinated on level terms or they should be separated. If the hills and the plains are to be linked in respect of legislative functions, the scheme outlined in Chapter IV seems greatly preferable.

CHAPTER VII—SPECIAL AREAS

176. The discussion in the three preceding chapters has concentrated on the areas which are part of the province of Assam and are administered as such. But the lands of the tribes include also certain areas which are not politically part of Assam, or which are not treated as such. Three of them belong to it naturally, since they cut across tribal boundaries, and form an economic unit with Assam. And they are linked with it administratively by the entrustment to the Governor as Agent to the Crown Representative or the Governor General in Council of responsibility for them and by the fact that this responsibility has been exercised through officers of the Assam cadres. These are (A) the Khasi States (B) Manipur (C) the Naga Tribal Area. The fourth area which consists of the Northern Hills is not legally separated

from Assam, but is treated in practice as a tribal area for which the Governor General in Council is responsible, the Governor of Assam acting as his Agent.

A. The Khasi States

177. There are 25 Khasi States. Collectively their area is 3,788 square miles and their population is 213,000 of whom over a third are Christians. All the States, therefore, are small and several of them are minute. Only 10 have a population of over 5,000 and 6 have less than 700. Their combined revenue in 1944 was about Rs. 4¹/₃ lakhs. One State, Mylliem, had revenue of 2 lakhs. Two others account for Rs. 1½ lakhs and the combined revenue of all the remaining 22 was less than a lakh. Portions of British India are interspersed with the States, and the greater part of Shillong lies within Mylliem State.

178. Administrative arrangements in most of the States are of the most rudimentary kind. The affairs of the State are normally vested in Myntris or elders who are elected, usually by particular clans, and who have a Siem at their head. The Siem is also, in nearly all cases, elected. Originally the idea of election was to decide who had the best right by heredity to succeed. But, although the hereditary idea has not quite disappeared, the election which is usually limited so far as the franchise is concerned, is now fairly open in respect of the candidates and is regulated largely by bribery in most cases. Crimes punishable with death or not less than 5 years' imprisonment are dealt with by the Assam police and come before Political Courts which are subordinate to the Governor's Court. These Courts also intervene in civil cases where there has been bias, prejudice or want of jurisdiction. The jurisdiction of the State Courts is limited to their own subjects: even cases involving other Khasis are excluded.

179. Taxation, except for bazar dues, is almost non-existent in most States, and 'nation-building activities', in so far as they

exist, are left mainly to other agencies. Thus education is largely left to Christian Missions, together with the Assam Government's schools in the patches of British India. Thanks to these, and to the position held by Khasi women, the standard reached is comparatively good. The few main roads are kept up by the Assam Government, which is vitally interested in the connections between Shillong and the plains, and they also maintain some other routes. Sir Keith Cantlie writes, "Maintenance of village paths by forced labour, employment of watchers for fruit groves, cleansing of markets, these with judicial and occasional religious functions comprise the total activities of the State authorities." Provisions for medical relief is scanty, except in Shillong. Despite this a fairly high standard of living is maintained without much exertion, on the part of the male population at least.

180. There can be no rational future for these States except merger with the adjoining areas of British India. Tentative plans for securing some form of federation of the States have been prepared; but as Sir Francis Wylie pointed out, they are collectively so small that even complete amalgamation would not produce a workable unit. Their creation was little more than an unfortunate accident, for they are, generally, the result of agreements made, when the British first penetrated the hills, by subordinate officers with local Khasis, most of whom might well have been regarded as village headmen, and to this day it would be difficult to determine all their common boundaries.

181. They are in fact artificial creations and there was for a long time doubt as to their status. The sanads given to the Siem are personal and they give no rights to their successors and can be (and have been) changed as occasion requires.* Sir Keith Cantlie, who gives an interesting discussion of past agreements and sanads in Chapters XVII to XXI of his "Notes on Khasi Law", writes:

"So wide are the powers of Government under the agreements that the Government of Bengal in 1867 and two Legal Remembrances and

---

*The extant agreements (Aitchisou's Treaties, Vol. XII) relate generally to subjects other than the system of Government.

212 Sir Andrew G. Clow

a Deputy Commissioner in 1910 considered that the States were a part of British India. It is unnecessary to set forth arguments showing that the contrary view was held at various times from 1835 till 1910, as, since that year, when an Act was extended under the Scheduled Districts Acts, the Foreign Jurisdiction Order of 1902 has been used as a vehicle for Acts, territory of the States being considered as outside British India".

182. Prior to 1937, when authority passed to the Governor as Agent to the Crown Representative, the States were a responsibility of the Government of Assam who treated them very much as parts of the province except that they took no taxation and gave them less attention than other parts. As late as 1927, they seemed disposed to assert that the Siems had no sovereignty and the Legal Remembrancer of the time (now Mr. Justice B. N. Rau) wrote:—

"I think it would be incorrect to say that the Siems have no 'sovereignty' whatever: if that were so, their territory would be part of British India. In fact their judicial powers, such as they are, are an exercise of sovereign rights: the fact that those powers are limited merely means that their sovereign rights extend up to a certain point, after which the sovereign rights of the British Government come into operation—in other words it is a case of division of sovereignty".

Their position under the Government of India Act, 1935, admits of no dubiety: but it is perhaps unfortunate that the framers of that Act drew no constitutional difference between Hyderabad or Mysore and a few Khasi villages.

183. The best method of proceeding would be to federate them in much the same manner as it was proposed to federate States under the Government of India Act, 1935, but this federation should be with the adjacent province and not with the Centre. If the hills were made a separate province, they would form part of that: if not they would be part of Assam. Thus they would be given representation in the legislature which would have authority over them, but the executive and judicial powers would, to begin with at least, be left much as they stand. The Siems who are not Princes but more like Presidents with limited jurisdiction,

would not nominate the representatives: that power would be given to the people. Already part of Mylliem State is in a British Indian constituency, although the provincial legislature has no authority over it. Residuary powers would have to be retained by the Governor or Government to ensure a reasonable measure of administration. The States should not be given the option of staying out of the federation.

B. Manipur

184. Manipur presents a more difficult problem. It is a State of 8,620 square miles in area, with a population of 512,000. Imphal, the capital, had 100,000 people in 1941 and includes a small British reserve. Apart from this reserve, the State falls into two areas, the Imphal plain, this is a comparatively small part of the area but has about two-thirds of the people, and the hills. The pre-war income of the State was about ten lakhs; inflation and dealings in supplies have about quadrupled it temporarily.

185. The plains are administered by the Maharaja with a Darbar, but various powers are vested in the Agent to the Crown Representative and his representative the Political Agent. In the hills and, indeed, over hillmen generally the Maharaja's authority is merely titular and the Darbar (apart from its President, an officer of the Indian Civil Service) has no authority at all. The administrative and judicial system is subordinate to the Governor as A.C.R.; but as in other hill areas, a considerable amount of authority is exercised by the peoples themselves. The people of the plains are sharply differentiated by religion and habits from those of the hills and any attempts by them to rule the hills might lead to serious trouble. Formerly the Manipuris tended to rely on the Kukis to keep the Nagas in subjection. The hills would probably welcome absorption in British India: the plain would not, although by no means enthusiastic about the present rule.

186. Here again the interests of the State point to federation with the neighbouring province, whatever form that takes.

The federation would, at first at least, be for only legislative functions. Executive and judicial functions, except in so far as it might be decided to retain the Governor's present powers with him or his Government, would vest in authorities within the State. Minor adjustments of territory with what is now British India would if possible be advantageous. In the hills, where conditions are very similar to those of British India with subdivisional officers appointed by the Governor, tribal councils should be developed. But these can, as in the rest of the hills, have only limited powers, and Government at a higher level cannot be vested in them.

187. The Maharaja's hereditary position would have to be respected and the problem here is part of the larger problem presented by the need of federating the States and provinces in India generally, and would have to depend to a considerable extent on the solution reached. But it is simplified to some extent by the restrictions placed on his powers, and the obvious line of development is to continue that process by a transfer of powers to Darbar and people, with the Maharaja in the position of a constitutional ruler. Thus in the plains provision could be made for the appointment of the Darbar (at present vested in His Highness and the Political Agent, acting for the Governor) by election.

188. The problem of linking the hills with the plains reproduces on a smaller scale but in an accentuated form the problem of the hills and plains in Assam. Although, as has been suggested, the Manipuris who fill the plain are of the same stock as the surrounding hill tribes, they themselves would deny this. Partly because of their conversion to Hinduism, which has made many of them "more orthodox than the orthodox", and partly because of different ways of life, there is no sympathy between the peoples, and the hill tribes could not be subjected to the rule of the plains without injustice and serious danger. But the divorce of the areas does not appear to be practical, and it would seem that they should look to an ultimate fusion. The best method of proceeding would probably be to give the hills a Darbar of their own initially; this might lead to greater integration later by the combination of the Darbars.

C. The Northern Hills

189. The Northern Hills, by which is meant all the mountainous country lying north and east of the Assam Valley down to about the Pangsau Pass, have an area of about 30,000 square miles. It is impossible to estimate the population with even approximate accuracy. Large parts have never even been visited, and the greater part of it is occupied by high ranges or thick forest and must be uninhabited. Local officers have estimated the Abor tribes at about 120,000 and the Mishmi tribes at perhaps half that figure. On the basis of these estimates and assuming that the other tribes have, on the average, the same density, the total population would be of the order of 400,000. All these figures involve a large amount of conjecture.

190. It will be clear from the preceding discussions that this large area presents a problem of its own. The bulk of it is little known: much is unexplored. The valleys and lower hills are peopled by tribes who, although akin to those in the other hills and sharing some of their customs, have no contacts with them, and very little with each other. Attempts at regular administration have only just begun, and although most of the area has governed itself in a primitive way from time immemorial, none of it is capable of participating in the representative Government of a province.

191. Although any amputation of the tribes is open to objection, it seems impracticable at present to treat these tribes on the same footing as the others, and there are good reasons for constituting the area as a federal agency. In the first place, Assam would not have the resources required to maintain a satisfactory administration and to secure the development which the tribes need. The area is equivalent to that of the whole of the Assam plains, and it is in a very backward state. Even slavery persists, modern medical aid is entirely lacking and literates are very few.

192. In the second place the area forms part of the external frontier of India, and is thus likely to raise questions affecting

foreign relations, especially as our administration is extended. Although Tibet agreed to the present boundary, she has shown a disposition to question it and has retained an interest in some areas lying south of it, while China never formally accepted the MacMahon Line. The area has also some strategic interest, the main consideration at present being that the peoples should be friendly. These considerations point to a continuance of the present system whereby policy and development in the area are the responsibility of the centre. The area would thus be a non-self-governing territory, and the provisions of Article 73 of the United Nations Charter would presumably be applicable to it, India having the responsibility for its administration.

193. At the same time some links should be maintained with Assam. It seems desirable that the superior officers for the area should form a joint cadre with those for the other hill areas and this will probably involve a joint cadre with Assam. Officers in the lower grades can be organized in separate cadres although it will be some time before local men can be secured to fill responsible posts. Part of the Assam Rifles will be required to serve in the area; to begin with, these will all be men from outside it, but a start should be made with local recruitment. The Governor of Assam should continue to act as Agent in respect of the area and to supervise the administration.

D. The Naga Tribal Area

194. This area of perhaps 3,000 square miles forms a long strip lying mainly between the Naga Hills district and Burma: it touches on the north the two plains districts of Sibsagar and Lakhimpur, and the Tirap Frontier Tract. The population is unknown; if the density were the same as in the Naga Hills district, it would be about 135,000. Such information as is available suggests a larger figure and 160,000 may not be far off the mark. If the proposal to include in India areas which have provisionally been treated

hitherto as part of Burma and which are inhabited by similar Nagas is adopted, the area and the population will probably be at least doubled. The combined area will be equivalent to a district, for which a new headquarters will be required.

195. No attempt has been made to administer this area, or to study it in detail. The area on the Burma side is even less known than on the Indian and part of it has not even been surveyed. There have been occasional expeditions, generally of a punitive nature, and the maintenance of American observer posts during the war has led to some penetration. But the people have been left almost entirely to themselves. There is probably a good deal of village warfare of a minor kind, in which head-hunting figures, with larger battles at intervals. In one raid recently 400 heads are said to have been taken. Human sacrifice has not entirely died out. Economically, the people are self-dependent and probably fairly comfortable in normal times; but in a recent famine a certain number died and such events may well have recurred from time to time.

196. The tract is divided into a controlled area and an uncontrolled area, but the term controlled is comparative, and the extent of control, which is not uniform, could not be easily defined. For example in only some parts of the controlled area has head-hunting been prohibited. Such control as is exercised is more an attempt to secure peace in the administered area across the border than an effort at administration within the area of control. But it has brought more settled conditions and some of the tribesmen, especially the Semas, a number of whom are Christians, are anxious to be brought within the administered area.

197. A considerable part of the tribal area could not participate in the Government or legislature of a province for some time. The large Konyak tribes in the north, for example, are almost all in a completely primitive state and this is true also of the Kalyo Kenyos. Both these tribes are strongly represented in what has hitherto been treated as Burma, and none of the Naga tribes there has reached the position of being able to share in self-government.

On the other hand the Semas and Changs to the south are fairly well advanced and should be joined to their kinsfolk on the provincial side of the boundary.

198. It would seem necessary therefore to divide the tribal area. Most of the south should be included in the province. The rest, together with any area taken over from the Burma authorities, can hardly be included. So far as the backwardness of the people is concerned, this area resembles the northern hills; much of the country is equally unknown, and all of it is undeveloped. Although it has not the same importance from the international point of view, there are thus grounds for treating it as a federal agency. It has always been a tribal area; and as the Konyaks, who are much the biggest group in it, have less of the democratic outlook than the other Naga tribes, their introduction to self-governing institutions will be more difficult. The main objection to this is that it continues, although with a different boundary, the present separation of the Nagas. But as has already been pointed out, the Nagas are not a people but a series of peoples, the arrangement proposed will give them a larger unity and the separation should be only temporary. Whatever boundary is drawn, it should, as far as possible, avoid the division of individual tribes: the present boundary pays little regard to tribal distribution.

CHAPTER VIII—THE CHOICE

199. If the argument outlined above is sound, the northern hills and part of the Naga tribal area should be treated, as they are at present, as a federal agency. For the rest of the Assam hills this would be one of the worst solutions and on the facts as they appear at present the choice can be confined to two possibilities, *viz.*:—

(*a*) A merger of the hills and plains of Assam in a manner which will conserve tribal rights and will recognize in an effective manner the different needs and outlook of the two areas;

(*b*) The constitution of separate provinces for the hills and for the plains, with some links on the administrative side.

In either case, tribal institutions would have a place in the constitution and would exercise a considerable measure of local autonomy.

200. It seems probable that before the choice has to be made, many fresh considerations will appear which will give extra weight to one of the alternatives or which may suggest something different. The solution of the issue of Pakistan, the treatment of other tribal areas, the position given to the States, the evolution of the new constitution, the arrangements made with the United Kingdom are all factors which have a bearing on the present problem and which may well put it in a new light, and call for fresh consideration. For the question here discussed relates only to a small part of India and if it is a grave error to treat the hills in isolation, it would be almost as foolish to assume that Assam as a whole can be treated as an independent problem.

201. If a choice had to be made now, the balance of advantage seems to lie with the first of the two alternatives. There is much that can be said for both, and an attempt has been made to set that out fairly on both sides. There is also much that can be said against both, for this is a problem which admits of no entirely satisfactory solution; and that too has been considered. The main difficulty is that the pace of advance in the plains has been too quick or that in the hills too slow to admit of any easy adjustment and that there is not, on the assumption which forms the basis of this study, the time that would be necessary to secure an entirely smooth transition. If unexpected events should secure adequate time, a continuance for a limited and defined period of something more nearly resembling the present system, with the early establishment of tribal councils in the hills and greater efforts to educate leaders of the people, would benefit both hills and plains in the end.

202. The arguments for and against both courses need not be repeated here. The reader can make his own assessment of them, and the judgment made above, which has not been reached without hesitation, is an individual one. But one consideration of importance, which has not been discussed previously, may be mentioned in conclusion; that is the long-term aim. On a long-term view it is difficult to see any future for the hills as a separate province. While they are by no means without resources, they seem too heterogeneous to form a satisfactory unity and too small, even if fully united, to sustain a healthy and progressive life of their own. The ultimate interests of both plains and hills lie in fusion.

203. If it is accepted that the ultimate aim should be a united province, it is a hazardous step to constitute two provinces now and one that should not be taken unless the advantages are seen to lie strongly on that side. Experience shows that it is much easier to divide States than to unite them; and there is little doubt that the setting up of two provinces would create vested interests in both areas which would oppose a union. Antagonisms tend to arise, economic barriers grow, and peoples drift apart rather than together. The hillmen, whose future depends on healthy intercourse with the wider world, and who have a good deal to contribute to it, might well find themselves shut up in their fastnesses with a petty and impoverished administration. Indeed it is conceivable that a stage might be reached when they wanted to join and would be unwelcome.

204. Assam is never likely to be as homogeneous as other provinces. The plains peoples are not so divided as those of the hills, but they are far from being a single people such as can be found in many equally large or larger areas in India. But this great collection of peoples, in hills and plains, have been set in a particularly well demarcated corner of the world and their welfare will depend on their proving able to live together. Assam should look to her diversity and to her capacity for toleration, which is greater than that of other provinces, to provide her strength.

APPENDIX

The Argument Summarised

The question considered is—Assuming complete Indian self-government at an early date what arrangements are feasible and appropriate for the tribesmen of Assam? Each of the following paragraphs summarises one chapter and the capital letters in brackets refer to the sections of that chapter.

CHAPTER I

(A) Assam and its associated territories consist of groups of mountains on the North, on the South and in the Centre with two separated Valleys. The total number of its tribal people is over three million. (B) The hillmen have had little contact with the plainsmen from most of whom they differ radically in origin, languages, culture and religion. The hillmen are not homogeneous but consist of a series of separated tribes. Those in the north have never been administered and the rest are at varying stages of progress and are in effect separate peoples. (C) The plains tribesmen, including recent immigrants, outnumber those of the hills. Their territories are not sharply defined and they have all been Hinduised to a considerable extent. They have minor affinities with the hillmen and there is a little overlapping of tribes between hills and plains. (D) The hills were penetrated at various times in the last 120 years with the object of assuring the security of the plains. Administration and Christianity have followed and brought civilization and pacification. But ignorance and lack of understanding have been responsible for a series of outbreaks and punitive expeditions.

CHAPTER II

(A) The valleys are subject to the ordinary form of ministerial government, the northern hills to no government and the other hills to a medley of constitutional arrangements, being split into excluded areas, partially excluded areas, States and tribal area. (B) The hills, to a large extent, govern themselves, law and order being largely left to the tribes whose tribal systems are, on the whole, distinctly democratic. (C) They deal themselves with all but the most serious crimes and nearly all civil disputes. Cases coming before official courts are few: these are dealt with by the Court of the Governor and courts subordinate to him. The hills have been largely officered by Europeans and Anglo-Indians, with a few hillmen. Whatever system of government be devised, they should have a separate cadre of "provincial" officers. Europeans will continue to be required at the higher level for some time. (D) The plains tribal peoples have not been noticeably injured by the introduction of ministerial government. The system of partial exclusion has had only partial success. The system of total exclusion has worked without friction and has been more effective. But on a longer view, there has been a tendency for the hills to lag behind. While the tribes have benefited from the absence of unwise interference and have been helped to better ways of life, there has been too little thought for the future and a distinctly static outlook in policy. In education particularly, Government have done little. Whatever form the Government takes, its head should have the assistance of an experienced administrator in charge of the hills.

Chapter III

(A) Although the hill tribes govern themselves to a large extent the form of government is strictly local. It is normally confined to village, and is limited to the primary functions of government, such as justice and the regulation of land. It should be extended by the institution of tribal councils, a system towards which some tribes have been feeling their way. But no such extension can provide for a government of the modern type or the progress which the tribes need. (B) The plains tribesmen are already participating in responsible government; the northern hillmen are incapable of doing so at present. The other hillmen, some of whom have already participated, lack experience and are back-ward educationally but have gifts of character and the instinct of democracy. They could furnish legislators, and with a proper system of selection, might provide some ministers. They would have much greater difficulty in forming a ministry of their own than in contributing to an all-Assam ministry. (C) Of the tribes-men capable of forming a considered judgment on the question the plains tribesmen and some of the hillmen would like union with Assam. The bulk of the hillmen would like the benefits of civilization with as little interference as possible. They do not want plains officers. (D) Their great lack of cohesion and the large number of linguistic divisions constitute a difficulty and it will be a long time before they could claim to be a people; even the Nagas could not make that claim. (E) There has been a ten-dency to treat the hills 'in vacuo' as if they could be permanently isolated. But their connections with the plains are important to them and have a relevance for the plains. Hills and plains are linked by geography, by economic necessities, by administrative history and arrangements and by a *lingua franca*.

CHAPTER IV

(A) The union of the hills with Assam has already proceeded some distance and a merger would meet some of the difficulties inherent in every other proposal, besides having advantages for the rest of Assam. But it has difficulties and dangers. (B) The cultural danger is not a grave one, but the political danger might be serious. The tribes of hills and plains would have some security in the fact that they would have nearly a third of the legislature and might hold the balance between Hindus and Muslims. But this would give precarious and inadequate security against pos-sible grave injuries in the sphere of legislation, *e.g.*, in criminal and civil law, land tenure and taxation, and against serious errors in administration. (C) Special arrangements would therefore be essential. If, as is assumed, the system of exclusion in legislation disappears, the constitution of separate upper chambers for hills and plains in place of the present upper chamber would be the least unsatisfactory way of meeting the difficulty. There could be a joint ministry but the hills and plains sections should be separately constituted and the plains ministers should not be allowed to outvote the hills ministers on hill matters. Differences over finance could be minimized by allocation of the central subvention between hills and plains. Each area would have its own subordinate cadres, only the higher official being on a common cadre. In the administrative sphere, matters concerning plains or hills would, as far as practicable, be the concern of plains or hills ministers respectively. (D) Assam might not retain its present boundaries. If Sylhet went back to Bengal the position of the tribes would be stronger, and a transfer of parts of the Assam Valley, now largely Bengali, would leave a province in which they could well hold their own. It is undesirable to include the Chittagong Hill tracts, and there is not a strong case for linking Tripura State, but an adjustment of boundaries so as to unite the Garos as far as possible should be considered.

Chapter V

(A) The idea has been mooted of constituting the hills, possibly together with the Burma hills, as a separate British colony, financed by the British taxpayer, perhaps with Indian assistance. It seems most unlikely that any such scheme would be accepted by either Britain or India. It would create a colony which would have to relapse into economic self-sufficiency of a primitive type and would have grave administrative difficulties. It would complicate the problem of Indian defence and represent a step backwards for some areas and postponement of responsibility in the others. (B) The hills have affinities with Burma and union with areas there would reduce the difficulty involved in creating so small a unit. But they must look for economic progress towards Assam rather than Burma, and the extension of Burma into the middle of the Assam plains would be most undesirable. Some adjustments of the boundary with Burma are desirable; but except in the event of Pakistan being established and including the whole of Assam, union with Burma need not be considered. Even in that event, it would be a step of doubtful wisdom. (C) The constitution of the hills as an agency under the Federal Government of India would meet some of the difficulties, but is open to the gravest objections. It would not remove the tribes from political influence, but would merely remove them from any share in that influence. This would have all the dangers of fusion with Assam with none of its benefits and would make the tribes politically impotent. The only lasting protection against mis-government lies in giving the tribes the largest measure of responsibility they are capable of discharging. The idea of a federal agency must be ruled out, except for areas which cannot participate in self-government. But a Central Board of experts could be of substantial assistance. (D) Professor Coupland's suggestion that treaty arrangements between India, Burma and Great Britain for joint system of defence might have associated with them some provision for the administration of the hills on both sides of the India-Burma border appears unsatisfactory and probably impractical. If it denies responsibility for self-government to the tribes, it is open to objection on that ground: if not, the problem of the form of government remains, and is complicated by the attempt to join areas whose natural development lies in different directions.

CHAPTER VI

(A) There is no provincial boundary in India so sharp as that dividing the Assam hills from the plains. This provides a strong argument for their constitution as a separate unit. The tribes have more right to the constitutional recognition of their autonomy than the rulers of Indian States and, whether they are included in Assam or form a separate unit, the authority of tribal institutions should be extended and should remain the foundation of Government. But there must be a provincial authority over which the tribes should have as much control as practicable, unless they are to be kept in a primitive state and their unity is to be prevented. (B) The provincial organization would require at first some special constitution. A small legislative body and ministry could be constituted, but there should be also an official minister and the Governor should have certain residuary powers. (C) The administrative difficulties of a province with a population roughly equivalent to that of one district, but scattered over an area equal to half-a-dozen, would be serious. They could be reduced by sharing certain parts of the administrative machine with Assam. There should be a common Governor for both provinces, with the capital of both at Shillong. (D) The idea of a sub-province with the tribes participating in a legislature of their own as well as in the Assam legislature has some attractions but is not sound, and the analogy of Ulster is inapplicable. If there is to be a legislative union the scheme in Chapter IV C is greatly preferable.

<h2 style="text-align:center">CHAPTER VII</h2>

(A) The 25 petty Khasi States can have no future except merger with the adjoining areas. The fact that the rulers have only personal *sanads* which can be and have been changed as need arises facilitates this. The States should be represented in the Assam legislature, as part of the most important one is already. The limited executive and judicial powers they have could, to begin with, be largely left to them. (B) Manipur consists of the plain administered by the Maharaja with a Darbar and the hills administered for him by officers under the Governor. The question of its future is linked up with that of the States generally. Its interests lie in federation with the neighbouring province, with an extension of popular government. The federation, in the first instance, would be for legislative functions only. (C) The Northern Hills are incapable of self-government and in view of the incapacity of a small province to develop them and their importance internationally they should constitute a federal agency. The Governor of Assam should continue to act as Agent of the Federal Government. (D) Part of the Naga Tribal Area should be taken under administration and included in the province. The rest of it, with the area taken over from Burma, might be included in the federal agency as a temporary measure.

CHAPTER VIII

For the rest of the hill areas a federal agency would be one of the worst solutions and the choice seems to lie between (1) schemes of the type outlined in Chapter IV C, involving the linking of the hills and plains in one province with some separate arrangement for each, and (2) schemes of the kind outlined in Chapter VI B and C, involving a separate hill province with some links on the administrative side. The balance of the argument seems to lie, in present circumstances, with the first alternative. The ultimate aim should be a single province and this is an additional consideration against separation now.

Some Notes on a Policy for the Hill Tribes of Assam

Philip F. Adams

INTRODUCTION

Although in this paper I shall continue myself to the problems presented by the hill peoples of Assam, it will not be perhaps, inappropriate to make a few remarks now on the general problem of the future of the backward peoples as a whole.

These people are in varying stages of development and have varying characteristics, histories, and cultures. The problems that they present admit of no general solution but must be arrived at for each individual unit after intensive study of all the factors involved. There is however one common factor that groups them together. They are as yet unable to compete on terms of equality with the more developed peoples with whom they are in contact. In the absence of any special treatment or protection they would inevitably suffer from exploitation and from extinction perhaps as cultural and social units. Protection is however only a negative aspect of policy which includes the establishment of law and order, and the provision of basic elementary needs. This must necessarily be accompanied by a positive and energetic programme for the social and economic betterment of the people, so that they may, in a measurable period of time, be enabled to compete and survive in the modern world. In the past, for a variety of reasons, among which must be included the lack of any positive interest in these people by Government, and the influence of a now largely outmoded school of anthropological thought, the negative aspect has perhaps received undue emphasis to the detriment of the essentially necessary positive policy. Protection must be viewed as a temporary measure for the transition period which an active development policy will seek to render as short as possible.

The future of the backward peoples has suffered considerably from the lack of any co-ordinated and consistent policy towards them. There is no one central authority specifically responsible for their welfare, development, or future. Policy has been left to the provinces concerned and has been in consequence unrelated to work in other areas, and lacking in any generally agreed objective. The absence of any central agency to advise, and stimulate activity on behalf of these people has tended to result in their receiving somewhat spasmodic attention, and their problems to be rather overshadowed by other more clamant political and administrative questions. It will be suggested later in this paper that it is desirable that some central authority should be created to co-ordinate the work of the provinces and to provide technical advice on specific problems.

It is now generally accepted by all civilised nations that the more developed peoples have a responsibility for the welfare of the less developed communities within their territorial jurisdiction, and that the development of these people cannot be left to chance or their own unaided efforts. This necessarily implies comprehensive planning, and, in consequence, the acquirement of detailed knowledge of the customs, culture, economic, and social organisations of the people concerned, together with the creation of administrative machinery adequate for the carrying out of a consistent and co-ordinated policy. Planning and policy are however alike of comparatively little use unless they secure the general support of the people concerned. A primary requisite therefore is the regular and effective ascertainment of public opinion—this is particularly essential with the more primitive societies who have no general method of voicing opinion. Local councils, tribal and extra-tribal, if suitably constituted and adequately representative, will be of value in this respect.

Equally necessary is that all executive agencies should be fully acquainted with the general objectives of policy and the broad framework of the method by which it is hoped to attain them. A position in which the executive has no guidance as to agreed objectives or policy cannot but be detrimental to the co-ordinated and consistent development of the people. The practice of the African colonies whereby a memorandum embodying the general objectives of Government and principles of policy is issued to all executive officers, has much to recommend it.

If it is agreed that evolution is preferable to revolution, then the best method by which to achieve stable social and economic progress is through, where possible, the adaptation and development of existing indigenous institutions. This is a method most likely to secure the support and co-operation of the people concerned, and least likely to result in social chaos and unrest. The major danger here is that an undue emphasis may be placed on the retention of traditional forms because they are traditional; whereas the determining factor must be whether or not the traditional method is adequate to the needs of the present and developing situation. Where it is not, then it must be either modified, adapted, or in the final resort replaced, by another. There is nothing intrinsically sacred about any traditional custom or institution. They have never been, nor could be, completely static. They must change with the changing needs of society if they are to discharge efficiently the functions for which they were created.

Finally it must always be remembered that the powers of Government, although considerable are limited in their ability to control or direct the development of a changing society. There is a variety of factors over which Government has little control which will exert their influence on the evolving pattern. Social, economic, and political ideas, and changes in neighbouring areas with which growing contact may be expected, the presence of traders and of Government servants themselves, religious conversion, and growth of an educated and middle class, are a few of the many factors which will be of significance. The final choice of what is to be accepted or rejected will remain with the people, and any efforts by Government to control their choice will meet with increasing resentment. The hill people may well, in spite of excellent advice and guidance, adopt customs and initiate changes which Government and the anthropologists regard as undesirable. But if they have been generally accepted as desirable by the people themselves it would be dangerous for Government to try to suppress or prohibit them. Power to protect and to offer advice and guidance Government has, but it must be wary of assuming from its omniscience a despotism, however benevolent in intention, which would only in time serve to alienate large sections of the people it was hoping to serve.

OBJECTIVES

It is important that the objectives towards which we are working should be defined in general terms, as these will necessarily influence policy considerably. Lines of development in certain spheres while of possibly immediate advantage, might well be harmful when seen in long term perspective against the background of the ends we are striving to attain, and might well lead to a situation inimical to their ultimate achievement. As an illustration, the support of autocratic authority might result in temporary advantages such as the reduction of litigation and faction, but might also in the long run engender growing opposition, splitting the people into two opposed parties to the detriment of the harmonious development of the community as a whole. On the other hand the delegation of local authority to tribal authorities may well result in decreased efficiency in the work delegated, and raise the possibility of bribery and nepotism. But if our aim is to provide training in the art of local self-government, administration, and politics, we must accept these consequences in order to attain our ends. All policy will have to be viewed with reference to this long term aspect, and not from the immediate result of particular acts.

The objectives to be attained might be classified under three heads—political, social and economic.

Political

In broad outline the possibilities are limited. The establishment of the hill areas as an independent unit or their union or linkage with Burma or India.

Although the hill tribes of Assam are of a distinct racial stock and have roughly similar social and economic organisation they in no way form a cohesive political unit. In most areas clan and village loyalty is paramount and tribal consciousness where existing is of recent development and fragile nature. The multiplicity of languages, and the lack of internal communications and trade between the different areas makes the development of any real sense of unity difficult at present. Financially the hills are heavily deficit areas and without external support could not maintain even the existing services provided by Government, scanty as they are, much less provide funds for their increase and for economic development. Even if these obstacles could be overcome the existence of such a poor and comparatively weak unit would always be dependent on the goodwill of its more powerful neighbours, and such independence would be of a nominal character only. In present circumstances the establishment of the hills as an independent area is impracticable, even if, and this is debatable, it was considered desirable.

Union with Burma also seems impracticable. It is difficult to see how Burma could administer any of the hill areas except those few contiguous to her frontier, and it is improbable that she would wish to shoulder the added financial liability that these areas must continue to be for some time to come. Communications are increasingly linking these areas economically and politically with India. Contact with Burma is, on the other hand, practically non-existent.

Everything points to the conclusion that their union or linkage must be with India, within whose political boundaries they are, and whose interest in such vitally strategic areas must always be considerable. What precise form the union or linkage will take it is now impossible to foresee. It will be necessary to arrive at some arrangement that allows for the cultural and racial differences of these areas with those of the plains within a frame-work of political unity. It is not a question of safeguards but the recognition that the hill and plains areas are distinct in character and problems—social, economic and political. Some arrangement that recognises this distinctiveness while establishing general political unity will have to be arrived at, if the relations of the two areas are to be harmonious and mutually helpful.

If it is with India that their ultimate union must be then it must be considered whether their relationship should be with the Central or Provincial Government. Some parts of the hill areas have been included within the sphere of the Provincial Government, and others partially so. The area as a whole is becoming, and must continue to become, especially economically, increasingly integrated with the province in general. There would be little advantage in the Central Government assuming a control which might delay or hinder this natural process. There is also, to support this view, the added argument that there are likely to be fewer people at the Centre with special knowledge and experience of the hill tribes, than would be found in the provincial sphere, and it seems likely that the hill peoples would be able to represent their needs more effectively in the province, of whose population they form a considerable portion, than at the Centre. Thus while the Centre could provide technical advice and information, and in general co-ordinate policy, the actual executive and administrative control should rest with the province. This would seem to indicate that the future of these peoples lies in their participation in the life of the province, as a community in their own right, so as to make their own distinctive contribution to the political, economic and cultural development of Assam.

Social

All social organisations, if they are to survive, must develop, change, and adapt themselves to the ever-changing situation within which they find themselves. The organisation suitable to a primitive and mainly self-sufficient, isolated community, over which hung the perpetual menace of recurrent local warfare and raiding, is not *prima facie* likely to be the one most suitable for the same community, increasingly educated, and in peaceable contact with other peoples, and within which new classes are arising and new economic incentives growing. Primitive society is already undergoing considerable change under the impact of these and other factors and as communications improve, trade increases, and education spreads this may be expected to continue. The new classes, of traders, Government servants, and the educated, who have no adequate representation or share in the traditional Government of their community may be expected to press for recognition of their claims, and it will be necessary to modify the organisation so that the more advanced elements can participate, together with the traditional authorities, in the governance of the people. Since change must come, and probably with increasing rapidity, it therefore follows that it is most undesirable that any measures should be taken that might tend to crystallise the existing structure of society or to make its adjustment to changing conditions more difficult. So long as we lack detailed knowledge of the community we can do little more than help to preserve its elasticity and adaptability, and at the most guide its main lines of development. This is admittedly of a negative nature but positive action is fraught with danger unless it is based on comprehensive knowledge at present not available.

One of the major problems for early decision is the general nature of the eventual social structure towards the development of which policy must be directed. There is in most primitive societies in contact with more advanced peoples a general trend towards the greater "individualisation" of activity and property. It is therefore of utmost importance to decide whether this trend is necessary or desirable. In other words, is it possible to revivify and develop a corporate organisation of society that will function as efficiently, economically and socially as would a similar society composed of individuals mostly concerned with pursuing their independent ends? If it should prove less efficient would this loss of efficiency be offset by any social advantage such as increased social stability, security, etc.? Before any answer can be attempted a detailed study of all the integrating factors in primitive society, such as the age group system, agricultural practice and land tenure, clan and kinship obligations, etc., would be necessary.

Economic

The economic objective must be decided not only in relation to economic consideration but also against the background of the agreed political and social objectives. On the purely economic side it might be the raising of the peoples standard of living to the maximum degree possible. But the need for social security and stability will modify this policy. A balance between cash and subsistence agriculture would have to be arrived at so that the community would not wholly be at the mercy of market fluctuations. The problem of individual enterprise would have to be viewed in relation to whether or not a co-operative society was the objective we were seeking to attain. On the other hand social and political objectives must be in some degree limited by economic considerations—forms of social and political organisation cannot hope to survive unless they provide the necessary setting for efficient economic activity.

Conclusions

It is suggested that the general objectives towards the attainment of which policy should be directed are:—

1. The linkage of the hill peoples with Assam in a way that will give effective recognition to their distinctive needs and problems, and the maximum control over their own affairs, within the general framework of provincial unity.

2. The maintenance of the elasticity of the social organisation, and the guiding of its development, so as to permit of its successful adaptation to the changing situation.
3. The raising of the standard of living of the people to the maximum possible having regard to such social considerations as stability, security, etc.

SOME FACTORS INFLUENCING POLICY

Transition Period

The peoples of the Tribal Areas are at present a Central responsibility. Administration has as yet hardly, if at all, touched them, and local wars and raiding still occur. The people are completely illiterate and have no conception of modern government, and hardly any knowledge of affairs outside their immediate locality. The first essential here is the gradual extension of administration on simple lines suited to the character of the people concerned. This must be followed by programme of economic and social development that will bring them to the level attained by neighbouring communities at the earliest possible date.

The peoples of the excluded and partially excluded areas are considerably in advance of those in the tribal areas. It will be possible in these areas to develop local self-governing bodies in a comparatively short space of time, but even here a measure of protection will be needed for the transition or developmental period.

It is suggested that it is necessary to consider the case of each racial group individually before determining the appropriate policy that will achieve the ends desired. A policy suitable for the Garos will not necessarily be satisfactory for the Nagas and Lushais, etc. There are however a few factors of general validity which may be discussed now.

The first is their position in regard to political training and experience. In most areas there is no unity of outlook or ideas between the different sections of the racial group. In the more advanced areas this is slowly emerging but is still of a fragile nature. This lack of unity has been the major hindrance to political development, and must first be overcome if these peoples are to play their proper part in the political life of the province. Unless the racial group develops some unity of outlook and purpose its representation in the provincial government will always be of a sectional and unsatisfactory character. To develop this unity and to provide training so as to render more easy their participation in the life of the province the development of a local authority is suggested. It is also argued that a system of this nature would be the most efficient and economical form of administration for the hill areas. The creation of such a system will require a little time as the wishes of the people must be consulted and the actual organisation will have to be modified to suit the differing characteristics of social organisation of the various peoples concerned. Moreover authority will have to be delegated slowly as the local council proves able and willing to exercise it. The final and most suitable organisation both from the point of view of efficiency and of acceptability to the people concerned cannot be determined until it has functioned for a period.

Another matter of major importance is the regularisation of land rights. The system of land tenure in the plains is unsuitable to the hills and a cheaper and more simple system will have to be evolved for the hills so as to secure the hillmen against the dangers of alienation and expropriation. Unless this is done the dangers of social unrest and disaffection are considerable.

In regard to economic development the hill areas are backward. A planned programme in regard to his must be initiated immediately if these areas are not to remain for ever deficit ones. In this period of development protection will be necessary against foreign merchants if the economic life of the area is not to be dominated by alien interests. A measure of controlled competition may be necessary to promote efficiency, but for the developmental stage uncontrolled competition would be as disastrous for the hill peoples as for any infant industry anywhere.

If the hill peoples are to play a full and equal part in the Province of Assam a period of rapid educational progress will be necessary, and if this aspect is not to delay their general advance too much it must be accompanied by a sustained programme of adult education. The importance of educational progress cannot be over-emphasised as there can be no equality, in any real sense of the word, between educationally advanced and backward peoples.

To ensure that the developmental work is carried out with the maximum expedition it is desirable to utilize, modified and adapted where necessary, the present form of administration which is understood and accepted by the people. The general policy would be for the District Officer to gradually delegate as many of his powers as practicable to local bodies, and to associate them increasingly with the formulation of police in the area.

Time Factor

It has been suggested that any programme envisaging the rapid development of backward peoples would entail the disruption of their social and economic systems and loss of their cultural identity. Examples are cited from Africa, the South Seas, and elsewhere. It is emphasised that progress must be gradual so that the people can assimilate the dangers and adapt them to their needs. There is however no known maximum or minimum rate of change for social organisations. Historically the rate has varied from period to period and country to country, and in more recent times Russia and Turkey provide examples of how quickly far-reaching changes in the basis of society can be assimilated under certain conditions after centuries of comparative stagnation.

It is not the speed of change that disrupts society but unco-ordinated change resulting from the lack of comprehensive planning, and from inadequate administrative and technical machinery. However, the greater the speed of change the greater will be the stresses and strains within the society, and the greater will be the difficulty of securing the support of the older and more conservative generations. Thus the rate of change is to a large extent limited by the amount of accurate knowledge we have of the present working of the society concerned, and by the adequacy of the administrative and technical services to secure that policy shall be consistent and effective.

Neighbouring areas are undergoing considerable change and development, and the leeway between the hill and plains peoples is possibly widening rather than narrowing. In this situation the inevitability of gradualness will not serve as an inspiration. The leeway must be made up in a period of rapid change and development.

Language

There are two aspects of the language problem. The first is that of the medium of instruction in the schools, and the second that of the lingua franca without which unity between the different communities will be impossible of achievement. It would be desirable, but not essential, if one language could perform both functions.

The importance of the native language as a means of preserving the culture of the people is now generally recognised. "The spiritual heritage of the community is to a large extent preserved in, and transmitted through, its native language." It is therefore most desirable that all possible encouragement should be given to the development of the various hill languages and any Government which assumes a responsibility towards these peoples must actively concern itself with the enrichment of their literature. But sooner or later comes the problem of a more general medium of instruction for an adequate number of text books, etc. cannot be translated into every hill language.

At present no one tribal language is used to any extent beyond the boundaries of the tribe concerned, and it would be most difficult if not impossible, to secure the acceptance of any one hill language as a general medium of instruction in all the hill areas. The choice would thus seem to lie between the adoption of either English or Assamese. The merits and demerits of each will have to be examined carefully, and in consultation with the people concerned, a decision reached at the earliest possible date so that educational progress is not hindered. If Assamese is finally chosen, then in view of the fact that English is at present in use, an interim period will be necessary to allow for the gradual change over so that there is the minimum of educational dislocation.

Education

A more vigorous and comprehensive educational programme is essential if the hill peoples are to be enabled to compete on even terms with other communities, and if the rapid changes are to be assimilated, and the resulting society is to be stable and progressive. As has been indicated previously the greater the speed of change, the greater will be the difficulty of securing the support of the older and more conservative elements. This opposition can only be overcome or lessened by propaganda and education. Adult education must be an essential part of any programme envisaging considerable changes in, and development of, primitive society.

Education has for too long been a thing apart from the ordinary home life of the children and has thus resulted in a growing division in the community between the educated and non-educated. It is necessary that the educational services should become an integral part of community life, and must cater not only for the children but for the adult members of society. Rural libraries and reading facilities are of vital importance if the literacy gained at school and in adult education is not to be lost. The content of the education to be given must be determined, and related to the culture, social organisation, and way of life of the people it is to serve.

Finance

The limiting factor in all schemes for the advancement of the hill peoples is finance. It is unlikely that within any near future the hill areas will be financially self-supporting, and progress and development must necessarily depend on the province of adequate funds. It will be difficult for the Province alone to shoulder the burden, and a strong case can be made out for a substantial contribution from the centre, both on the ground of general responsibility for the welfare of the backward communities, and on the ground that defensive and political considerations require a contended and loyal population in these vital areas.

POLICY

Political and Administrative Training

As has been indicated previously, if the hill peoples are to be associated with other communities in the province on terms of equality, it is necessary that they should receive some measure of political and administrative training so that they may play a fair part in any Government including them within its jurisdiction. It is suggested that this can best be achieved by the creation of a local authority system and by increasingly associating the representatives of the people with the formulation of policy.

In most of the hill areas the village authority or panchayat continues to exercise unimpaired its control over village life and the vast majority of disputes are finally settled by it. The constitution of the village authority varies from tribe to tribe and is except in a few cases fundamentally democratic. It will be necessary to constitutionalise autocracy where found by reviving or developing conciliar activity, the seeds of which are usually present, in one form or another, in the political structure. Apart from this it is essential that for good and effective administration nothing should be done to weaken the authority of this primary administrative unit.

Together with the maintenance of the village authority must come the development of representative councils embracing wider units such as the tribe and racial group. Among some of the peoples particularly the Nagas, this development has already taken place, and there are councils representing all the main tribes and a Naga National Council representing the tribes collectively. These councils are a new creation for which there are no traditional or indigenous parallels for guidance, and they will require sympathetic guidance and support for some years if they are not to founder on the rocks of inexperience and inter-village and inter-tribal jealousies. It will therefore be necessary for Government to see that this sympathy and guidance is provided, and every District Office should receive instructions that their sound development should be his main preoccupation.

It is suggested that the primary electoral body for the establishment of tribal and inter-tribal councils should be the village authority and not the individual voter. The advantage of this would be the strengthening of the position of the village authority, and the probability that a better type of leader would be thrown up. Financial responsibility is an integral element in political training, and subject to necessary auditing and general control, the local authority should have as large a discretionary power over the allocation of funds at its disposal as possible. In Africa it has been found that the institution of native treasuries has done much to stimulate this sense of financial responsibility. Local authorities should also be entrusted with as much executive authority as they are willing and able to exercise, and while the amount which can be delegated may vary from people to people it should be Government's aim to entrust them with the maximum amount possible even though this does entail an element of risk. It is only by making mistakes that they will learn. Executive authority will be novel to tribal authorities and considerable experimentation will be necessary to evolve suitable machinery for the control of staff and supervision of work.

The village authority has already considerable judicial powers and the majority of cases occurring in the village are settled by it. It is desirable that nothing should be done to weaken this authority, but for the settlement of inter-village, inter-tribal, and more serious cases the establishment of tribal and inter-tribal courts are necessary.

It is suggested that at the village level no separation of judicial and executive powers is either desirable or practicable. Any serious abuse of power is most unlikely as all sections of the village are represented on the village council and the close personal and clan relationships existing in the community provide a considerable safeguard against victimisation. The case for separation becomes much stronger when we consider the position of the tribal and inter-tribal authorities. Firstly the safeguards existing at the village level become less effective; secondly the qualities necessary to a judge, an intimate knowledge of customary law and experience in the settlement of cases, are not necessarily possessed by an executive agent, although they may be; thirdly the tribal authority will not be in continuous session while the tribal court will have to sit for the regular disposal of cases; and lastly, the tribal authority may have to prosecute people for disobeying its lawful orders, and it is not desirable that it should be both prosecutor and judge. On the whole therefore I incline to the view that judicial and executive powers should be separated above the village level.

The mere exercise of local authority will not in itself provide sufficient political training. In order to give some idea of the broader problems and factors influencing policy it will be necessary to associate the representatives of the people with the framing of policy. This may be done in the first place by making it obligatory for the District Officer to consult the representative bodies in matters of general importance to the district and in other subjects to be specified. At a higher level the creation of an advisory council for all the hill areas would be a useful medium by which the more general problems affecting the hills could be reviewed and considered. If truly representative it would reflect accurately the opinion of the hill peoples and would provide Government with invaluable advice concerning proposed legislation and policy so far as it affected the areas represented by the council.

Social Development

The social structure of the hill peoples is already undergoing considerable change under the impact of a variety of factors among which are the spread of education, improved communications resulting in greater contacts with other people, the used of salaried or middle classes, etc. This process may be expected to continue and increase in momentum. A social organisation created to meet the needs of a primitive and largely self-sufficient community cannot be expected to be adequate to the needs of a society that is becoming increasingly integrated with the general and economic life of the province and within which new classes are arising who have no adequate representation or share in the traditional government of their community. It is to be emphasised here that any policy which does not secure the fullest possible co-operation from the more advanced elements in the society will lack efficiency and its achievements permanence.

As a society changes the authority controlling it must also change, and different qualities will be demanded of its leaders. In a society where custom and tradition are the ultimate sanctions, and war an ever-present menace to life and property, leaders versed in traditional lore and experienced in negotiation are necessary. The unity of the community in the face of constant external danger is a primary consideration. As the danger of warfare diminishes, and as the strength of custom and tradition is lowly undermined a new type of leadership is required. As Westerman remarks, there is a growing number of people who "find it unreasonable to have to bow to the orders of rulers who have had far less experience of the world and of life than they themselves possess, and who are far from always benevolent and unselfish patriarchs". Dependence for the selection of leaders on age, status, and lineage, becomes less satisfactory, and merit and ability must play an increasingly important part. It is therefore desirable that the basis of local authority should where it is not already fully representative of all section of the community be broadened so as to admit, if the peoples so desire, those whose character and ability warrant it, although their appointment might not have the sanction of tradition.

With a policy of rapid advance and progress for the hill peoples considerable changes in the bases of their social structure must be anticipated, and it is therefore essential that the general principles guiding the changes should be fully understood so that, when required, sympathetic advice and assistance can be given. Above all my measures that would tend to crystallise the existing structure and make its adaptation to changing circumstances more difficult must be avoided.

The position of the hereditary Lushai chief is a point in illustration. Generally speaking prior to administration the power of the chief was fairly limited and his privileges were accompanied by various corresponding obligations. He could not with impunity ignore the advice of the elders of the village, his liberty of action was circumscribed by tradition and custom, and any desire to exploit the ordinary villager for his own profit was held in check by the possibility of the villager emigrating to another village and consequently weakening his own. There was in fact an elaborate system of checks that on the whole guarded the commoner against tyranny reasonably well.

This balance has now been disturbed and cannot be retrieved and a new one is necessary. Tradition and custom have now a less compelling sanction, the development of settled agriculture, such as terraced rice fields, and the growing scarcity of land, make the emigration of the cultivator more difficult and arduous, Government recognition of the Chief as the village authority has tended to increase his power *vis-a-vis* the elders. While these factors have tended to increase the power of the Chief other new factors have tended to undermine his position. The chief enjoyed much of his prestige on account of his leadership in war which has now been stopped, some of his villagers are often more educated or experienced in affairs than he is himself and question his authority and orders, the scarcity of land has stopped the practice of the younger sons setting up new villages for themselves and has resulted in a perpetual scramble for power than continually divides the village into hostile groups each supporting their own claim, the unsuccessful claimants are always a potential source of faction in the village and thereby diminish the authority of the Chief. On the whole the factors diminishing the authority of the Chief have proved stronger and the tendency has been for the Chief to try to get Government support to maintain his privileges while decreasing his obligations.

If my general argument is accepted then Government must avoid any measures that would confirm the Chief in all his privileges and check the general tendency. We should seek rather, as has been suggested previously, to constitutionalise the Chief's position by giving recognition to the elders. Instead of the Chief being recognised as the village authority it should be initially, the Chief in Council and from this beginning a more adequate village authority among the Lushais might evolve.

Any positive action towards guiding the development of primitive society is dependent on detailed and exhaustive knowledge of all aspects of the life of the community, which can only be acquired by anthropological field work over a considerable period. Without this exact knowledge we can do little more than to influence the broad trends in the direction of the objectives we are striving to attain.

Economic Development

In considering policy in regard to economic development it would be well to divide the problem into two parts—the external market and the internal market.

Supplying an external market is largely dependent on transport and communication. The greater the relative cost of transport the greater will be difficulty of finding profitable markets. That the development of communications must precede or accompany the economic development of the areas, and cannot wait until later, is obvious.

The development of some kind of power is essential, and the most obvious method is the utilisation of the abundant water-power in the hills. In Nepal and the Shan States, as well as other areas, every village has one or more water-wheels to supply cheap power, and which can easily be maintained by the local inhabitants. It will be necessary to secure a grant to experiment until the most suitable form of wheel is arrived at, but the resulting benefit to the hills will be out of all proportion to the initial cost involved. The husking of paddy, the crushing of sugarcane and of mustard seed, are only a few of the immediate uses for which this power can be utilised.

It will also have to be decided whether economic enterprise should be left in the hands of individuals or organised on co-operative lines. Subject to further study I would suggest that the latter method is best suited to the hills where communal activity and responsibility is still a vital force in the lives of the people. If this is so this would necessitate the immediate training of a number of hillmen in co-operative theory and practice, the appointment of a supervisory staff, and the adaptation of co-operative rules to suit the differing conditions in the hills. It will probably be relatively easy to direct economic development along co-operative lines but much more difficult to transform a developed individualistic economy.

Agriculture must continue to be the main occupation of the hill areas and the growing of cash crops the most general way of securing money. The old system of barter is gradually dying and the demand for cash to buy goods produced in other areas, to educate children, to pay taxes, etc., is increasing and will continue to increase. The most profitable crops will be those for which the hills have special advantages for growing or are able to grow at seasons when the plains are unable to do so—vegetables, fruits, etc. Where the plains can compete on level terms the additional transport charges will tip the balance against the hills.

The development of any large scale industries in the hill areas is a speculative proposition on which expert advice is the first requisite. It would in the first place probably be preferable, and more advantageous to the people concerned, to develop small scale industries for which cheap and abundant water-power, referred to above, would be available and suitable. The possibilities of cottage industries as means of raising the standard of living of the ordinary villagers needs to be explored forthwith.

The internal market while limited is none the less important. Where the demand is relatively small large scale production cannot compete with village industries. The making of tribal cloths, ceremonial cloths, particular ornaments, etc., is not likely to suffer from external competition. Transport charges while unfavourable to the external market favour the internal one, and where the cost of production is comparable with or only slightly higher than that in the plains, the hillman will be able to compete successfully in the local market. *Gur*, mustard oil, cured tobacco, etc., are some of the articles which the local producer will probably be able to sell in competition with plains productions in the local market with success. Similarly where the village industry is carried on as a part-time occupation, as the weaving of cloth and the making of baskets and earthenware pots, with improved methods, there should be a considerable market for the products locally. Finally although the importance of barter is diminishing there will, so long as money is relatively scarce, always be a certain amount of trade by this method which will remain in the hands of the local producers.

As has been mentioned previously, one of the most important matters for decision is the feasibility of securing the development of these areas on a co-operative basis. On *prima facie* grounds there would appear every hope of success, as community feeling is still very strong, and a large part of village life already functions on traditionally co-operative lines. The employment of an expert to study the problem now, and to advise on the most suitable methods of co-operative organisation in the hills is an urgent need.

MACHINERY

Central Government

If the problems of the hill peoples are to be dealt with adequately then the technical advice and assistance of experts in primitive education, law, agriculture, land tenure, co-operation, etc., is essential. The provision of such a staff of experts is beyond the means of each individual province, and could most suitably be provided by the Central Government. It is therefore suggested that the welfare and development of the backward peoples as a whole should be a matter of concern for the Central Government, and that an advisory department should be created specifically responsible for the co-ordination of policy, and the provision of technical assistance and advice on particular problems. This department would make available to all provinces the information gained from experience in each, as well as that gained in other countries confronted with the same problems. It would undertake independent surveys as well as surveys at the request of particular provincial Governments, and make public its reports. It would also advise the Central Government in cases where contributions were requested by provincial Governments for expenditure on the development of the backward peoples.

It is here necessary to discuss the role of the expert *vis-a-vis* the administrator. The expert's task is to provide factual reports on particular problems and to advise Government on the probable consequences of any particular line of action. It is however for the administration to determine policy in the light of all the relevant facts provided by the expert. It is therefore suggested that the department should be mainly staffed by administrators, and that, as is done by the British Colonial Office, experts be engaged from time to time to report on specific problems.

Provincial Government

Some provincial administrative machinery is necessary to co-ordinate hill policy and to see that it is effectively carried out. The present position whereby the only connecting link between the Governor and the District Officers is the Governor's Secretary, a non-touring officer whose time is fully engaged in administrative routine and office work, is most unfortunate.

It is suggested that an advisory committee for the hill areas should be created to formulate and review policy and to make recommendations as to future action. Representatives of the hill peoples and of Government would be on this committee which might provide the beginning for the development of a Hills Council. Wherever particular racial groups have established representative institutions the members of the Committee would be elected by these bodies. In other cases the members would, for the time being, have to be nominated after consulting the wishes of the people concerned as fully as possible.

As has been suggested above if a policy of active development is to be made effective in the hill areas the administrative machinery, suitable perhaps in the past, will need urgent overhaul. The problem arising in both the Tribal Areas and the Excluded and Partially Excluded Areas are of the same nature although differing in degree, consequent upon the different stages of advance reached by the various peoples, and policy for both areas must needs be co-ordinated. From the point of view of the people it would be preferable that all the peoples came under one administration and not, as at present, be divided between the Centre and the Province. Politically however the Centre must always be keenly interested in the Northern Hills in particular, where questions of external policy are involved. For the time being the necessary co-ordination can probably be secured by one officer being appointed to supervise the administration in all the hill areas with two deputies—one for the Tribal Areas and another for the Excluded and Partially Excluded Areas. These three officers would be members of the advisory committee proposed above.

It is also necessary that the Provincial Government should recruit more hillmen to the services not on the basis of population but on the basis of hill posts to be filled. While there is no objection to plains people filling hill posts and hillmen filling plains posts it is an inescapable fact that this is liked neither by the plains officer nor the hill officer. It means considerable added expense to both, as it usually involves the maintenance of two establishments, especially when the officer has children to be educated, lack of social amenities, and, in the case of hill posts, arduous touring for which only a hillman is suited.

District Administration

As has been suggested before the District Officers play an active part in the development of representative local self-governing bodies. It is necessary that the development of tribal councils should not result in the intensifying of tribal jealousies and separistic tendencies. It is therefore essential to establish both tribal and inter-tribal authorities at the same time to check any possible tendencies of this nature. The controlled development of local units might otherwise result in the growth of parochial and exclusive loyalties that could not but be detrimental to the progress of the people as a whole.

Together with the delegation of authority to the local bodies must come the association of the representatives of the people with the formulation of policy in the area. A small advisory committee might be formed to sit with the District Officer from time to time to consider matters of general importance to the district.

It is also worthy of consideration whether in the more advanced areas subdivisional councils could not be developed to take over the functions of the Subdivisional Officers.

CONCLUSIONS

The preceding note has as its intention the presentation of some of the points on which a decision must be reached if a consistent and satisfactory hill policy is to be formulated and carried out.

It is first necessary to clarify the objectives towards which policy must be directed, and then to decide on the best method of attaining them, and the administrative machinery required for the execution of the policy agreed upon. Before it is possible to arrive at any decisions, full account must be taken of the cultural, social and economic organisation of the peoples, and the present position of, and trends within, the communities concerned. Finally, and of most importance, is the prior ascertainment of the wishes of the people themselves.

It has been suggested in the note that the most economical, efficient, and acceptable method of administration of the hill areas would be the creation of a fully representative local authority system enjoying the maximum amount of delegated authority feasible, and closely associated with the provincial administration. It is recognised that all areas cannot be dealt with in precisely the same way, and that differing racial groups are in widely different stages of development, and that therefore the transition and development period must vary in each case, but that every effort must be made to render it as short as possible. To do this will require the united efforts of the people concerned supported by sympathetic and effective help from Government both in finance and administrative staff.

The essential point is that if their progress and development is not to be delayed Government must, at the earliest possible date, arrive at a settled policy towards the hill peoples of Assam.

About the Editor and Contributors

EDITOR

David R. Syiemlieh joined the Department of History, North-Eastern Hill University (NEHU) in 1979. He was the Head of the Department of History, 2002–2005. He was Honorary Director of the Indian Council of Social Science Research–North Eastern Regional Centre (ICSSR-NERC). A member and for many years treasurer and secretary of the North East India History Association, he was nominated in 2005 as Council Member of the Indian Council of Historical Research (ICHR), New Delhi and served two terms as Member of the ICHR. Professor Syiemlieh is also former Vice-Chancellor, Rajiv Gandhi University. He has won numerous awards and scholarships such as J.J.M. Nichols-Roy Award; National Scholarship; Jawaharlal Nehru Book Award and NEHU Gold Medal for First Position in MA; Charles Wallace India Trust Grant; India-France Cultural Exchange Programme; and Senior Fulbright Fellowship at Notre Dame University, USA.

Professor Syiemlieh has edited numerous books including volumes of *Proceedings of the North East India History Association*. With numerous published articles in journals/edited volumes, some of his authored books include *British Administration in Meghalaya* (1989), *A Brief History of the Catholic Church in Nagaland* (1990), *They Dared to Hope* (1999) and *Survey of Research in History on North East India 1970–1990* (2000).

Professor Syiemlieh is presently Member, Union Public Service Commission.

CONTRIBUTORS

Philip F. Adams arrived in India as a young Indian Civil Service (ICS) officer on 14 December 1937 and was among the last cadre of officers that was recruited for service. He was for several years attached to the Assam administration and posted as assistant commissioner of the Naga Hills District in charge of the Mokokchung Subdivision. Together with Charles Pawsey, the deputy commissioner, they were responsible for the administration of these hills during the entire war years. Pawsey was knighted for the effort of administering these hills during the difficult war years. Adams received a Master of the British Empire (MBE). Adams was for several months secretary to the Governor of Assam, a position he filled after J. P. Mills put in his papers. Adams published *Some Notes on a Policy for the Hills Tribes of Assam*, Shillong, 1947, 10 days before India's Independence, by which date he had resigned from service. He remained as secretary to assist Sir Akbar Hydari, the first Indian Governor of Assam. Adams subsequently left India for service in East Africa.

Sir Andrew G. Clow (1890–1957) joined the Indian Civil Service (ICS) in 1914 and was initially posted in the United Provinces. He was an authority on labour conditions in India. He was member of the Viceroy's Executive Council in 1939. He took over as Governor of Assam from Sir Robert N. Reid in May 1942. His tenure as governor covered the war years, the last phase of the Indian national movement, the political adjustments and postwar reconstruction. Yet he had the time to write *The Future Government of the Assam Tribal Peoples*, Shillong, 1945. He handed over charge of the province of Assam to Sir Akbar Hydari in May 1947.

James P. Mills (1890–1960) graduated from Winchester College and Corpus Christi College, Oxford. He entered the Indian Civil Service (ICS) in 1913 and like J. H. Hutton before him, spent much of his administrative career in the Naga Hills first as a sub-division officer and later as the district's deputy commissioner. He used his administrative experience to author two monographs on the Nagas, *The Lhota Nagas*, 1922 and *The Ao Nagas*, 1926 and a number of articles on the anthropology of the region. In 1930, he became Honorary Director of Ethnology, Assam. Two years later, he was promoted as Secretary to the Government of Assam. An important assignment he held for several years was Adviser to the Governor of Assam for Tribal Areas and States. He retired from the ICS in mid-1947, just before India's Independence. With his service as colonial administrator and his interest in anthropology built up during his service in India, he joined the faculty of Anthropology in the School of Oriental and African Studies, University of London, serving the institution from 1947 till 1954.

Sir Robert N. Reid (1883–1964) was appointed to the Indian Civil Service in 1907 and served for many years in Bengal. Awarded the KCSI and KCIE medals, he took over as Governor of Assam in March 1937. He handed over charge to Sir Andrew G. Clow in May 1942. He was acting governor of Bengal, February to June 1939. A prolific writer he wrote extensively of the region. His first publication was *A Note on the Future of the Present Excluded, Partially Excluded and Tribal Areas of Assam,* Shillong, 1941. A year later, he wrote *History of the Frontier Areas Bordering on Assam,* Shillong, an update of Alexander Mackenzie's *A History of the Relations of the Government with the Hill Tribes of North East Frontier of Bengal* (Calcutta, 1884). An unpublished manuscript is with the British Library, India and Oriental Collection. Titled "Assam and the North East Frontier of India", Reid wrote this after his retirement and returned home in 1946. Before his death in 1964, he had put together his biography which was published posthumously as *Years of Change in Bengal and Assam,* in 1966, with a Foreword by Ian Stephens. Sir Robert Reid is known to have befriended the tribal people of Assam and took up their cause during his retirement. He was for sometime China Relations Officer.